STEP 3

WORD
Bridge
3600

Intro

Word Bridge 3600의 수준별 학습
중학교 필수 단어에서 특목고 대비를 위한 단어까지 총 3,600 단어가 단계별로 레벨업되어 있습니다.
자신의 수준에 맞추어서 차근차근 어휘력을 다져나갈 수 있도록 하였습니다.

귀로 듣고, 입으로 따라하기
단어마다 문법과 구문법칙이 응용된 모범예문을 원어민의 정확한 발음으로 듣고 따라하다 보면 암기 효과를
두 배로 올릴 수 있도록 하였습니다.

영영정의를 통한 의미 이해
단어의 주요 의미를 영영으로 정의해 놓고 연관된 예문을 제시함으로써 그 의미를 더욱 정확하게 이해할 수
있도록 하였습니다.

반복, 반복 쏙쏙 암기
눈으로 암기하는 단어는 오래 기억되지 못합니다. 듣기, 말하기, 쓰기 등을 활용한 다양한 연습 형태를 통해
반복적으로 단어를 학습할 수 있도록 하였습니다.

교재의 구성

본 교재는 단계별로 총 5권으로 구성되어 있습니다.

각 권은 10 Part로, 각 Part는 모두 4 unit으로 구성되어 있습니다.

Listen and repeat
주요 학습 파트로 새로운 단어 18개와 단어를 활용한 모범예문이 수록되어 있으며 듣기 학습이 포함되어 있습니다.

Exercise / Review
주요 학습에서 익힌 단어와 예문을 활용하여 문제를 풀어보고 암기 합니다.

▼ Step 1

Unit 1

🎧 Listen and repeat. Track 1

01 abbey   n 대수도원, 대성당   a large church in which monks or nuns live
   [ǽbi]   He was buried in Westminster **Abbey**.
                                      그는 웨스트민스터 성당에 안장되었다.

02 aboard   ad 해외로 / prep ~을 타고   in or to another country or countries
   [əbɔ́ːrd]   What do you think of traveling **abroad**?
                                      해외로 여행하는 것에 대해 어떻게 생각하니?

03 anxious   a 열망하는   wanting something very much
   [ǽŋkʃəs]   Parents are **anxious** for the welfare of their children.
                                      부모는 자식의 행복을 열망한다.

04 apt   a ~하는 경향이 있는, 적절한   suitable in a particular situation
   [æpt]   I thought 'complex' was an **apt** description of the book.

▼ Step 2

n 대수도원, 대성당   a large church in which monks or nuns live
                     He was buried in Westminster **Abbey**.
                     그는 웨스트민스터 성당에 안장되었다.

ad 해외로 / prep ~을 타고   in or to another country or countries
                           What do you think of traveling **abroad**?
                           해외로 여행하는 것에 대해 어떻게 생각하니?

a 열망하는   wanting something very much
              Parents are **anxious** for the welfare of their children.
              부모는 자식의 행복을 열망한다.

a ~하는 경향이 있는, 적절한   suitable in a particular situation
                             I thought 'complex' was an **apt** description of the book.
                             나는 '콤플렉스'가 이 책에 대한 적절한 설명이라고 생각했다.

▼ Step 3

🎧 Listen and repeat. Track 2

10 celebrate   v 경축하다, 찬양하다   to show an event by doing som
   [séləbrèit]   It is **celebrating** its tenth year on the air.
                                      방송 10주년째를 기념하고 있다.

11 chemical   n 화학 / a 화학의   connected with chemistry
   [kémikəl]   It will show a **chemical** reaction soon.
                                     그것은 곧 화학 반응을 보일 것이다.

12 conference n 회담, 회의   a large official meeting to discuss impor
   [kánfərəns]   There was an international **conference** on globa
                                     지구 온난화에 관한 국제 회의가 있었다.

13 control   n 지배 / v 통제하다, 억제하다   the act of managing som

▼ Step 4

14. We hope that you will be able to quickly _____
    우리는 당신이 하루빨리 이러한 변화에 대처하시기를 바랍니다.

15. What do you think of traveling _____?
    해외로 여행하는 것에 대해 어떻게 생각하니?

16. However, this _____ is somewhat incomplete.
    그러나 이 정의는 조금 불완전하다.

17. It will show a _____ reaction soon.
    그것은 곧 화학 반응을 보일 것이다.

18. I'll give you _____ to my house.
    너에게 우리 집으로 가는 방향을 알려주겠다.

Hint
bloom   conference   celebrate   awake   cattle   chemical   a
control decoration   definition abbey   cope   anxious

▼ Step 5

B. Fill in the word and meaning.

Word	Meaning		Meaning	Word
01 blank		01	대수도원	
02 aboard		02	해외로, ~을 타고	
03 decoration		03	열망하는	
04 celebrate		04	~하는 경향이 있는, 적절한	
05 abbey		05	청중, 관객	
06 chemical		06	깨우다, 깨어 있는	
07 definition		07	공백, 백지의	
08 anxious		08	꽃이 피다	
09 cope		09	소	
10 bloom		10	경축하다, 찬양하다	
11 direction		11	화학, 화학의	
12 awake		12	회당, 회의	
13 convenient		13	지배, 통제하다, 억제하다	
14 audience		14	편리한	

▼ Step 6

🎧 **C. Listen, write the word and meaning.** (Track 3)

Word	Meaning		Word
01		10	
02		11	
03		12	
04		13	
05		14	
06		15	
07		16	
08		17	
09		18	

▼ Step 7

A. Read and fill in the word and meaning.

word	definition	meaning
	cows and bulls that are kept as farm animals	
	a large church in which monks or nuns live	
	instructions about how to do something or get to a place	
	to show an event by doing something special on it	
	in or to another country or countries	
	connected with chemistry	
	to deal successfully with something difficult	
	to produce flowers	
	useful, easy to do	

교재의 학습방법

- **Step 1 - 새 단어 귀로 들으며 익히기**
  새 단어와 예문을 원어민의 발음으로 들으며 익힌다.

- **Step 2 - 단어 뜻 암기하기**
  영영 정의를 익히면서 단어의 정확한 의미를 이해하고, 예문을 해석하면서 예문 속에서 단어의 쓰임을 학습합니다.

- **Step 3 - 입으로 따라하며 암기하기**
  다시 한 번 CD를 들으면서 큰 소리로 따라합니다. 예문을 따라하면서 통째로 암기합니다.

- **Step 4 - 문장 완성하기**
  주어진 단어 힌트를 이용하여 암기한 예문을 완성합니다.

- **Step 5 - 단어와 뜻 채우기**
  제시된 영어 단어는 뜻을 우리 말로 쓰고, 단어의 뜻이 제시되어 있으면 영어 단어를 쓰면서 복습합니다.

- **Step 6 - 듣고 단어와 뜻 채우기**
  CD를 듣고 정확한 발음을 익히며 영어 단어와 뜻을 쓰면서 반복 학습합니다.

- **Step 7 - 단어 암기 확인**
  영영 정의를 읽고 암기한 영어 단어와 뜻을 쓰면서 확인 학습을 합니다.

Contents

part 1

Unit 1	6
Unit 2	10
Review 1	14
Unit 3	16
Unit 4	20
Review 2	24

part 2

Unit 5	26
Unit 6	30
Review 3	34
Unit 7	36
Unit 8	40
Review 4	44

part 3

Unit 9	46
Unit 10	50
Review 5	54

Unit 11	56
Unit 12	60
Review 6	64

part 4

Unit 13	66
Unit 14	70
Review 7	74
Unit 15	76
Unit 16	80
Review 8	84

part 5

Unit 17	86
Unit 18	90
Review 9	94
Unit 19	96
Unit 20	100
Review 10	104

WORD BRIDGE 3600

part 6

Unit 21	106
Unit 22	110
Review 11	114
Unit 23	116
Unit 24	120
Review 12	124

part 7

Unit 25	126
Unit 26	130
Review 13	134
Unit 27	136
Unit 28	140
Review 14	144

part 8

Unit 29	146
Unit 30	150
Review 15	154

Unit 31	156
Unit 32	160
Review 16	164

part 9

Unit 33	166
Unit 34	170
Review 17	174
Unit 35	176
Unit 36	180
Review 18	184

part 10

Unit 37	186
Unit 38	190
Review 19	194
Unit 39	196
Unit 40	200
Review 20	204
Total Test	207
Answer Key	229

Unit 1

🎧 Listen and repeat. (Track 1)

01 abbey [ǽbi]
n 대수도원, 대성당   a large church in which monks or nuns live
He was buried in Westminster **Abbey**.
그는 웨스트민스터 성당에 안장되었다.

02 abroad [əbrɔ́ːd]
ad 해외로, 널리   in or to another country or countries
What do you think of traveling **abroad**?
해외로 여행하는 것에 대해 어떻게 생각하니?

03 anxious [ǽŋkʃəs]
a 열망하는   wanting something very much
Parents are **anxious** for the welfare of their children.
부모는 자식의 행복을 열망한다.

04 apt [æpt]
a ~하는 경향이 있는, 적절한   suitable in a particular situation
I thought 'complex' was an **apt** description of the book.
나는 '콤플렉스'가 이 책에 대한 적절한 설명이라고 생각했다.

05 audience [ɔ́ːdiəns]
n 청중, 관객   all the people who are watching a play, concert, speech, etc
The **audience** was wild with excitement.
관객들은 흥분해서 사나워졌다.

06 awake [əwéik]
v 깨우다 / a 깨어 있는   to wake up; not asleep
The coffee will help him stay **awake**.
그가 깨어 있을 수 있게 도와줄 것이다.

07 blank [blæŋk]
a 공백의, 백지의   empty printed or recorded on it
He tore a **blank** page from his notebook.
그는 자기 공책에서 빈 페이지 한 장을 뜯어냈다.

08 bloom [bluːm]
v 꽃이 피다   to produce flowers
Azaleas **bloom** all over the bank.
강둑에는 온통 진달래가 펴 있다.

09 cattle [kǽtl]
n 소   cows and bulls that are kept as farm animals
Cattle, sheep and goats have a pair of horns.
소, 양 그리고 염소에게는 한 쌍의 뿔이 있다.

---

key words
monk n 수사 / nun v 수녀 / bury v 묻다, 장례식을 하다 / description n 기술, 서술
excitement v 흥분, 격양 / tear v 찢다 / azalea n 진달래 / bank n 둑, 제방 / horn n 뿔

🎧 Listen and repeat. Track 2

10 celebrate [séləbrèit]
v 경축하다, 찬양하다   to show an event by doing something special on it
It is **celebrating** its tenth year on the air.
방송 10주년째를 기념하고 있다.

11 chemical [kémikəl]
n 화학 / a 화학의   connected with chemistry
It will show a **chemical** reaction soon.
그것은 곧 화학 반응을 보일 것이다.

12 conference [kánfərəns]
n 회당, 회의   a large official meeting to discuss important matters
There was an international **conference** on global warming.
지구 온난화에 관한 국제 회의가 있었다.

13 control [kəntróul]
n 지배 / v 통제하다, 억제하다   the act of managing something
The man is signaling that the fire is under **control**.
그 남자는 불이 통제되고 있다는 신호를 보내고 있다.

14 convenient [kənvíːnjənt]
a 편리한   useful, easy to do
Modern technology makes our living much more **convenient**.
현대 과학 기술은 우리 생활을 훨씬 더 편리하게 만들고 있다.

15 cope [koup]
v 대처하다, 극복하다   to deal successfully with something difficult
We hope that you will be able to quickly **cope** with this change.
우리는 당신이 하루빨리 이러한 변화에 대처하시기를 바랍니다.

16 decoration [dèkəréiʃən]
n 장식, 훈장   the style in which something is decorated
I've bought the Christmas **decorations**.
나는 크리스마스에 쓸 장식물들을 샀다.

17 definition [dèfəníʃən]
n 정의, 한정   the act of stating the meanings of words and phrases
However, this **definition** is somewhat incomplete.
그러나 이 정의는 조금 불완전하다.

18 direction [dirékʃən]
n 방향, 지도, 감독   instructions about how to do something or get to a place
I'll give you **directions** to my house.
너에게 우리 집으로 가는 방향을 알려주겠다.

key words
reaction n 반작용, 반응 / global a 세계적인, 지구전체의 / signal v 신호하다
incomplet a 불완전한 / instruction n 지시, 설명

Exercise

A. Complete the sentence.

1. The _____ was wild with excitement.
   관객들은 흥분해서 사나워졌다.

2. There was an international _____ on global warming.
   지구 온난화에 관한 국제 회의가 있었다.

3. He tore a _____ page from his notebook.
   그는 자기 공책에서 빈 페이지 한 장을 뜯어냈다.

4. Parents are _____ for the welfare of their children.
   부모는 자식의 행복을 열망한다.

5. I thought 'complex' was an _____ description of the book.
   나는 '콤플렉스'가 이 책에 대한 적절한 설명이라고 생각했다.

6. Azaleas _____ all over the bank.
   강둑에는 온통 진달래가 펴 있다.

7. _____, sheep and goats have a pair of horns.
   소, 양 그리고 염소에게는 한 쌍의 뿔이 있다.

8. I've bought the Christmas _____.
   나는 크리스마스에 쓸 장식물들을 샀다.

9. It is _____ its tenth year on the air.
   방송 10주년째를 기념하고 있다.

10. He was buried in Westminster _____.
    그는 웨스트민스터 성당에 안장되었다.

11. The man is signaling that the fire is under _____.
    그 남자는 불이 통제되고 있다는 신호를 보내고 있다.

12. Modern technology makes our living much more _____.
    현대 과학 기술은 우리 생활을 훨씬 더 편리하게 만들고 있다.

13. The coffee will help him stay _____.
    그가 깨어 있을 수 있게 도와 줄 것이다.

14. We hope that you will be able to quickly _____ with this change.
    우리는 당신이 하루빨리 이러한 변화에 대처하시기를 바랍니다.

15. What do you think of traveling _____?
    해외로 여행하는 것에 대해 어떻게 생각하니?

16. However, this _____ is somewhat incomplete.
    그러나 이 정의는 조금 불완전하다.

17. It will show a _____ reaction soon.
    그것은 곧 화학 반응을 보일 것이다.

18. I'll give you _____ to my house.
    너에게 우리 집으로 가는 방향을 알려주겠다.

Hint

bloom　conference　celebrate　awake　cattle　chemical　abroad　blank　direction
control　decoration　definition　abbey　cope　anxious　audience　apt　convenient

Unit 1

Exercise

B. Fill in the word and meaning.

	Word	Meaning
01	blank	
02	abroad	
03	decoration	
04	celebrate	
05	abbey	
06	chemical	
07	definition	
08	anxious	
09	cope	
10	bloom	
11	direction	
12	awake	
13	convenient	
14	audience	
15	cattle	
16	control	
17	conference	
18	apt	

	Meaning	Word
01	대수도원, 대성당	
02	해외로, 널리	
03	열망하는	
04	~하는 경향이 있는, 적절한	
05	청중, 관객	
06	깨우다, 깨어 있는	
07	공백의, 백지의	
08	꽃이 피다	
09	소	
10	경축하다, 찬양하다	
11	화학, 화학의	
12	회당, 회의	
13	지배, 통제하다, 억제하다	
14	편리한	
15	대처하다, 극복하다	
16	장식, 훈장	
17	정의, 한정	
18	방향, 지도, 감독	

🎧 **C. Listen, write the word and meaning.** (Track 3)

	Word	Meaning		Word	Meaning
01			10		
02			11		
03			12		
04			13		
05			14		
06			15		
07			16		
08			17		
09			18		

Unit 2

🎧 Listen and repeat. Track 4

01 dislike
[disláik]
v 싫어(미워)하다   to think that somebody / something is unpleasant
She **dislikes** any form of exercise.
그녀는 어떤 형태의 운동이든 싫어한다.

02 distance
[dístəns]
n 거리, 간격   the amount of space between two places or things
It's difficult to find **distances** with one eye closed.
한쪽 눈을 감은 채 사물의 거리감을 알아내는 것은 어렵다.

03 dizzy
[dízi]
a 현기증 나는 / v 현기증 나게 하다   feeling that you are not able to balance
I get easily short of breath and **dizzy**.
나는 자주 숨이 차고 현기증이 납니다.

04 erupt
[irʌ́pt]
v 분출하다   to be thrown out from the volcano
They dread that the volcano may **erupt** again.
그들은 화산이 다시 폭발하지 않을까 무서워하고 있다.

05 evil
[íːvəl]
a 나쁜, 사악한   having a harmful effect; morally bad
In the play Bill is portrayed as an **evil** king.
그 연극에서 빌은 사악한 왕으로 묘사된다.

06 exactly
[igzǽktli]
ad 정확하게, 엄밀히   precisely, completely correct
However, no one knows **exactly** who invented them.
하지만, 누가 만들었는지는 아무도 정확히 알 수 없다.

07 flight
[flait]
n 비상, 비행   the act of flying
Do you have a **flight** this evening?
오늘 저녁에 비행편이 있나요?

08 float
[flout]
v 뜨다, 표류하다   to move slowly on water
The log **floated** down the stream.
통나무는 개울을 떠내려갔다.

09 fold
[fould]
v 접다   to bend something so that one part lies on top of another part
He **folded** the letter before putting it into the envelope.
그는 편지를 봉투에 넣기 전에 그것을 접었다.

key words
throw v 발사하다, 던지다 / dread v 두려워하다 / portray v 그리다, 묘사하다 / stream n 시내, 개울

🎧 Listen and repeat. Track 5

10 graze [greiz]
v 풀을 뜯어 먹(게 하)다 to eat grass that is growing in a field
There were cows **grazing** by the river.
소들이 강가에서 풀을 뜯어 먹고 있었다.

11 grief [gri:f]
n 슬픔, 비탄 great sadness
He showed **grief** over his daughter's death.
그는 딸의 죽음으로 슬픔에 빠졌다.

12 handicap [hǽndikæ̀p]
n 신체장애, 불이익 impossible to use a particular part of body
The loss of my arm hasn't been as great a **handicap** as you have expected.
내가 팔을 잃은 것은 네가 생각했던 것만큼 큰 신체장애가 되지 않는다.

13 identification [aidèntəfikéiʃən]
n 신분증명(서), 신원확인 the process of recognizing who somebody is
A passport is a traveler's primary means of **identification**.
여권은 여행자들이 신분을 증명할 수 있는 가장 중요한 수단이다.

14 ignore [ignɔ́:r]
v 무시하다 to pay no attention to somebody / something
She **ignored** her doctor's advice about drinking and smoking less.
그녀는 술과 담배를 줄이라는 의사의 충고를 무시했다.

15 imaginary [imǽdʒənèri]
a 상상의, 가상의 existing only in your mind
What is an '**Imaginary** Field Trip'?
'가상 현장 학습'이 무엇인가요?

16 kingdom [kíŋdəm]
n 왕국 a country ruled by a king
Its name came from a **kingdom** of ancient Korea.
이것의 이름은 고대 한국의 한 왕국에서부터 전해져 내려왔다.

17 knot [nat]
n 매듭 / v 매다 a join made by tying together two pieces
If you tie the **knot** that way, it might not be safe.
매듭을 그런 식으로 맨다면, 튼튼하지 않을 수도 있다.

18 knowledge [nάlidʒ]
n 지식, 학식 the information that you gain through education
All our **knowledge** is derived from experience.
우리의 지식은 모두 경험에서부터 온다.

key words
recognize v 알아보다, 인지하다 / derive v 끌어내다, ~에서 나와있다

Unit 2

Exercise

A. Complete the sentence.

1. In the play Bill is portrayed as an _____ king.
   그 연극에서 빌은 사악한 왕으로 묘사된다.

2. It's difficult to find _____ with one eye closed.
   한쪽 눈을 감은 채 사물의 거리감을 알아내는 것은 어렵다.

3. She _____ her doctor's advice about drinking and smoking less.
   그녀는 술과 담배를 줄이라는 의사의 충고를 무시했다.

4. They dread that the volcano may _____ again.
   그들은 화산이 다시 폭발하지 않을까 무서워하고 있다.

5. However, no one knows _____ who invented them.
   하지만, 누가 만들었는지는 아무도 정확히 알 수 없다.

6. The log _____ down the stream.
   통나무는 개울을 떠내려갔다.

7. There were cows _____ by the river.
   소들이 강가에서 풀을 뜯어 먹고 있었다.

8. All our _____ is derived from experience.
   우리의 지식은 모두 경험에서부터 온다.

9. I get easily short of breath and _____.
   나는 자주 숨이 차고 현기증이 납니다.

10. He _____ the letter before putting it into the envelope.
    그는 편지를 봉투에 넣기 전에 그것을 접었다.

11. She _____ any form of exercise.
    그녀는 어떤 형태의 운동이든 싫어한다.

12. He showed _____ over his daughter's death.
    그는 딸의 죽음으로 슬픔에 빠졌다.

13. The loss of my arm hasn't been as great a _____ as you have expected.
    내가 팔을 잃은 것은 네가 생각했던 것만큼 큰 신체장애가 되지 않는다.

14. A passport is a traveler's primary means of _____.
    여권은 여행자들이 신분을 증명할 수 있는 가장 중요한 수단이다.

15. Do you have a _____ this evening?
    오늘 저녁에 비행편이 있나요?

16. What is an '_____ Field Trip'?
    '가상 현장 학습'이 무엇인가요?

17. Its name came from a _____ of ancient Korea.
    이것의 이름은 고대 한국의 한 왕국에서부터 전해져 내려왔다.

18. If you tie the _____ that way, it might not be safe.
    매듭을 그런 식으로 맨다면, 튼튼하지 않을 수도 있다.

Hint

| handicap | imaginary | fold | dislike | kingdom | dizzy | float | knot | identification |
| exactly | knowledge | erupt | graze | distance | flight | evil | ignore | grief |

Exercise

B. Fill in the word and meaning.

	Word	Meaning
01	dizzy	
02	evil	
03	dislike	
04	flight	
05	graze	
06	distance	
07	ignore	
08	knot	
09	erupt	
10	knowledge	
11	identification	
12	kingdom	
13	exactly	
14	imaginary	
15	grief	
16	fold	
17	handicap	
18	float	

	Meaning	Word
01	싫어(미워)하다	
02	거리, 간격	
03	현기증 나는, 현기증 나게 하다	
04	분출하다	
05	나쁜, 사악한	
06	정확하게, 엄밀히	
07	비상, 비행	
08	뜨다, 표류하다	
09	접다	
10	풀을 뜯어 먹(게 하)다	
11	슬픔, 비탄	
12	신체장애, 불이익	
13	신분증명, 신원확인	
14	무시하다	
15	상상의, 가상의	
16	왕국	
17	매듭, 매다	
18	지식, 학식	

🎧 **C. Listen, write the word and meaning.** (Track 6)

	Word	Meaning		Word	Meaning
01			10		
02			11		
03			12		
04			13		
05			14		
06			15		
07			16		
08			17		
09			18		

Review 1

A. Read and fill in the word and meaning.

word	definition	meaning
	cows and bulls that are kept as farm animals	
	a large church in which monks or nuns live	
	instructions about how to do something or get to a place	
	to show an event by doing something special on it	
	in or to another country or countries	
	connected with chemistry	
	to deal successfully with something difficult	
	to produce flowers	
	useful, easy to do	
	a large official meeting to discuss important matters	
	wanting something very much	
	the act of managing something	
	the act of stating the meanings of words and phrases	
	suitable in a particular situation	
	the style in which something is decorated	
	empty printed or recorded on it	
	all the people who are watching a play, concert, speech, etc	
	to wake up, not asleep	

Hint
bloom   conference   celebrate   awake   cattle   chemical   abroad   blank   direction
control   decoration   definition   abbey   cope   anxious   audience   apt   convenient

B. Read and fill in the word and meaning.

word	definition	meaning
dislike	to think that somebody / something is unpleasant	
identification	the process of recognizing who somebody is	
grief	great sadness	
handicap	impossible to use a particular part of body	
ignore	to pay no attention to somebody / something	
distance	the amount of space between two places or things	
graze	to eat grass that is growing in a field	
fold	to bend something so that one part lies on top of another part	
imaginary	existing only in your mind	
dizzy	feeling that you are not able to balance	
kingdom	a country ruled by a king	
erupt	to be thrown out from the volcano	
float	to move slowly on water	
knot	a join made by tying together two pieces	
flight	the act of flying	
evil	having a harmful effect; morally bad	
knowledge	the information that you gain through education	
exactly	precisely, completely correct	

Hint

handicap imaginary fold dislike kingdom dizzy float knot identification
exactly knowledge erupt graze distance flight evil ignore grief

Unit 3

🎧 Listen and repeat. Track 7

01 load [loud]
n 짐 / v 짐을 싣다   something that is waiting to be carried
The donkey carries a heavy **load** on his back.
당나귀는 등에 무거운 짐을 실어 나른다.

02 local [lóukəl]
a 장소의, 지방의   of a particular place near you
The man is reading a **local** newspaper near a door.
그 남자는 문 옆에서 지방 신문을 읽고 있다.

03 lower [lóuər]
v 낮추다 / a 낮은(아래)쪽의   to make something less in amount, quality, etc
Could you **lower** the price a little?
가격을 약간 낮추어 주실 수 있나요?

04 message [mésidʒ]
n 전갈, 통신(문)   a written piece of information that you send to a person
Please call me as soon as possible or leave a **message**.
가능한 한 빨리 나에게 전화를 주던지 메시지를 남겨 줘.

05 microphone [máikrəfòun]
n 마이크   an electrical equipment that is used for making sounds louder
The **microphone** doesn't seem to be working.
마이크가 작동하지 않는 것 같아요.

06 microscope [máikrəskòup]
n 현미경   an equipment that makes very small objects look big
This **microscope** magnifies an object up to eight hundred times.
이 현미경은 물체를 800배까지 확대한다.

07 normal [nɔ́ːrməl]
a 정상의, 표준적인   standard, usual or ordinary
Your blood pressure is just a little above **normal**.
당신의 혈압은 정상보다 조금 높습니다.

08 northern [nɔ́ːrðərn]
a 북쪽에 있는   in or from the north of a place
The **northern** part of the country is mountainous.
그 나라의 북부는 산이 많다.

09 notice [nóutis]
n 주의, 주목 / v 알아채다, 주의하다   to pay attention to or knowing about something
She **noticed** his pretended sympathy.
그녀는 그의 거짓 동정을 눈치 챘다.

key words
work v 작동하다 / magnify v 확대하다 / pressure n 압력
mountainous a 산이 많은, 산지의 / pretended a 거짓의, 겉치레의 / sympathy n 동정

🎧 Listen and repeat. Track 8

10 patch
[pætʃ]
n 헝겊조각, 부스러기   a piece of material that you use to cover a hole in clothes
I sewed **patches** on the knees of my jeans.
나는 청바지의 무릎부분에 헝겊 조각을 덧대었다.

11 patient
[péiʃənt]
n 환자 / a 인내심이 강한   a person who is receiving medical treatment
More than fifteen **patients** were waiting to see the doctor.
의사의 진찰을 받기 위해 기다리는 환자들이 15명도 넘었다.

12 percent
[pərsént]
n 퍼센트   one part in every hundred
You get 10 **percent** off if you pay cash.
현금으로 지불하시면 10퍼센트 싸게 드립니다.

13 predict
[pridíkt]
v 예언하다, 예보하다   to say that something will happen in the future
The man is **predicting** the future.
그 남자는 미래를 예언하고 있다.

14 prepare
[pripɛ́ər]
v 준비하다   to get ready
The supervisor is going to **prepare** a new schedule.
감독자는 새로운 스케줄을 준비하려고 한다.

15 preserve
[prizə́:rv]
v 보전하다, 보호하다   to keep something safe
Salt is used to **preserve** food.
소금은 음식물을 보존하는 데 사용된다.

16 rapidly
[rǽpidli]
ad 빠르게, 재빨리   happening very quickly
The postwar birth rate increased **rapidly**.
전후의 출생률은 급속히 증가했다.

17 rather
[rǽðər]
ad 오히려, 다소   quite; to some extent
They would **rather** use a machine on it.
그들은 오히려 기계를 사용해 그 일을 하는 것이 낫다.

18 reach
[ri:tʃ]
v 도착하다, 뻗치다   to arrive at a place
The person who first **reaches** the finish line is the winner.
결승선에 먼저 도착하는 사람이 승자가 된다.

---

key words
sew v 꿰매다, 박다 / supervisor n 감독자 / postwar a 전후의

Exercise

A. Complete the sentence.

1. The _____ doesn't seem to be working.
   마이크가 작동하지 않는 것 같아요.

2. The donkey carries a heavy _____ on his back.
   당나귀는 등에 무거운 짐을 실어 나른다.

3. I sewed _____ on the knees of my jeans.
   나는 청바지의 무릎부분에 헝겊 조각을 덧대었다.

4. She _____ his pretended sympathy.
   그녀는 그의 거짓 동정을 눈치 챘다.

5. Salt is used to _____ food.
   소금은 음식물을 보존하는 데 사용된다.

6. Please call me as soon as possible or leave a _____.
   가능한 한 빨리 나에게 전화를 주던지 메시지를 남겨 줘.

7. The postwar birth rate increased _____.
   전후의 출생률은 급속히 증가했다.

8. This _____ magnifies an object up to eight hundred times.
   이 현미경은 물체를 800배까지 확대한다.

9. They would _____ use a machine on it.
   그들은 오히려 기계를 사용해 그 일을 하는 것이 낫다.

10. Your blood pressure is just a little above _____.
    당신의 혈압은 정상보다 조금 높습니다.

11. The _____ part of the country is mountainous.
    그 나라의 북부는 산이 많다.

12. Could you _____ the price a little?
    가격을 약간 낮추어 주실 수 있나요?

13. More than fifteen _____ were waiting to see the doctor.
    의사의 진찰을 받기 위해 기다리는 환자들이 15명도 넘었다.

14. You get 10 _____ off if you pay cash.
    현금으로 지불하시면 10퍼센트 싸게 드립니다.

15. The man is _____ the future.
    그 남자는 미래를 예언하고 있다.

16. The man is reading a _____ newspaper near a door.
    그 남자는 문 옆에서 지방 신문을 읽고 있다.

17. The supervisor is going to _____ a new schedule.
    감독자는 새로운 스케줄을 준비하려고 한다.

18. The person who first _____ the finish line is the winner.
    결승선에 먼저 도착하는 사람이 승자가 된다.

Hint

| preserve | rather | normal | patient | local | reach | northern | microphone | predict |
| message | prepare | load | notice | lower | rapidly | percent | microscope | patch |

Unit 3

Exercise

B. Fill in the word and meaning.

	Word	Meaning
01	normal	
02	patient	
03	preserve	
04	load	
05	prepare	
06	notice	
07	rapidly	
08	local	
09	predict	
10	microphone	
11	northern	
12	microscope	
13	reach	
14	patch	
15	message	
16	rather	
17	percent	
18	lower	

	Meaning	Word
01	짐, 짐을 싣다	
02	장소의, 지방의	
03	낮추다, 낮은(아래)쪽의	
04	전갈, 통신(문)	
05	마이크	
06	현미경	
07	정상의, 표준적인	
08	북쪽에 있는	
09	주의, 주목, 알아채다, 주의하다	
10	헝겊조각, 부스러기	
11	환자, 인내심이 강한	
12	퍼센트	
13	예언하다, 예보하다	
14	준비하다	
15	보전하다, 보호하다	
16	빠르게, 재빨리	
17	오히려, 다소	
18	도착하다, 뻗치다	

C. Listen, write the word and meaning. (Track 9)

	Word	Meaning		Word	Meaning
01			10		
02			11		
03			12		
04			13		
05			14		
06			15		
07			16		
08			17		
09			18		

Unit 4

🎧 Listen and repeat. (Track 10)

01 request [rikwést]
n 요구 / v 요구하다　an act of asking for something
I'm going to make a **request** for a larger desk.
나는 더 큰 책상을 요구할 것이다.

02 require [rikwáiə:r]
v 요구하다, 필요로 하다　to need something; to demand something
A more active person will **require** even more water.
보다 활동적인 사람은 더 많은 물을 필요로 한다.

03 rescue [réskju:]
n 구조 / v 구조하다　to save somebody from a danger
He **rescued** a child from drowning.
그는 물에 빠진 아이를 구조했다.

04 scary [skéəri]
a 무서운　making you feel afraid
Was the movie as **scary** as people say?
영화가 사람들이 말하는 것처럼 무섭던가요?

05 scientific [sàiəntífik]
a 과학적인　connected with science
Hangeul is the most **scientific** writing system in the world.
한글은 세계에서 가장 과학적인 문자 체계이다.

06 scream [skri:m]
v 소리치다　to cry out loudly in a high voice
The girl **screamed** and yelled in pain.
그 소녀는 아파서 비명을 질렀다.

07 soldier [sóuldʒə:r]
n 군인　a member of an army
Soldiers sank exhausted on the ground all together.
군인들은 모두 지쳐서 땅 위에 늘어져 버렸다.

08 soul [soul]
n 영혼, 정신　the inner part of a person containing their deepest thoughts
Body and **soul** are indivisible relation.
육체와 영혼은 불가분의 관계이다.

09 specialist [spéʃəlist]
n 전문가, 전문의　a person with deep knowledge of a particular subject
She's a **specialist** in cattle disease.
그녀는 가축의 병에 관한 전문가이다.

---

key words
drown v 물에 빠지다 / yell v 고함치다 / sink v 쓰러지다, 기진하다
exhausted a 지칠 대로 지친 / indivisible a 불가분의 / disease n 질병 / cattle n 가축, 축우

🎧 Listen and repeat. (Track 11)

10 stream [striːm]
v 흐르다   to flow in large amounts
Tears were **streaming** down his face.
그의 얼굴에 눈물이 흘러 내렸다.

11 stretch [stretʃ]
v 뻗다, 늘이다   to pull something so that it becomes longer or wider
The rubber band **stretches**.
고무 밴드는 늘어난다.

12 structure [strʌ́ktʃər]
n 구조, 조직   the way that the parts of something are put together
A lot of the park **structures** are built of wood, steel and glass.
많은 공원 구조물들이 목재, 철강, 유리로 구성되어 있다.

13 textbook [tékstbùk]
n 교과서   a book that teaches a subject in schools
The **textbook** was adopted in several schools.
그 교과서는 몇몇 학교에서 채택되었다.

14 thread [θred]
n 실, 바느질 실   a long thin piece of cotton, wool, etc.
The **thread** is tangled.
실이 엉클어졌다.

15 threaten [θrétn]
v 협박하다, 위협하다   to warn that you may hurt, kill somebody
There are many issues which **threaten** world peace.
세계 평화를 위협하는 문제들이 많다.

16 twist [twist]
v 뒤틀다, 꼬다   to bend or turn something into a particular shape
She **twisted** her long hair into a knot.
그녀는 긴 머리카락을 꼬아서 매듭 지었다.

17 upset [ʌpsét]
v 뒤집어엎다, 당황케 하다   to make somebody worry or feel unhappy
She was **upset** by his impolite remarks.
그녀는 그의 무례한 말들에 당황해했다.

18 upside [ʌ́psàid]
n 윗면, 위쪽   the top part of something
You should hold the **upside** of the picture.
당신은 그림의 위쪽을 잡아야 합니다.

---

key words
adopt v 채택하다 / tangle v 엉키다 / knot n 매듭 / impolite a 무례한 / remark n 소견, 비평

Unit 4

Exercise

A. Complete the sentence.

1. Was the movie as _____ as people say?
   영화가 사람들이 말하는 것처럼 무섭던가요?

2. I'm going to make a _____ for a larger desk.
   나는 더 큰 책상을 요구할 것이다.

3. The rubber band _____.
   고무 밴드는 늘어난다.

4. She was _____ by his impolite remarks.
   그녀는 그의 무례한 말들에 당황해 했다.

5. A more active person will _____ even more water.
   보다 활동적인 사람은 더 많은 물을 필요로 한다.

6. _____ sank exhausted on the ground all together.
   군인들은 모두 지쳐서 땅 위에 늘어져 버렸다.

7. He _____ a child from drowning.
   그는 물에 빠진 아이를 구조했다.

8. There are many issues which _____ world peace.
   세계 평화를 위협하는 문제들이 많다.

9. Hangeul is the most _____ writing system in the world.
   한글은 세계에서 가장 과학적인 문자 체계이다.

10. She's a _____ in cattle disease.
    그녀는 가축의 병에 관한 전문가이다.

11. A lot of the park _____ are built of wood, steel and glass.
    많은 공원 구조물들이 목재, 철강, 유리로 구성되어 있다.

12. The _____ was adopted in several schools.
    그 교과서는 몇몇 학교에서 채택되었다.

13. The girl _____ and yelled in pain.
    그 소녀는 아파서 비명을 질렀다.

14. She _____ her long hair into a knot.
    그녀는 긴 머리카락을 꼬아서 매듭 지었다.

15. Tears were _____ down his face.
    그의 얼굴에 눈물이 흘러 내렸다.

16. The _____ is tangled.
    실이 엉클어졌다.

17. Body and _____ are indivisible relation.
    육체와 영혼은 불가분의 관계이다.

18. You should hold the _____ of the picture.
    당신은 그림의 위쪽을 잡아야 합니다.

Hint

structure   soul   twist   scary   request   scream   thread   stream   threaten
require   upset   soldier   rescue   stretch   textbook scientific upside   specialist

Exercise

B. Fill in the word and meaning.

	Word	Meaning
01	rescue	
02	scientific	
03	request	
04	stream	
05	structure	
06	require	
07	soul	
08	textbook	
09	upside	
10	soldier	
11	thread	
12	specialist	
13	upset	
14	twist	
15	scream	
16	threaten	
17	stretch	
18	scary	

	Meaning	Word
01	요구, 요구하다	
02	요구하다, 필요로 하다	
03	구조, 구조하다	
04	무서운	
05	과학적인	
06	소리치다	
07	군인	
08	영혼, 정신	
09	전문가, 전문의	
10	흐르다	
11	뻗다, 늘이다	
12	구조, 조직	
13	교과서	
14	실, 바느질 실	
15	협박하다, 위협하다	
16	뒤틀다, 꼬다	
17	뒤집어엎다, 당황케 하다	
18	윗면, 위쪽	

🎧 C. Listen, write the word and meaning. (Track 12)

	Word	Meaning		Word	Meaning
01			10		
02			11		
03			12		
04			13		
05			14		
06			15		
07			16		
08			17		
09			18		

Review 2

A. Read and fill in the word and meaning.

word	definition	meaning
	to pay attention to or knowing about something	
	of a particular place near you	
	a piece of material that you use to cover a hole in clothes	
	to arrive at a place	
	something that is waiting to be carried	
	a person who is receiving medical treatment	
	quite; to some extent	
	to make something less in amount, quality, etc	
	happening very quickly	
	one part in every hundred	
	a written piece of information that you send to a person	
	to keep something safe	
	an electrical equipment that is used for making sounds louder	
	in or from the north of a place	
	to say that something will happen in the future	
	an equipment that makes very small objects look big	
	to get ready	
	standard, usual or ordinary	

Hint

| preserve | rather | normal | patient | local | reach | northern | microphone | predict |
| message | prepare | load | notice | lower | rapidly | percent | microscope | patch |

B. Read and fill in the word and meaning.

word	definition	meaning
	an act of asking for something	
	to flow in large amounts	
	a person with deep knowledge of a particular subject	
	the top part of something	
	to need something, to demand something	
	the inner part of a person containing their deepest thoughts	
	a book that teaches a subject in schools	
	to save somebody from a danger	
	the way that the parts of something are put together	
	a long thin piece of cotton, wool, etc.	
	making you feel afraid	
	to warn that you may hurt, kill somebody	
	a member of an army	
	to pull something so that it becomes longer or wider	
	to bend or turn something into a particular shape	
	connected with science	
	to make somebody worry or feel unhappy	
	to cry out loudly in a high voice	

Hint

structure   soul   twist   scary   request   scream   thread   stream   threaten
require   upset   soldier   rescue   stretch   textbook scientific upside   specialist

Unit 5

🎧 Listen and repeat. Track 13

01 academy [əkǽdəmi]
n 학교, 학원   a school for special training
His son is in a military **academy** now.
그의 아들은 지금 육군 사관 학교에 있어요.

02 addition [ədíʃən]
n 추가, 부가   adding something
In **addition**, exercise can help you sleep better at night.
게다가 운동을 하면 밤에 단잠을 잘 수 있다.

03 appointment [əpɔ́intmənt]
n 약속, 임명   an arrangement to see somebody at a particular time
The family is setting up an **appointment**.
가족들이 약속을 정하고 있다.

04 approval [əprúːvəl]
n 찬성, 승인   showing that you think something is good; agreement
Everybody gave their **approval** to the proposal.
모두 그 제안에 찬성을 표했다.

05 bay [bei]
n 만   a part of the coast where the land goes in to form a curve
The sailboats are crossing the **bay**.
돛단배들이 만을 건너고 있다.

06 behavior [bihéivjər]
n 행동, 행실   the way that you act or behave
His **behavior** was nothing short of criminal.
그의 행위는 범죄 행위나 다름없다.

07 boring [bɔ́ːriŋ]
a 지루한, 따분한   not at all interesting
That's the most **boring** book in the world.
그 책은 세상에서 가장 지루한 책이에요.

08 bound [baund]
n 경계, 범위 / **a** ~행의   a line that marks the limits of something and divides it
I saw the **bounds** of heaven and earth.
나는 하늘과 땅의 경계를 보았다.

09 central [séntrəl]
a 중앙의, 중심적인   in the center of something
They bombed the **central** part of the city.
그들은 도시 중심부를 폭격했다.

key words
arrangement **n** 합의 / proposal **n** 제의, 계획 / short **a** 불충분한, 미치지 못하는
criminal **a** 범죄의 / bomb **v** 폭탄을 투하하다

🎧 Listen and repeat. (Track 14)

10 certain [sə́:rtən]
a 확실한, 일정한   completely sure
Officials emphasized that they could not be **certain**.
공무원들은 확신할 수 없다는 점을 강조했다.

11 compact [kəmpǽkt]
n 밀집한 / **n** 압축하다   small or take up very little space
The equipment in that case is packed in a **compact** way.
그 상자 안의 장비는 빽빽하게 담겨있다.

12 complaint [kəmpléint]
n 불평   a statement that you are not satisfied with something
Complaints can also be filed by telephone.
불만 사항은 전화로도 받고 있습니다.

13 correct [kərékt]
a 옳은, 정확한 / **v** 고치다   with no mistakes; right
All your answers were **correct**.
당신이 한 대답이 모두 옳았다.

14 credit [krédit]
n 신용거래, 칭찬 / **n** 믿다   a way of buying goods or services and not paying for them until later
What's the **credit** limit on your **credit** card?
당신의 신용카드의 신용거래 한도는 얼마입니까?

15 cradle [kréidl]
n 요람   a small bed for a baby
She is rocking the baby's **cradle**.
그녀는 아기의 요람을 흔들고 있다.

16 depart [dipá:rt]
v 출발하다   to leave a place at the beginning of a journey
Flight 808 is scheduled to **depart** at 9:00 in the morning.
808기는 오전 9시에 출발할 예정이다.

17 depend [dipénd]
v 의지하다, 믿다   to be trusted; rely on
We **depend** upon the mass media for daily news.
우리는 매일 일어나는 뉴스를 알기 위해 매스컴에 의존한다.

18 depressed [diprést]
a 우울한, 내리 눌린   very unhappy for a long period of time
My boyfriend just broke up with me and I feel **depressed**.
나는 최근에 남자 친구에게 실연을 당해 우울하다.

---

key words
emphasize **v** 강조하다 / file **v** 신청하다 / rock **v** 가볍게 흔들다 / rely **v** 의지하다 / daily **a** 매일의, 날마다의

Unit 5

Exercise

A. Complete the sentence.

1. In _____, exercise can help you sleep better at night.
   게다가 운동을 하면 밤에 단잠을 잘 수 있다.

2. She is rocking the baby's _____.
   그녀는 아기의 요람을 흔들고 있다.

3. That's the most _____ book in the world.
   그 책은 세상에서 가장 지루한 책이에요.

4. What's the _____ limit on your _____ card?
   당신의 신용카드의 신용거래 한도는 얼마입니까?

5. The family is setting up an _____.
   가족들이 약속을 정하고 있다.

6. Flight 808 is scheduled to _____ at 9:00 in the morning.
   808기는 오전 9시에 출발할 예정이다.

7. His _____ was nothing short of criminal.
   그의 행위는 범죄 행위나 다름없다.

8. They bombed the _____ part of the city.
   그들은 도시 중심부를 폭격했다.

9. His son is in a military _____ now.
   그의 아들은 지금 육군 사관 학교에 있어요.

10. Officials emphasized that they could not be _____.
    공무원들은 확신할 수 없다는 점을 강조했다.

11. The equipment in that case is packed in a _____ way.
    그 상자 안의 장비는 빽빽하게 담겨있다.

12. I saw the _____ of heaven and earth.
    나는 하늘과 땅의 경계를 보았다.

13. _____ can also be filed by telephone.
    불만 사항은 전화로도 받고 있습니다.

14. All your answers were _____.
    당신이 한 대답이 모두 옳았다.

15. Everybody gave their _____ to the proposal.
    모두 그 제안에 찬성을 표했다.

16. We _____ upon the mass media for daily news.
    우리는 매일 일어나는 뉴스를 알기 위해 매스컴에 의존한다.

17. The sailboats are crossing the _____.
    돛단배들이 만을 건너고 있다.

18. My boyfriend just broke up with me and I feel _____.
    나는 최근에 남자 친구에게 실연을 당해 우울하다.

Hint

| central | boring | certain | cradle | credit | complaint | bound | academy | depressed |
| addition | depend | correct | bay | approval | behavior | depart | compact | appointment |

Exercise

B. Fill in the word and meaning.

	Word	Meaning
01	bay	
02	complaint	
03	academy	
04	behavior	
05	cradle	
06	addition	
07	correct	
08	boring	
09	depart	
10	bound	
11	approval	
12	credit	
13	depend	
14	compact	
15	depressed	
16	certain	
17	central	
18	appointment	

	Meaning	Word
01	학교, 학원	
02	추가, 부가	
03	약속, 임명	
04	찬성, 승인	
05	만	
06	행동, 행실	
07	지루한, 따분한	
08	경계, 범위, ~행의	
09	중앙의, 중심적인	
10	확실한, 일정한	
11	밀집한, 압축하다	
12	불평	
13	옳은, 정확한, 고치다	
14	신용거래, 칭찬, 믿다	
15	요람	
16	출발하다	
17	의지하다, 믿다	
18	우울한, 내리 눌린	

🎧 **C. Listen, write the word and meaning.** (Track 15)

	Word	Meaning		Word	Meaning
01			10		
02			11		
03			12		
04			13		
05			14		
06			15		
07			16		
08			17		
09			18		

Unit 6

🎧 Listen and repeat. Track 16

01 disagree
[dìsəgríː]
v 의견이 다르다   to have a different opinion
He often **disagrees** with his father about politics.
그는 정치에 관해 그의 아버지와 종종 의견이 다르다.

02 doubt
[daut]
n 의심, 의혹 / v 의심하다   to feel uncertain
He had never **doubted** her support.
그는 그녀의 후원에 대해 의심한 적이 결코 없다.

03 dough
[dou]
n 가루 반죽   a mixture of flour, water, etc.
Gather **dough** into a ball and place it in a greased bowl.
반죽을 둥그렇게 만들어 기름을 두른 그릇에 담는다.

04 exist
[igzíst]
v 존재하다, 생존하다   to be real; to live
Many forms of life **exist** on the ocean floor.
해저에는 많은 종류의 생물이 서식하고 있다.

05 expect
[ikspékt]
v 기대하다   to think that somebody / something will come
She was **expecting** a letter from the bank this morning.
오늘 아침 그녀는 은행에서 올 편지를 기대하고 있었다.

06 experiment
[ikspérəmənt]
n 실험, 시험   a scientific test that is done to get proof of something
The scientist is planning to begin a new **experiment**.
그 과학자는 새로운 실험을 시작할 계획 중이다.

07 force
[fɔːrs]
n 힘, 영향(력)   physical strength or power
The police used **force** to break up the demonstration.
경찰은 시위대를 해산시키기 위해 힘을 사용했다.

08 forecast
[fɔ́ːrkæst]
n 예상, 예보   saying what will probably happen in the future
I don't believe the weather **forecast**.
나는 날씨 예보를 믿지 않는다.

09 forgive
[fəːrgív]
v 용서하다   to stop being angry for something that someone has done wrong
I can't **forgive** his behavior last night.
나는 지난 밤에 그가 한 행동을 용서할 수가 없다.

key words
politics n 정치 / grease v 기름을 바르다 / proof n 증거, 증명 / demonstration n 시위 운동

🎧 Listen and repeat. Track 17

10 frequent
[fríːkwənt]
a 자주 일어나는, 빈번한   to happen often
Fires are **frequent** at this time of the year.
해마다 이맘때면 화재가 빈번하다.

11 harm
[haːrm]
n 해, 손해   damage or injury
Everyone knows the **harm** of tobacco.
담배가 해롭다는 것은 모두가 아는 사실이다.

12 harmful
[háːrmfəl]
a 해로운   causing harm
A sudden drop in temperature is **harmful** to most cereal crops.
기온이 갑자기 떨어지는 일은 대부분의 곡물에게 해롭다.

13 impressive
[imprésiv]
a 인상적인, 감동을 주는   causing a feeling of admiration
His work experience and education are **impressive**.
그의 경력과 학력은 인상적이다.

14 indeed
[indíd]
ad 참으로, 과연   really; certainly
Indeed, I'd like very much to meet him.
사실, 그를 너무 만나고 싶어요.

15 informal
[infɔ́ːrməl]
a 비공식의, 약식의   suitable for a relaxed occasion
Our meetings are **informal**, and usually well-attended.
저희 회의는 비공식 행사이며 대개 참석률이 높습니다.

16 labor
[léibər]
n 노동, 노동자   work, usually of a hard, physical kind or workers
Nobody now despises honest **labor**.
오늘날 정직한 노동을 우습게 보는 사람은 없다.

17 lamb
[læm]
n 어린양   a young sheep
He is as mild as a **lamb**.
그는 양처럼 순하다.

18 lawn
[lɔːn]
n 잔디(밭)   an area of grass in a garden or park
Landscapers are putting in a new **lawn**.
조경사들이 새 잔디를 심는 중이다.

key words
admiration **n** 감탄 / suitable **a** 적당한 / well-attended **a** 출석률이 좋은
despise **v** 경멸하다, 멸시하다 / landscaper **n** 조경사

Exercise

A. Complete the sentence.

1. Gather _____ into a ball and place it in a greased bowl.
   반죽을 둥그렇게 만들어 기름을 두른 그릇에 담는다.

2. Everyone knows the _____ of tobacco.
   담배가 해롭다는 것은 모두가 아는 사실이다.

3. Landscapers are putting in a new _____.
   조경사들이 새 잔디를 심는 중이다.

4. She was _____ a letter from the bank this morning.
   오늘 아침 그녀는 은행에서 올 편지를 기대하고 있었다.

5. He often _____ with his father about politics.
   그는 정치에 관해 그의 아버지와 종종 의견이 다르다.

6. His work experience and education are _____.
   그의 경력과 학력은 인상적이다.

7. The scientist is planning to begin a new _____.
   그 과학자는 새로운 실험을 시작할 계획 중이다.

8. He is as mild as a _____.
   그는 양처럼 순하다.

9. The police used _____ to break up the demonstration.
   경찰은 시위대를 해산시키기 위해 힘을 사용했다.

10. He had never _____ her support.
    그는 그녀의 후원에 대해 의심한 적이 결코 없다.

11. I don't believe the weather _____.
    나는 날씨 예보를 믿지 않는다.

12. Fires are _____ at this time of the year.
    해마다 이맘때면 화재가 빈번하다.

13. _____, I'd like very much to meet him.
    사실, 그를 너무 만나고 싶어요.

14. A sudden drop in temperature is _____ to most cereal crops.
    기온이 갑자기 떨어지는 일은 대부분의 곡물에게 해롭다.

15. Our meetings are _____, and usually well-attended.
    저희 회의는 비공식 행사이며 대개 참석률이 높습니다.

16. I can't _____ his behavior last night.
    나는 지난 밤에 그가 한 행동을 용서할 수가 없다.

17. Many forms of life _____ on the ocean floor.
    해저에는 많은 종류의 생물이 서식하고 있다.

18. Nobody now despises honest _____.
    오늘날 정직한 노동을 우습게 보는 사람은 없다.

Hint

forecast lamb   dough   indeed   force   exist   disagree   harmful   frequent
informal forgive expect   doubt   lawn   harm   labor   impressive experiment

Exercise

B. Fill in the word and meaning.

	Word	Meaning
01	expect	
02	disagree	
03	frequent	
04	forecast	
05	indeed	
06	doubt	
07	forgive	
08	informal	
09	force	
10	lamb	
11	harmful	
12	lawn	
13	experiment	
14	labor	
15	impressive	
16	exist	
17	harm	
18	dough	

	Meaning	Word
01	의견이 다르다	
02	의심, 의혹, 의심하다	
03	가루 반죽	
04	존재하다, 생존하다	
05	기대하다	
06	실험, 시험	
07	힘, 영향(력)	
08	예상, 예보	
09	용서하다	
10	빈번한	
11	해, 손해	
12	해로운	
13	인상적인, 감동을 주는	
14	참으로, 과연	
15	비공식의, 약식의	
16	노동, 노동자	
17	어린양	
18	잔디(밭)	

C. Listen, write the word and meaning. (Track 18)

	Word	Meaning		Word	Meaning
01			10		
02			11		
03			12		
04			13		
05			14		
06			15		
07			16		
08			17		
09			18		

Review 3

A. Read and fill in the word and meaning.

word	definition	meaning
	a line that marks the limits of something and divides it	
	a small bed for a baby	
	in the center of something	
	adding something	
	not at all interesting	
	a school for special training	
	completely sure	
	to leave a place at the beginning of a journey	
	a way of buying goods or services and not paying for them until later	
	an arrangement to see somebody at a particular time	
	the way that you act or behave	
	small or take up very little space	
	showing that you think something is good; agreement	
	to be trusted; rely on	
	a statement that you are not satisfied with something	
	a part of the coast where the land goes in to form a curve	
	with no mistakes; right	
	very unhappy for a long period of time	

Hint

central   boring   certain   cradle   credit   complaint   bound   academy   depressed
addition   depend   correct   bay   approval   behavior   depart   compact   appointment

B. Read and fill in the word and meaning.

word	definition	meaning
	saying what will probably happen in the future	
	to happen often	
	to stop being angry for something that someone has done wrong	
	damage or injury	
	to have a different opinion	
	really; certainly	
	a scientific test that is done to get proof of something	
	physical strength or power	
	causing harm	
	causing a feeling of admiration	
	to think that somebody / something will come	
	work, usually of a hard, physical kind or workers	
	suitable for a relaxed occasion	
	a young sheep	
	to feel uncertain	
	an area of grass in a garden or park	
	to be real; to live	
	a mixture of flour, water, etc.	

Hint
forecast lamb dough indeed force exist disagree harmful frequent
informal forgive expect doubt lawn harm labor impressive experiment

Unit 7

🎧 Listen and repeat. Track 19

01 loyal [lɔ́iəl]
a 성실한, 충실한   remaining faithful to somebody / something
Because they're **loyal** to their master.
그것들은 주인에게 충성스럽기 때문이야.

02 lump [lʌmp]
n 덩어리, 혹   a piece of something hard or solid
There were **lumps** in the sauce.
소스 속에 덩어리들이 있었다.

03 lunar [lú:nər]
a 달의, 태음의   connected with the moon
A **lunar** halo signifies rain.
달무리는 비가 올 징조이다.

04 mild [maild]
a 온순한, 따뜻한   not very cold, and therefore pleasant
Italy has a **mild** climate.
이탈리아의 날씨는 온화하다.

05 mission [míʃən]
n 임무, 사명   an important official job that a person is given to do
Our **mission** is to promote peace among the nations.
국제 평화를 촉진하는 것이 우리의 사명이다.

06 mistake [mistéik]
n 잘못, 틀림   an action that is not correct
I made a serious **mistake**.
나는 중대한 실수를 했다.

07 obey [oubéi]
v 복종하다   to do what you are told to do
I cannot **obey** him in every particular.
그 사람의 명령을 하나에서 열까지 다 복종할 수는 없다.

08 occupation [àkjəpéiʃən]
n 직업, 업무   a job or profession
Please state your **occupation** on the form.
그 양식에 당신의 직업을 기입해 주세요.

09 offer [ɔ́(:)fər]
v 제공하다 / **n** 제안, 제공   to say that you are willing to give something
Tours of Mozart's birthplace are **offered** every half hour.
모차르트 생가를 방문하는 관광은 30분마다 제공된다.

key words
remain **v** 남다 / halo **n** 무리 / signify **v** ~의 전조가 되다 / promote **v** 진전시키다 / birthplace **n** 출생지

🎧 Listen and repeat. (Track 20)

10 personal [pə́ːrsənəl]
a 개인의, 본인 스스로의   your own
Being overweight is not simply a **personal** problem.
비만은 단지 개인적인 문제만이 아닙니다.

11 phrase [freiz]
n 구, 관용구   a group of words without a finite verb
This **phrase** may be understood when it is read from the bottom up.
이 구절은 거꾸로부터 읽어야 이해가 된다.

12 pirate [páiərət]
n 해적   a person on a ship who attacks other ships at sea
Pirates pillaged the towns along the coast.
해적들이 연안의 도시들을 노략질하였다.

13 press [pres]
v 누르다, 강조하다   to push something closely
Press a button, **press** the pedals, and turn the wheel to test them.
단추를 누르고 페달을 밟고 휠을 돌려 테스트하십시오.

14 prize [praiz]
n 상품, 상   an award that is given to a person who wins a competition
He won the first **prize** in the essay contest.
그는 현상 논문에서 1등 상을 탔어.

15 probable [prábəbəl]
a 있음직한, 예상되는   likely to happen, to be true
What is the **probable** cost?
비용이 어느 정도로 예상됩니까?

16 reaction [riːǽkʃən]
n 반응, 반작용   what you do as a result of something that has happened
The common **reaction** to jokes is to laugh.
농담에 대한 일반적인 반응은 웃는 것이다.

17 reality [riːǽləti]
n 진실, 사실   the true situation that actually exist
It is sometimes hard to face **reality**.
때로는 진실을 직시하기가 어렵다.

18 recipe [résəpìː]
n 처방(전), 조리법   a set of instructions that tells you how to cook something
One banana and five strawberries are needed in the **recipe**.
바나나 1개와 딸기 5개의 과일이 이 요리법에 필요하다.

key words
overweight a 중량이 초과된 / finite a 정형의 / pillage v 약탈하다 / face v 직시하다

Unit 7

Exercise

A. Complete the sentence.

1. Because they're _____ to their master.
   그것들은 주인에게 충성스럽기 때문이야.

2. Italy has a _____ climate.
   이탈리아의 날씨는 온화하다.

3. He won the first _____ in the essay contest.
   그는 현상 논문에서 1등 상을 탔다.

4. Our _____ is to promote peace among the nations.
   국제 평화를 촉진하는 것이 우리의 사명이다.

5. Being overweight is not simply a _____ problem.
   비만은 단지 개인적인 문제만이 아닙니다.

6. I cannot _____ him in every particular.
   그 사람의 명령을 하나에서 열까지 다 복종할 수는 없다.

7. _____ pillaged the towns along the coast.
   해적들이 연안의 도시들을 노략질하였다.

8. I made a serious _____.
   나는 중대한 실수를 했다.

9. Please state your _____ on the form.
   그 양식에 당신의 직업을 기입해 주세요.

10. Tours of Mozart's birthplace are _____ every half hour.
    모차르트 생가를 방문하는 관광은 30분마다 제공된다.

11. This _____ may be understood when it is read from the bottom up.
    이 구절은 거꾸로부터 읽어야 이해가 된다.

12. It is sometimes hard to face _____.
    때로는 진실을 직시하기가 어렵다.

13. There were _____ in the sauce.
    소스 속에 덩어리들이 있었다.

14. _____ a button, _____ the pedals, and turn the wheel to test them.
    단추를 누르고 페달을 밟고 휠을 돌려 테스트하십시오.

15. What is the _____ cost?
    비용이 어느 정도로 예상됩니까?

16. The common _____ to jokes is to laugh.
    농담에 대한 일반적인 반응은 웃는 것이다.

17. A _____ halo signifies rain.
    달무리는 비가 올 징조이다.

18. One banana and five strawberries are needed in the _____.
    바나나 1개와 딸기 5개의 과일이 이 요리법에 필요하다.

Hint

| personal | obey | prize | mild | probable | lump | phrase | mission | loyal |
| reaction | lunar | press | offer | occupation | recipe | mistake | pirate | reality |

Exercise

B. Fill in the word and meaning.

	Word	Meaning
01	mission	
02	loyal	
03	press	
04	offer	
05	prize	
06	mild	
07	reaction	
08	occupation	
09	probable	
10	lunar	
11	reality	
12	personal	
13	recipe	
14	pirate	
15	mistake	
16	phrase	
17	obey	
18	lump	

	Meaning	Word
01	성실한, 충실한	
02	덩어리, 혹	
03	달의, 태음의	
04	온순한, 따뜻한	
05	임무, 사명	
06	잘못, 틀림	
07	복종하다	
08	직업, 업무	
09	제공하다, 제안, 제공	
10	개인의, 본인 스스로의	
11	구, 관용구	
12	해적	
13	누르다, 강조하다	
14	상품, 상	
15	있음직한, 예상되는	
16	반응, 반작용	
17	진실, 사실	
18	처방(전), 조리법	

🎧 C. Listen, write the word and meaning. (Track 21)

	Word	Meaning		Word	Meaning
01			10		
02			11		
03			12		
04			13		
05			14		
06			15		
07			16		
08			17		
09			18		

Unit 8

🎧 Listen and repeat. Track 22

01 response [rispáns]
n 응답, 반응   a spoken answer or a reaction to something
We look forward to your prompt **response**.
당신의 신속한 응답을 기대합니다.

02 result [rizʌ́lt]
n 결과, 성과   something that happens because of something else
The **result** was better than I had expected.
그 결과는 나의 예상 보다 좋았다.

03 reuse [ri:jú:z]
v 다시 이용하다, 재생하다   to use something again
We help communities reduce, **reuse** or recycle unwanted materials.
우리는 지역 사회의 쓰레기들을 줄이고 재생하고 재활용할 수 있도록 도울 것입니다.

04 seal [si:l]
n 바다표범   a sea animal that eats fish and lives around coasts
Seals are awkward on land but graceful in the water.
바다표범은 육지에서는 꼴사납지만 물속에서는 우아하다.

05 secretary [sékrətèri]
n 비서, 서기   a person who works in an office for another person
Have you met our new **secretary**?
새로 온 비서 만나 봤어요?

06 senseless [sénslis]
a 무감각의, 인사불성의   without feeling; unconscious
He knocked a person **senseless**.
그는 어떤 사람을 인성불성이 되도록 때렸다.

07 spank [spæŋk]
v 찰싹 때리다   to hit somebody on their bottom as a punishment
I'll come up there and **spank** you.
내가 가서 너를 때려줄 거야.

08 species [spí:ʃi(:)z]
n 종류, 종   a group into which animals, plants, etc.
Every year some of these **species** disappear.
해마다 이들 종들 중 일부는 멸종한다.

09 spicy [spáisi]
a 향신료를 넣은, 향긋한   strongly flavored with spices
The cat seemed to hate **spicy** foods.
고양이는 향신료를 넣은 음식을 싫어하는 듯 했다.

---

key words
prompt a 신속한 / awkward a 섣부른, 눈치 없는 / knock v 때리다 / disappear v 사라지다

🎧 Listen and repeat. (Track 23)

10 subject [sʌ́bdʒikt]
n 주제, 과목   an area of knowledge studied in a school
We learn many **subjects** in school.
우리는 학교에서 여러 과목을 배웁니다.

11 subtract [səbtrǽkt]
v 빼다, 감하다   to take a number or an amount away from others
Subtract the smaller number from the larger number.
큰 숫자에서 작은 숫자를 빼라.

12 succeed [səksí:d]
v 성공하다   to achieve something that you have been trying to do
It is surely no accident that he **succeeded**.
그의 성공은 결코 우연이 아니다.

13 tightly [taitli]
ad 단단히   closely and firmly
She kept her eyes **tightly** closed.
그녀는 두 눈을 단단히 감고 있었다.

14 tone [toun]
n 음질, 음색, 어조   the quality of somebody's voice
He said it in an angry **tone**.
그는 화난 어조로 말했다.

15 tour [tuə:r]
n 관광 여행   a journey during which you visit several places
I'm calling about the position for a **tour** guide.
관광 여행 가이드 자리가 있나 보려고 전화 했습니다.

16 valuable [vǽlju:əbəl]
a 귀중한, 값비싼   worth a lot of money
People who have lost something **valuable** advertise it in the newspaper.
귀중품을 분실한 사람은 그것을 신문에 광고 합니다.

17 via [váiə]
prep ~경유로   through a place
Last week I received the shipment **via** surface mail.
지난주에 저는 선박 우편을 통해 물품을 받았습니다.

18 volcano [valkéinou]
n 화산   a mountain which hot melted gas, steam, and ash come out
I have never seen an active **volcano**.
나는 지금까지 활화산을 본 적이 없다.

---

key words
firmly **ad** 굳게 / advertise **v** 광고하다 / surface **a** 수상의

Unit 8   41

Exercise

A. Complete the sentence.

1. I'll come up there and _____ you.
   내가 가서 너를 때려줄 거야.

2. We help communities reduce, _____ or recycle unwanted materials.
   우리는 지역 사회의 쓰레기들을 줄이고 재생하고 재활용할 수 있도록 도울 것입니다.

3. _____ are awkward on land but graceful in the water.
   바다표범은 육지에서는 꼴사납지만 물속에서는 우아하다.

4. She kept her eyes _____ closed.
   그녀는 두 눈을 단단히 감고 있었다.

5. Every year some of these _____ disappear.
   해마다 이들 종들 중 일부는 멸종한다.

6. _____ the smaller number from the larger number.
   큰 숫자에서 작은 숫자를 빼라.

7. It is surely no accident that he _____.
   그의 성공은 결코 우연이 아니다.

8. He said it in an angry _____.
   그는 화난 어조로 말했다.

9. We learn many _____ in school.
   우리는 학교에서 여러 과목을 배웁니다.

10. We look forward to your prompt _____.
    당신의 신속한 응답을 기대합니다.

11. I'm calling about the position for a _____ guide.
    관광 여행 가이드 자리가 있나 보려고 전화 했습니다.

12. He knocked a person _____.
    그는 어떤 사람을 인성불성이 되도록 때렸다.

13. People who have lost something _____ advertise it in the newspaper.
    귀중품을 분실한 사람은 그것을 신문에 광고 합니다.

14. The cat seemed to hate _____ foods.
    고양이는 향신료를 넣은 음식을 싫어하는 듯 했다.

15. Have you met our new _____?
    새로 온 비서 만나 봤어요?

16. The _____ was better than I had expected.
    그 결과는 나의 예상 보다 좋았다.

17. Last week I received the shipment _____ surface mail.
    지난주에 저는 선박 우편을 통해 물품을 받았습니다.

18. I have never seen an active _____.
    나는 지금까지 활화산을 본 적이 없다.

Hint

species	volcano	seal	result	secretary	tone	subject	response	spank
reuse	spicy	via	tightly	senseless	subtract	valuable	succeed	tour

Exercise

B. Fill in the word and meaning.

	Word	Meaning
01	seal	
02	tightly	
03	response	
04	spicy	
05	tone	
06	secretary	
07	valuable	
08	volcano	
09	senseless	
10	subtract	
11	result	
12	subject	
13	via	
14	spank	
15	tour	
16	species	
17	succeed	
18	reuse	

	Meaning	Word
01	응답, 반응	
02	결과, 성과	
03	다시 이용하다, 재생하다	
04	바다표범	
05	비서, 서기	
06	무감각의, 인사불성의	
07	찰싹 때리다	
08	종류, 종	
09	향신료를 넣은, 향긋한	
10	주제, 과목	
11	빼다, 감하다	
12	성공하다	
13	단단히	
14	음질, 음색, 어조	
15	관광 여행	
16	귀중한, 값비싼	
17	~경유로	
18	화산	

C. Listen, write the word and meaning. (Track 24)

	Word	Meaning		Word	Meaning
01			10		
02			11		
03			12		
04			13		
05			14		
06			15		
07			16		
08			17		
09			18		

Unit 8

Review 4

A. Read and fill in the word and meaning.

word	definition	meaning
	a job or profession	
	a set of instructions that tells you how to cook something	
	an action that is not correct	
	the true situation that actually exist	
	to do what you are told to do	
	to say that you are willing to give something	
	your own	
	remaining faithful to somebody/something	
	a group of words without a finite verb	
	a piece of something hard or solid	
	a person on a ship who attacks other ships at sea	
	an important official job that a person is given to do	
	to push something closely	
	what you do as a result of something that has happened	
	not very cold, and therefore pleasant	
	likely to happen, to be true	
	connected with the moon	
	an award that is given to a person who wins a competition	

Hint

personal   obey   prize   mild   probable   lump   phrase   mission   loyal
reaction   lunar   press   offer occupation   recipe mistake   pirate   reality

B. Read and fill in the word and meaning.

word	definition	meaning
	strongly flavored with spices	
	through a place	
	a group into which animals, plants, etc.	
	a spoken answer or a reaction to something	
	worth a lot of money	
	an area of knowledge studied in a school	
	to take a number or an amount away from others	
	something that happens because of something else	
	to hit somebody on their bottom as a punishment	
	a journey during which you visit several places	
	without feeling; unconscious	
	a mountain which hot melted gas, steam, and ash come out	
	to use something again	
	to achieve something that you have been trying to do	
	closely and firmly	
	a sea animal that eats fish and lives around coasts	
	the quality of somebody's voice	
	a person who works in an office for another person	

Hint

species   volcano   seal   result   secretary   tone   subject   response   spank
reuse   spicy   via   tightly   senseless   subtract   valuable   succeed   tour

Unit 9

🎧 Listen and repeat. (Track 25)

01 adjust [ədʒʌ́st]
v 조정하다, 맞추다 — to make something work better
How do you **adjust** the video quality?
비디오 화질을 어떻게 조정하나요?

02 admiral [ǽdmərəl]
n 해군 대장, 제독 — an officer of very high rank in the navy
The **admiral** retired from the navy.
그 제독은 해군에서 퇴역했다.

03 arrival [əráivəl]
n 도착, 도달 — an act of coming
Let's see if our client is waiting for us at **arrivals**.
도착 장소에 가서 고객이 우릴 기다리고 있는지 봅시다.

04 assignment [əsáinmənt]
n 할당, 담당, 숙제 — a task that somebody is given to do
I'm sorry but I couldn't finish your **assignment** due on the 21st.
죄송하지만 이번 달 21일까지의 과제물을 다 못 끝냈어요.

05 badly [bǽdli]
ad 대단히, 나쁘게 — seriously; severely
Optimists are said to maintain that all is well when things are going **badly**.
낙관론자들은 일들이 나쁘게 되어갈 때도 모든 것이 좋다고 주장한다고 한다.

06 better [bétər]
a 보다 좋은 / ad 보다 좋게 — in a more excellent
The redder paint is **better** for the building.
그 건물에는 더 빨간 색의 페인트가 어울린다.

07 branch [bræntʃ]
n 가지 — a part of a tree that grows out from the main stem
The **branches** needed to be sawn off.
나뭇가지는 톱으로 잘라내야 했다.

08 breathe [bri:ð]
v 호흡하다 — to take air into your lungs and send it out again
I'd give my life to only see you **breathe** again.
당신이 다시 숨 쉬는 것을 볼 수만 있다면 내 목숨이라도 바치겠어요.

09 charity [tʃǽrəti]
n 자비, 자선 — kindness and sympathy towards other people
I gave every penny I had to **charity**.
나는 주머니를 털어 자선 단체에 기부했다.

---

key words
retire v 은퇴하다 / severely ad 심하게 / optimist n 낙관론자 / stem n 줄기 / saw v 톱질하다 / lung n 폐

🎧 Listen and repeat. Track 26

10 cheat [tʃiːt]
v 기만하다, 속이다 / n 속임수 to trick or deceive somebody
The shopkeeper **cheated** customers by giving them too little change.
그 가게 주인은 거스름돈을 덜 주는 것으로 고객들을 속였다.

11 complete [kəmpliːt]
a 완전한 / v 완성하다 including all parts; to make something whole
The construction of a building is **completed**.
건물 공사가 완료 되었다.

12 comprehension [kàmprihénʃən]
n 이해, 이해력 the ability to understand
The existence of God is beyond human **comprehension**.
신의 존재는 인간이 이해할 수 없는 것이다

13 crazy [kréizi]
a 미친 not sensible; mentally ill
Keep away from her, she's **crazy**.
그녀는 제정신이 아니니 피해 있으세요.

14 create [kriéit]
v 창조하다, 고안하다 to make something happen or exist
We are planning to **create** new jobs in the area.
우리는 이 지역에 새로운 일자리를 창출할 계획입니다.

15 cricket [kríkit]
n 크리켓 a game played on grass by two teams of 11 players
They scored a hundred points at **cricket**.
그들은 크리켓에서 100점을 땄다.

16 depression [dipréʃən]
n 우울, 불경기 a period when the economic situation is bad
Prosperity and **depression** move in cycles.
경기와 불경기는 순환한다.

17 depth [depθ]
n 깊이, 깊음 the distance down from the top to the bottom of something
The hole should be 3cm in **depth**.
구멍은 깊이가 3cm 정도 되어야 한다.

18 descendant [diséndənt]
n 자손, 후예 the people in later generations
I want you to keep in mind that we should keep the earth clean for our **descendants**.
저는 여러분들이 우리들의 후손을 위해 지구를 깨끗이 보존해야 한다는 것을 명심해 주시기를 바랍니다.

key words
trick v 속이다 / shopkeeper n 상인 / change n 잔돈 / existence n 존재 / beyond prep ~의 범위를 넘어서 / mentally ad 정신적으로 / prosperity n 번영, 성공 / generation n 세대

Unit 9 47

Exercise

A. Complete the sentence.

1. I gave every penny I had to _____.
   나는 주머니를 털어 자선 단체에 기부했다.

2. The construction of a building is _____.
   건물 공사가 완료 되었다.

3. Let's see if our client is waiting for us at _____.
   도착 장소에 가서 고객이 우릴 기다리고 있는지 봅시다.

4. Keep away from her, she's _____.
   그녀는 제정신이 아니니 피해 있으세요.

5. I'm sorry but I couldn't finish your _____ due on the 21st.
   죄송하지만 이번 달 21일까지의 과제물을 다 못 끝냈어요.

6. Optimists are said to maintain that all is well when things are going _____.
   낙관론자들은 일들이 나쁘게 되어갈 때도 모든 것이 좋다고 주장한다고 한다.

7. The hole should be 3cm in _____.
   구멍은 깊이가 3cm 정도 되어야 한다.

8. The shopkeeper _____ customers by giving them too little change.
   그 가게 주인은 거스름돈 덜 주는 것으로 고객들을 속였다.

9. The _____ needed to be sawn off.
   나뭇가지는 톱으로 잘라내야 했다.

10. I'd give my life to only see you _____ again.
    당신이 다시 숨 쉬는 것을 볼 수만 있다면 내 목숨이라도 바치겠어요.

11. How do you _____ the video quality?
    비디오 화질을 어떻게 조정하나요?

12. The existence of God is beyond human _____.
    신의 존재는 인간이 이해할 수 없는 것이다.

13. We are planning to _____ new jobs in the area.
    우리는 이 지역에 새로운 일자리를 창출할 계획입니다.

14. The redder paint is _____ for the building.
    그 건물에는 더 빨간 색의 페인트가 어울린다.

15. They scored a hundred points at _____.
    그들은 크리켓에서 100점을 땄다.

16. Prosperity and _____ move in cycles.
    경기와 불경기는 순환한다.

17. The _____ retired from the navy.
    그 제독은 해군에서 퇴역했다.

18. I want you to keep in mind that we should keep the earth clean for our _____.
    저는 여러분들이 우리들의 후손을 위해 지구를 깨끗이 보존해야 한다는 것을 명심해 주시기를 바랍니다.

Hint

complete badly   assignment   cricket   cheat   better   crazy   admiral   depression
breathe   create descendant   branch   depth   adjust   arrival charity   comprehension

Exercise

B. Fill in the word and meaning.

	Word	Meaning
01	cheat	
02	adjust	
03	badly	
04	admiral	
05	comprehension	
06	branch	
07	complete	
08	depression	
09	better	
10	descendant	
11	create	
12	depth	
13	breathe	
14	crazy	
15	assignment	
16	cricket	
17	charity	
18	arrival	

	Meaning	Word
01	조정하다, 맞추다	
02	해군 대장, 제독	
03	도착, 도달	
04	할당, 담당, 숙제	
05	대단히, 나쁘게	
06	보다 좋은, 보다 좋게	
07	가지	
08	호흡하다	
09	자비, 자선	
10	기만하다, 속이다, 속임수	
11	완전한, 완성하다	
12	이해, 이해력	
13	미친	
14	창조하다, 고안하다	
15	크리켓	
16	우울, 불경기	
17	깊이, 깊음	
18	자손, 후예	

🎧 C. Listen, write the word and meaning. (Track 27)

	Word	Meaning		Word	Meaning
01			10		
02			11		
03			12		
04			13		
05			14		
06			15		
07			16		
08			17		
09			18		

Unit 10

🎧 Listen and repeat. (Track 28)

01 earmuff [íərmʌf]
n 귀덮개 — either of a pair of covering for the ears
My little sister cried all day for me to buy her a pair of **earmuffs**.
나의 어린 여동생은 방한용 귀덮개를 사달라고 온 종일 울었다.

02 earn [əːrn]
v (생활비를) 벌다, 획득하다 — to get money for work that you do
But what I really need to do is to **earn** more.
그러나 정말로 필요한 건 돈을 더 많이 버는 거예요.

03 education [èdʒukéiʃən]
n 교육, 양성 — a process of teaching and learning in schools
Girls used to receive only a superficial **education**.
과거에 여성들은 피상적인 교육만 받곤 했다.

04 fable [féibəl]
n 우화, 전설, 꾸며낸 이야기 — a traditional story that teaches a moral lesson
Everyone must have read Aesop's **Fables** when they were young.
모든 사람들이 어릴 때 틀림없이 이솝우화를 읽었을 것이다.

05 factual [fǽktʃuəl]
a 사실의, 실제의 — based on or containing things that are true or real
We all enjoy stories of giants and dragons even though we do not regard them as **factual**.
실제로 존재한다고 여기지 않으면서도 우리는 거인과 용의 이야기를 즐겨 읽는다.

06 failure [féiljər]
n 실패, 부족, 쇠약 — lack of success in doing something
Success or **failure** makes no difference to me.
성공하든지 실패하든지 나에겐 별 차이가 없다.

07 frank [fræŋk]
a 솔직한, 명백한 — honest and direct in what you say
Your answer is not **frank**.
너의 대답은 솔직하지 못하다.

08 freedom [fríːdəm]
n 자유, 면제 — the right to do what you want without anyone stopping you
He was deprived of his **freedom**.
그는 자유를 빼앗겼다.

09 friendship [fréndʃip]
n 우정 — a relationship between friends
This meeting will promote the **friendship** that has long existed between the two countries.
이 회담은 양국 간의 오랜 우호 관계를 한층 더 강화할 것이다.

---

key words
superficial a 표면상의 / deprive v 박탈하다 / relationship n 관계 / promote v 증진하다

🎧 Listen and repeat. Track 29

10 harmony [háːrməni]
n 조화, 화합   a state of peaceful existence and agreement
The Korean flag shows the perfect beauty of balance and **harmony**.
한국의 국기는 균형과 조화의 완벽한 아름다움을 보여주고 있어.

11 hatch [hætʃ]
v 까다, 부화하다   to come out of an egg
It takes three weeks for eggs to **hatch**.
알이 부화하는데 3주일이 걸립니다.

12 health [helθ]
n 건강   the condition of a person's body or mind
Doctors say our emotional health is closely connected to our physical **health**.
의사들은 우리의 정서적 건강이 신체적 건강과 밀접하게 관련 있다고 말한다.

13 ingredient [ingríːdiənt]
n 성분, 재료   one of the things from which something is made
Using basic **ingredients**, he was able to create an unbelievably delicious meal.
그는 기본 재료만을 사용해 믿기지 않을 정도로 맛있는 음식을 만들어 낼 수 있었다.

14 inner [ínər]
a 안의, 정신적인   inside; towards to the center of a place
Yoga is said to restore one's **inner** balance.
요가는 사람의 내적 균형을 회복시켜 준다고 한다.

15 insist [insíst]
v 강요하다, 주장하다   to say strongly
She **insisted** on her innocence.
그녀는 결백을 주장했다.

16 lawyer [lɔ́ːjər]
n 법률가, 변호사   a person who is qualified to advise people about the law
He is a **lawyer** of good reputation.
그는 평판이 좋은 변호사이다.

17 least [liːst]
a 가장 작은(적은) / **n** 최소, 최저   smallest in size, degree, etc.
I am asking for permission to hire at **least** four workers.
최소한 4명을 채용할 수 있도록 허락해 주십시오.

18 lend [lend]
v 빌려주다   to allow somebody to use something for a short time
I have always made it a principle never to borrow nor to **lend** money.
나의 원칙은 돈을 빌리거나 빌려 주지 않는 것이다.

key words
emotional **a** 정서의 / innocence **n** 결백, 무죄 / reputation **n** 평판, 명성 / principle **n** 원칙

Unit 10 51

Exercise

A. Complete the sentence.

1. Your answer is not _____.
   너의 대답은 솔직하지 못하다.
2. My little sister cried all day for me to buy her a pair of _____.
   나의 어린 여동생은 방한용 귀덮개를 사달라고 온 종일 울었다.
3. Girls used to receive only a superficial _____.
   과거에 여성들은 피상적인 교육만 받곤 했다.
4. Everyone must have read Aesop's _____ when they were young.
   모든 사람들이 어릴 때 틀림없이 이솝우화를 읽었을 것이다.
5. Yoga is said to restore one's _____ balance.
   요가는 사람의 내적 균형을 회복시켜 준다고 한다.
6. Success or _____ makes no difference to me.
   성공하든지 실패하든지 나에겐 별 차이가 없다.
7. This meeting will promote the _____ that has long existed between the two countries.
   이 회담은 양국 간의 오랜 우호 관계를 한층 더 강화할 것이다.
8. The Korean flag shows the perfect beauty of balance and _____.
   한국의 국기는 균형과 조화의 완벽한 아름다움을 보여주고 있어.
9. He is a _____ of good reputation.
   그는 평판이 좋은 변호사이다.
10. It takes three weeks for eggs to _____.
    알이 부화하는데 3주일이 걸립니다.
11. But what I really need to do is to _____ more.
    그러나 정말로 필요한 건 돈을 더 많이 버는 거예요.
12. Doctors say our emotional health is closely connected to our physical _____.
    의사들은 우리의 정서적 건강이 신체적 건강과 밀접하게 관련 있다고 말한다.
13. Using basic _____, he was able to create an unbelievably delicious meal.
    그는 기본 재료만을 사용해 믿기지 않을 정도로 맛있는 음식을 만들어 낼 수 있었다.
14. We all enjoy stories of giants and dragons even though we do not regard them as _____.
    실제로 존재한다고 여기지 않으면서도 우리는 거인과 용의 이야기를 즐겨 읽는다.
15. She _____ on her innocence.
    그녀는 결백을 주장했다.
16. I am asking for permission to hire at _____ four workers.
    최소한 4명을 채용할 수 있도록 허락해 주십시오.
17. He was deprived of his _____.
    그는 자유를 빼앗겼다.
18. I have always made it a principle never to borrow nor to _____ money.
    나의 원칙은 돈을 빌리거나 빌려 주지 않는 것이다.

Hint

| lawyer | freedom | ingredient | fable | inner | earn | factual | harmony | earmuff |
| lend | friendship | education | insist | failure | health | least | frank | hatch |

Exercise

B. Fill in the word and meaning.

	Word	Meaning
01	frank	
02	harmony	
03	earn	
04	hatch	
05	education	
06	inner	
07	fable	
08	least	
09	friendship	
10	lend	
11	freedom	
12	lawyer	
13	failure	
14	insist	
15	health	
16	factual	
17	ingredient	
18	earmuff	

	Meaning	Word
01	귀덮개	
02	(생활비를) 벌다, 획득하다	
03	교육, 양성	
04	우화, 전설, 꾸며낸 이야기	
05	사실의, 실제의	
06	실패, 부족, 쇠약	
07	솔직한, 명백한	
08	자유, 면제	
09	우정	
10	조화, 화합	
11	까다, 부화하다	
12	건강	
13	성분, 재료	
14	안의, 정신적인	
15	강요하다, 주장하다	
16	법률가, 변호사	
17	가장 작은(적은), 최소, 최저	
18	빌려주다	

🎧 C. Listen, write the word and meaning. (Track 30)

	Word	Meaning		Word	Meaning
01			10		
02			11		
03			12		
04			13		
05			14		
06			15		
07			16		
08			17		
09			18		

Review 5

A. Read and fill in the word and meaning.

word	definition	meaning
descendant	the people in later generations	
charity	kindness and sympathy towards other people	
depth	the distance down from the top to the bottom of something	
breathe	to take air into your lungs and send it out again	
adjust	to make something work better	
cheat	to trick or deceive somebody	
depression	a period when the economic situation is bad	
complete	including all parts; to make something whole	
admiral	an officer of very high rank in the navy	
comprehension	the ability to understand	
branch	a part of a tree that grows out from the main stem	
cricket	a game played on grass by two teams of 11 players	
crazy	not sensible; mentally ill	
arrival	an act of coming	
better	in a more excellent	
assignment	a task that somebody is given to do	
create	to make something happen or exist	
badly	seriously; severely	

Hint
complete   badly   assignment   cricket   cheat   better   crazy   admiral   depression
breathe   create   descendant   branch   depth   adjust   arrival   charity   comprehension

B. Read and fill in the word and meaning.

word	definition	meaning
	either of a pair of covering for the ears	
	lack of success in doing something	
	to get money for work that you do	
	inside; towards to the center of a place	
	honest and direct in what you say	
	one of the things from which something is made	
	the condition of a person's body or mind	
	the right to do what you want without anyone stopping you	
	to come out of an egg	
	a traditional story that teaches a moral lesson	
	a process of teaching and learning in schools	
	to allow somebody to use something for a short time	
	based on or containing things that are true or real	
	a person who is qualified to advise people about the law	
	to say strongly	
	smallest in size, degree, etc.	
	a state of peaceful existence and agreement	
	a relationship between friends	

Hint

lawyer   freedom   ingredient   fable   inner   earn   factual   harmony   earmuff
lend   friendship education   insist failure health least   frank   hatch

Unit 11

🎧 Listen and repeat. (Track 31)

01 magazine [mǽgəzíːn]
n 잡지   a book with a paper cover that you can buy every week or month
The **magazine** is a monthly and is produced by a staff of twelve.
그 잡지는 월간지로 12명이 만든다.

02 mainly [méinli]
ad 주로, 대개   mostly
I did a bit of shopping but **mainly** I just relaxed on the beach.
쇼핑을 조금 하긴 했지만 주로 해변에서 휴식을 취했습니다.

03 major [méidʒər]
a 주요한, 큰   very large or important
It's valid only in six **major** cities.
그것은 주요 도시 여섯 곳에서만 유효합니다.

04 marriage [mǽridʒ]
n 결혼   the relationship between a husband and wife
Their **marriage** ended in divorce.
그들의 결혼은 이혼으로 끝났다.

05 modern [mádəːrn]
a 현대의, 근대의   of the present time or recent times
Pollution is one of the major problems in the **modern** world.
공해는 현대 세계의 중요한 문제들 중 하나이다.

06 movement [múːvmənt]
n 운동, 활동   an act of moving the body
This gives us clear information of the **movements** of the graduates.
이것을 보면 졸업생들의 활동에 관한 분명한 정보를 알 수 있다.

07 operate [ápərèit]
v 작동하다, 작용하다   to work in a particular way
These switches **operate** the central heating.
이 스위치들로 중앙 난방을 작동 시킨다.

08 orbit [ɔ́ːrbit]
n 궤도 / v 궤도를 돌다   a curved path followed by a planet or an object
The spacecraft went into **orbit** around the earth.
우주선은 지구 궤도에 진입했다.

09 oyster [ɔ́istər]
n 굴   a large flat shellfish
Oysters are found in shallow water along seacoasts.
굴은 해안을 따라 얕은 물에서 발견된다.

key words
monthly n 월간지 / staff n 직원, 부원 / relax v 피로를 풀다 / valid a 유효한
divorce n 이혼 / spacecraft n 우주선 / shallow a 얕은

🎧 Listen and repeat. (Track 32)

10 pitch [pitʃ]
v 던지다, (천막을) 치다   to throw something
I went to the ball game last night and Moyer **pitched** a great game.
어제 밤에 야구장에 갔는데 Moyer가 공을 잘 던졌다.

11 pity [píti]
n 동정, 애석한 일   a feeling of sympathy and sadness
It is a **pity** that he can't come to the party.
그가 파티에 올 수 없다니 애석한 일이다.

12 pleasant [pléznt]
a 즐거운, 좋은   enjoyable or pleasing
Perfume is also a **pleasant** natural smell.
향수는 기분 좋은 천연의 냄새이기도 하다.

13 professional [prəféʃənəl]
a 직업의, 전문의 / **n** 전문가   connected with a job that needs special skill
The book is very informative and **professional**.
그 책은 아주 유익하고 전문적이다.

14 prove [pruːv]
v 증명하다, 시험하다   to use facts, etc. to show that something is true
We can **prove** her innocence.
우리는 그녀의 결백을 입증할 수 있다.

15 proverb [právəːrb]
n 속담, 격언   a well-known sentence that gives advice
Remember the **proverb**, 'Look before you leap'.
'돌다리도 두들겨 보고 건너라' 는 속담을 잊지 마라.

16 recommend [rèkəménd]
v 추천하다, 권하다   to tell somebody that something is good
We **recommend** oil changes every four months.
오일을 4개월마다 바꾸실 것을 권해드립니다.

17 reduction [ridʌ́kʃən]
n 감소, 축소   action of making something less or smaller
There was a sharp **reduction** in the number of students in the school.
그 학교에 다니는 학생 수의 급격한 감소가 있었다.

18 refer [rifə́ːr]
v 언급하다, 지시하다   to mention particular subject or person
What exactly are you **referring** to?
정확히 어떤 걸 말씀하시는 거죠?

key words
perfume **n** 향수 / informative **a** 유익한, 정보의 / leap **v** 뛰어 넘다

Exercise

A. Complete the sentence.

1. We can _____ her innocence.
   우리는 그녀의 결백을 입증할 수 있다.

2. The _____ is a monthly and is produced by a staff of twelve.
   그 잡지는 월간지로 12명이 만든다.

3. Perfume is also a _____ natural smell.
   향수는 기분 좋은 천연의 냄새이기도 하다.

4. I did a bit of shopping but _____ I just relaxed on the beach.
   쇼핑을 조금 하긴 했지만 주로 해변에서 휴식을 취했습니다.

5. The spacecraft went into _____ around the earth.
   우주선은 지구 궤도에 진입했다.

6. Their _____ ended in divorce.
   그들의 결혼은 이혼으로 끝났다.

7. There was a sharp _____ in the number of students in the school.
   그 학교에 다니는 학생 수의 급격한 감소가 있었다.

8. Pollution is one of the major problems in the _____ world.
   공해는 현대 세계의 중요한 문제들 중 하나이다.

9. This gives us clear information of the _____ of the graduates.
   이것을 보면 졸업생들의 활동에 관한 분명한 정보를 알 수 있다.

10. These switches _____ the central heating.
    이 스위치로 중앙 난방을 작동 시킨다.

11. _____ are found in shallow water along seacoasts.
    굴은 해안을 따라 얕은 물에서 발견된다.

12. I went to the ball game last night and Moyer _____ a great game.
    어제 밤에 야구장에 갔는데 Moyer가 공을 잘 던졌다.

13. What exactly are you _____ to?
    정확히 어떤 걸 말씀하시는 거죠?

14. It is a _____ that he can't come to the party.
    그가 파티에 올 수 없다니 애석한 일이다.

15. It's valid only in six _____ cities.
    그것은 주요 도시 여섯 곳에서만 유효합니다.

16. Remember the _____, 'Look before you leap'.
    '돌다리도 두들겨 보고 건너라' 는 속담을 잊지 마라.

17. We _____ oil changes every four months.
    오일을 4개월마다 바꾸실 것을 권해드립니다.

18. The book is very informative and _____.
    그 책은 아주 유익하고 전문적이다.

Hint

| orbit | marriage | movement | pitch | magazine | operate | oyster | prove | professional |
| refer | proverb | reduction | pity | pleasant | mainly | major | modern | recommend |

Exercise

B. Fill in the word and meaning.

	Word	Meaning
01	marriage	
02	orbit	
03	magazine	
04	pitch	
05	modern	
06	professional	
07	recommend	
08	major	
09	proverb	
10	oyster	
11	prove	
12	reduction	
13	pity	
14	refer	
15	movement	
16	pleasant	
17	operate	
18	mainly	

	Meaning	Word
01	잡지	
02	주로, 대개	
03	주요한, 큰	
04	결혼	
05	현대의, 근대의	
06	운동, 활동	
07	작동하다, 작용하다	
08	궤도, 궤도를 돌다	
09	굴	
10	던지다, (천막을) 치다	
11	동정, 애석한 일	
12	즐거운, 좋은	
13	직업의, 전문의, 전문가	
14	증명하다, 시험하다	
15	속담, 격언	
16	추천하다, 권하다	
17	감소, 축소	
18	언급하다, 지시하다	

C. Listen, write the word and meaning. (Track 33)

	Word	Meaning		Word	Meaning
01			10		
02			11		
03			12		
04			13		
05			14		
06			15		
07			16		
08			17		
09			18		

Unit 11

Unit 12

🎧 Listen and repeat. (Track 34)

01 reward
[riwɔ́:rd]
n 보수, 포상 / v 보답하다   a thing that you are given because you have done something good
This **reward** means a lot to me.
이 상은 나에게 많은 의미를 준다.

02 roam
[roum]
v 거닐다, 돌아다니다   to walk an area without any direction
He **roamed** about the street for hours.
그는 몇 시간이고 거리를 어슬렁거렸다.

03 romance
[roumǽns]
n 로맨스, 연애   a relationship between two people who are in love with each other
His **romance** is much gossiped about.
그의 연애에 대한 소문이 자자하다.

04 series
[síəri:z]
n 연속, 시리즈   several events of a similar kind that happen one after the other
He wrote a **series** of historical facts.
그는 역사적 사실에 대한 시리즈를 썼다.

05 serious
[síəriəs]
a 진지한, 중대한   that must be treated as important
You made a **serious** mistake.
당신은 중대한 실수를 했다.

06 share
[ʃɛə:r]
v 분배하다, 공유하다   to divide something between two or more people
We **shared** the pizza out between the four of us.
우리는 피자를 네 명이 먹을 수 있게 분배했다.

07 spill
[spil]
v 엎지르다   to flow over the edge of a container
The man has **spilled** coffee on the page.
남자가 종이 위에 커피를 엎질렀다.

08 spoil
[spɔil]
v 망쳐놓다   to change something good into something bad
A succession of accidents **spoiled** our automobile trip.
연속된 사고가 우리 자동차 여행을 망쳤다.

09 squeeze
[skwi:z]
v 짜내다, 압착하다   to get liquid out of something by twisting it hard
They are **squeezing** the fruit.
그들은 과즙을 짜내고 있다.

---

key words
gossip v 수근거리다 / succession n 연속

🎧 Listen and repeat. Track 35

10 success
[səksés]
n 성공, 성취 — the fact that you have achieved what you want
Success and hard work go together.
성공에는 고생이 따르기 마련이다.

11 sudden
[sʌ́dn]
a 돌연한, 갑작스러운 — happening quickly and unexpectedly
He was shocked about her **sudden** change.
그는 그녀의 갑작스러운 변화에 충격을 받았다.

12 summarize
[sʌ́məràiz]
v 요약하다 — to give a summary of something
It may be **summarized** as follows.
그것은 대강 다음과 같이 요약될 수 있다.

13 tourist
[túərist]
n 여행자, 관광객 — a person who is travelling a place for pleasure
The **tourists** are getting off the bus.
관광객들이 버스에서 내리고 있다.

14 trade
[treid]
v 거래하다, 무역하다 / **n** 무역 — the activity of buying and selling between countries
Excuse me, does that bus go to the **Trade** Center?
실례지만 저 버스 무역 센터 갑니까?

15 traditional
[trədíʃənəl]
a 전통적인, 관습의 — having a custom or belief that has continued for a long time
Hanbok is Korean **traditional** dress.
한복은 한국의 전통적인 의상이다.

16 vow
[vau]
n 맹세, 서약 — a serious promise to do something
I am under a **vow** not to smoke again.
나는 다시는 흡연하지 않기로 맹세했다.

17 wealth
[welθ]
n 부, 재산 — a large amount of property that a person owns
What is **wealth** without health?
건강이 없는 재물은 무슨 가치가 있겠는가?

18 weigh
[wei]
v 무게를 재다 — to measure how heavy something is
He **weighed** vegetables on a balance.
그는 야채를 저울에 달았다.

key words
shock **v** 충격을 주다 / summary **n** 요약, 개요 / promise **v** 약속하다 / balance **n** 저울

Exercise

A. Complete the sentence.

1. He wrote a _____ of historical facts.
   그는 역사적 사실에 대한 시리즈를 썼다.

2. Hanbok is Korean _____ dress.
   한복은 한국의 전통적인 의상이다.

3. You made a _____ mistake.
   당신은 중대한 실수를 했다.

4. We _____ the pizza out between the four of us.
   우리는 피자를 네 명이 먹을 수 있게 분배했다.

5. This _____ means a lot to me.
   이 상은 나에게 많은 의미를 준다.

6. The man has _____ coffee on the page.
   남자가 종이 위에 커피를 엎질렀다.

7. He _____ vegetables on a balance.
   그는 야채를 저울에 달았다.

8. A succession of accidents _____ our automobile trip.
   연속된 사고가 우리 자동차 여행을 망쳤다.

9. They are _____ the fruit.
   그들은 과즙을 짜내고 있다.

10. What is _____ without health?
    건강이 없는 재물은 무슨 가치가 있겠는가?

11. I am under a _____ not to smoke again.
    나는 다시는 흡연하지 않기로 맹세했다.

12. _____ and hard work go together.
    성공에는 고생이 따르기 마련이다.

13. His _____ is much gossiped about.
    그의 연애에 대한 소문이 자자하다.

14. He was shocked about her _____ change.
    그는 그녀의 갑작스러운 변화에 충격을 받았다.

15. The _____ are getting off the bus.
    관광객들이 버스에서 내리고 있다.

16. It may be _____ as follows.
    그것은 대강 다음과 같이 요약될 수 있다.

17. He _____ about the street for hours.
    그는 몇 시간이고 거리를 어슬렁거렸다.

18. Excuse me, does that bus go to the _____ Center?
    실례지만 저 버스 무역 센터 갑니까?

Hint

| spoil | trade | series | weigh | roam | serious | summarize | wealth | spill |
| tourist | reward | sudden | romance | success | traditional | share | vow | squeeze |

Exercise

B. Fill in the word and meaning.

	Word	Meaning
01	serious	
02	reward	
03	sudden	
04	summarize	
05	romance	
06	spoil	
07	tourist	
08	squeeze	
09	vow	
10	series	
11	wealth	
12	success	
13	weigh	
14	roam	
15	traditional	
16	spill	
17	trade	
18	share	

	Meaning	Word
01	보수, 포상, 보답하다	
02	거닐다, 돌아다니다	
03	로맨스, 연애	
04	연속, 시리즈	
05	진지한, 중대한	
06	분배하다, 공유하다	
07	엎지르다	
08	망쳐놓다	
09	짜내다, 압착하다	
10	성공, 성취	
11	돌연한, 갑작스러운	
12	요약하다	
13	여행자, 관광객	
14	거래하다, 무역하다, 무역	
15	전통적인, 관습의	
16	맹세, 서약	
17	부, 재산	
18	무게를 재다	

C. Listen, write the word and meaning. (Track 36)

	Word	Meaning		Word	Meaning
01			10		
02			11		
03			12		
04			13		
05			14		
06			15		
07			16		
08			17		
09			18		

Review 6

A. Read and fill in the word and meaning.

word	definition	meaning
reduction	action of making something less or smaller	
professional	connected with a job that needs special skill	
magazine	a book with a paper cover that you can buy every week or month	
pleasant	enjoyable or pleasing	
recommend	to tell somebody that something is good	
prove	to use facts, etc. to show that something is true	
mainly	mostly	
pitch	to throw something	
proverb	a well-known sentence that gives advice	
pity	a feeling of sympathy and sadness	
major	very large or important	
oyster	a large flat shellfish	
refer	to mention particular subject or person	
marriage	the relationship between a husband and wife	
orbit	a curved path followed by a planet or an object	
modern	of the present time or recent times	
operate	to work in a particular way	
movement	an act of moving the body	

Hint

orbit　marriage　movement　pitch　magazine　operate　oyster　prove　professional
refer　proverb　reduction　pity　pleasant　mainly　major　modern　recommend

B. Read and fill in the word and meaning.

word	definition	meaning
share	to divide something between two or more people	
reward	a thing that you are given because you have done something good	
serious	that must be treated as important	
traditional	having a custom or belief that has continued for a long time	
roam	to walk an area without any direction	
series	several events of a similar kind that happen one after the other	
romance	a relationship between two people who are in love with each other	
spill	to flow over the edge of a container	
trade	the activity of buying and selling between countries	
summarize	to give a summary of something	
tourist	a person who is travelling a place for pleasure	
spoil	to change something good into something bad	
weigh	to measure how heavy something is	
squeeze	to get liquid out of something by twisting it hard	
wealth	a large amount of property that a person owns	
success	the fact that you have achieved what you want	
vow	a serious promise to do something	
sudden	happening quickly and unexpectedly	

Hint

spoil   trade   series   weigh   roam   serious   summarize   wealth   spill
tourist   reward   sudden   romance   success   traditional   share   vow   squeeze

Unit 13

🎧 Listen and repeat. (Track 37)

01 affect [əfékt]
v 영향을 주다, 감동시키다   to produce a change in somebody / something
The new law may **affect** our business.
새로운 법률은 우리의 사업에 영향을 줄지도 모른다.

02 against [əgénst]
prep ~에 기대어서, 반대하여   disagreeing with somebody / something
She felt that everybody was **against** her.
그녀는 모든 사람들이 그녀를 반대한다고 느꼈다.

03 agency [éidʒənsi]
n 대리점, 대리권   a business which provides a service
He is moved back to the city to open an insurance **agency**.
그는 보험 대리점을 열기 위해 도시로 돌아왔다.

04 athletic [æθlétik]
a 운동의, 체육의   connected with sports
He joined an **athletic** association.
그는 운동 경기 협회에 가입했다.

05 billion [bíljən]
n 10억   1000000000; a thousand million
There are nine zeroes in a **billion**.
10억에는 0이 9개가 있다.

06 biologist [baiálədʒist]
n 생물학자   a scientist who studies biology
Biologists have expressed concern about the animal.
생물학자들은 그 동물에 대한 염려를 표명했다.

07 broadcast [brɔ́:dkæst]
v 방송하다 / n 방송   sending out programmes on television or radio
The **broadcast** was recorded, not live.
그 방송은 생방송이 아니라 녹화된 것이었다.

08 bulb [bʌlb]
n 구, 전구   the glass part that fits into an electric lamp, etc.
Do we have any more light **bulbs**?
백열전구 좀 더 가지고 있어요?

09 cheek [tʃi:k]
n 뺨, 볼   either side of the face below the eyes
His **cheeks** were red from the cold.
그의 볼은 추위 때문에 붉어졌다.

---

key words
insurance n 보험 / association n 협회, 연합 / either a 어느 한 쪽의

🎧 Listen and repeat. Track 38

10 childhood
[tʃáildhùd]
n 어린 시절   the period of somebody's life when they are children
He has been sickly from **childhood**.
그는 어렸을 때부터 잔병을 늘 앓아 왔다.

11 condition
[kəndíʃən]
n 조건, 상태, 지위   the state that somebody is in
His **condition** improved more than yesterday.
그는 어제보다 상태가 호전되었다.

12 conductor
[kəndʌ́ktər]
n 안내자, 지휘자   a person who stands in front of an orchestra
The **conductor** holds a baton.
지휘자가 지휘봉을 쥐고 있다.

13 crosswalk
[krɔ́:swɔ̀:k]
n 횡단보도   a place where pedestrians can cross a street
The men are approaching a **crosswalk**.
남자들이 횡단보도에 다다르고 있다.

14 crumb
[krʌm]
n 작은 조각, 빵부스러기   a very small piece of food, especially of bread
Don't throw away a **crumb** of bread.
빵부스러기를 던지지 마.

15 dash
[dæʃ]
v 돌진하다, 내던지다   to go somewhere very quickly
We all **dashed** for shelter when it started to rain.
비가 내리기 시작하자 우리 모두는 대피소로 돌진했다.

16 difficulty
[dífikʌ̀lti]
n 곤란, 어려움   a problem; a situation that causes problems
It is a task of extreme **difficulty**.
그것은 무척 어려운 과제이다.

17 diligent
[dílədʒənt]
a 근면한, 부지런한   showing care and effort in your duties
I certify that he is a **diligent** student.
나는 그가 근면한 학생임을 보증한다.

18 dimension
[diménʃən]
n 치수, 차원, 규모   a measurement in space
Could you take the **dimensions** of the room?
방의 치수를 재주실 수 있습니까?

key words
sickly a 자주 앓는, 병약한 / pedestrian n 보행자 / shelter n 대피소 / certify v 보증하다

Unit 13

Exercise

A. Complete the sentence.

1. The new law may _____ our business.
   새로운 법률은 우리의 사업에 영향을 줄지도 모른다.

2. He has been sickly from _____.
   그는 어렸을 때부터 잔병을 늘 앓아 왔다.

3. There are nine zeroes in a _____.
   10억에는 0이 9개가 있다.

4. His _____ improved more than yesterday.
   그는 어제보다 상태가 호전되었다.

5. It is _____ the rules.
   그것은 규칙 위반이다.

6. We all _____ for shelter when it started to rain.
   비가 내리기 시작하자 우리 모두는 대피소로 돌진했다.

7. He is moved back to the city to open an insurance _____.
   그는 보험 대리점을 열기 위해 도시로 돌아왔다.

8. The men are approaching a _____.
   남자들이 횡단보도에 다다르고 있다.

9. I certify that he is a _____ student.
   나는 그가 근면한 학생임을 보증한다.

10. He joined an _____ association.
    그는 운동 경기 협회에 가입했다.

11. _____ have expressed concern about the animal.
    생물학자들은 그 동물에 대한 염려를 표명했다.

12. Do we have any more light _____?
    백열전구 좀 더 가지고 있어요?

13. His _____ were red from the cold.
    그의 볼은 추위 때문에 붉어졌다.

14. Don't throw away a _____ of bread.
    빵 부스러기를 던지지 마.

15. It is a task of extreme _____.
    그것은 무척 어려운 과제이다.

16. The _____ was recorded, not live.
    그 방송은 생방송이 아니라 녹화된 것이었다.

17. Could you take the _____ of the room?
    방의 치수를 재주실 수 있습니까?

18. The _____ holds a baton.
    지휘자가 지휘봉을 쥐고 있다.

Hint

| difficulty | conductor | broadcast | cheek | billion | affect | crosswalk | athletic | bulb |
| condition | dimension | agency | crumb | dash | biologist | childhood | diligent | against |

Exercise

B. Fill in the word and meaning.

	Word	Meaning
01	billion	
02	affect	
03	cheek	
04	dash	
05	against	
06	broadcast	
07	difficulty	
08	conductor	
09	athletic	
10	crumb	
11	bulb	
12	crosswalk	
13	biologist	
14	diligent	
15	condition	
16	dimension	
17	childhood	
18	agency	

	Meaning	Word
01	영향을 주다, 감동시키다	
02	~에 기대어서, 반대하여	
03	대리점, 대리권	
04	운동의, 체육의	
05	10억	
06	생물학자	
07	방송하다, 방송	
08	구, 전구	
09	뺨, 볼	
10	어린 시절	
11	조건, 상태, 지위	
12	안내자, 지휘자	
13	횡단보도	
14	작은 조각, 빵부스러기	
15	돌진하다, 내던지다	
16	곤란, 어려움	
17	근면한, 부지런한	
18	치수, 차원, 규모	

🎧 C. Listen, write the word and meaning. (Track 39)

	Word	Meaning		Word	Meaning
01			10		
02			11		
03			12		
04			13		
05			14		
06			15		
07			16		
08			17		
09			18		

Unit 14

🎧 Listen and repeat. Track 40

01 effect [ifékt]
n 효과, 영향 / v 초래하다   a change that is caused by something
The medicine took instant **effect**.
그 약은 즉시 효과를 나타냈다.

02 elbow [élbou]
n 팔꿈치   the joint between the upper and lower parts of the arm
Keep your **elbows** off the table.
팔꿈치를 식탁에 올려놓지 마세요.

03 electronic [ilèktránik]
a 전자(학)의   using many small parts that control a small electric current
He has a difficulty in dealing with an **electronic** equipment.
그는 전자 장비를 다루는데 어려움이 있다.

04 fashionable [fǽʃənəbəl]
a 유행의, 유행을 따른   following a style that is popular at a particular time
It is **fashionable** to wear small watches now.
요즈음은 작은 시계를 차는 것이 유행이다.

05 fasten [fǽsn]
v 묶다, 고정하다   to fix or tie something to something
Fasten this badge on your jacket.
재킷에 이 명찰을 고정 시키세요.

06 favor [féivər]
n 호의, 부탁 / v 호의를 보이다   approval or support for somebody / something
Can I ask you a **favor**?
부탁하나 해도 될까요?

07 folk [fouk]
n 사람들 / a 서민의, 민속의   people in general
Some **folk** are never satisfied.
어떤 사람들은 결코 만족할 줄 모른다.

08 future [fjúːtʃər]
n 미래, 장래   the time that will come after the present
What will happen in the **future**?
미래에 어떤 일이 일어날까?

09 generation [dʒènəréiʃən]
n 동시대의 사람들, 세대   all the people in a family or country who were born at about the same time
This photograph shows three **generations** of my family.
이 사진은 우리 가족의 3세대를 모두 보여준다.

---

key words
instant a 즉시의 / joint n 접합 부분, 관절 / badge n 배지, 명찰

🎧 Listen and repeat. (Track 41)

10 helmet [hélmit]
n 헬멧   a type of hard hat that protects the head
The woman is buying a bicycle **helmet**.
여자가 자전거용 헬멧을 구입하고 있다.

11 hire [haiər]
v 고용하다, 임대하다 / n 고용, 임대료   to give somebody a job by paying him / her
It's a shame we can't **hire** them both.
둘 다 채용할 수 없는 게 유감이네요.

12 identity [aidéntəti]
n 신원, 정체성   who or what a person or a thing is
There are few clues to the **identity** of the killer.
살인범의 신원을 알 수 있는 단서가 거의 없다.

13 intention [inténʃən]
n 의향, 의지, 목적   what you plan to do; your aim
I have no **intention** of ignoring your rights.
당신의 권리를 무시할 의사는 없다.

14 interaction [intərǽkʃən]
n 상호 작용   that involves people having an influence on each other
All **interaction** is based on commands entered by the user.
모든 상호 작용은 사용자가 입력한 명령을 기반으로 한다.

15 invite [inváit]
v 초청하다, 권유하다   to ask somebody to come to a event
The man **invited** both of his sons for dinner.
남자는 두 아들 모두 저녁 식사에 초대했다.

16 length [leŋkθ]
n 길이   the measurement of something from one end to the other
The **length** of this box is twice its breadth.
이 상자의 길이는 폭의 두 배가 된다.

17 level [lévəl]
n 수평, 수준   a position or rank in a scale of importance
Are you keeping an eye on your cholesterol **level**?
당신은 자신의 콜레스테롤 수치에 신경을 쓰고 있습니까?

18 liberty [líbə:rti]
n 자유   the freedom to live your life in the way that you want
The visitors were given the **liberty** to wander about the city.
방문자들은 그 도시를 자유롭게 돌아다닐 수 있도록 허가받았다.

key words
aim n 목적 / influence n 영향(력) / command n 명령 / breadth n 폭 / wander v 돌아다니다

Unit 14 71

Exercise

A. Complete the sentence.

1. He has a difficulty in dealing with an _____ equipment.
   그는 전자 장비를 다루는데 어려움이 있다.

2. It's a shame we can't _____ them both.
   둘 다 채용할 수 없는 게 유감이네요.

3. I have no _____ of ignoring your rights.
   당신의 권리를 무시할 의사는 없다.

4. It is _____ to wear small watches now.
   요즈음은 작은 시계를 차는 것이 유행이다.

5. _____ this badge on your jacket.
   재킷에 이 명찰을 고정 시키세요.

6. What will happen in the _____?
   미래에 어떤 일이 일어날까?

7. This photograph shows three _____ of my family.
   이 사진은 우리 가족의 3세대를 모두 보여준다.

8. The woman is buying a bicycle _____.
   여자가 자전거용 헬멧을 구입하고 있다.

9. The _____ of this box is twice its breadth.
   이 상자의 길이는 폭의 두 배가 된다.

10. There are few clues to the _____ of the killer.
    살인범의 신원을 알 수 있는 단서가 거의 없다.

11. The medicine took instant _____.
    그 약은 즉시 효과를 나타냈다.

12. All _____ is based on commands entered by the user.
    모든 상호 작용은 사용자가 입력한 명령을 기반으로 한다.

13. The man _____ both of his sons for dinner.
    남자는 두 아들 모두 저녁 식사에 초대했다.

14. Some _____ are never satisfied.
    어떤 사람들은 결코 만족할 줄 모른다.

15. Are you keeping an eye on your cholesterol _____?
    당신은 자신의 콜레스테롤 수치에 신경을 쓰고 있습니까?

16. Keep your _____ off the table.
    팔꿈치를 식탁에 올려놓지 마세요.

17. The visitors were given the _____ to wander about the city.
    방문자들은 그 도시를 자유롭게 돌아다닐 수 있도록 허가 받았다.

18. I was wondering if I could ask you a _____.
    부탁 하나 해도 될까요?

Hint

| future | intention | favor | interaction | identity | liberty | elbow | fasten | generation |
| effect | electronic | level | fashionable | folk | invite | hire | length | helmet |

Exercise

B. Fill in the word and meaning.

	Word	Meaning
01	elbow	
02	folk	
03	interaction	
04	effect	
05	invite	
06	future	
07	electronic	
08	length	
09	generation	
10	hire	
11	fasten	
12	helmet	
13	liberty	
14	favor	
15	level	
16	identity	
17	intention	
18	fashionable	

	Meaning	Word
01	효과, 영향, 초래하다	
02	팔꿈치	
03	전자(학)의	
04	유행의, 유행을 따른	
05	묶다, 고정하다	
06	호의, 부탁, 호의를 보이다	
07	사람들, 서민의, 민속의	
08	미래, 장래	
09	동시대의 사람들, 세대	
10	헬멧	
11	고용하다, 임대하다, 고용	
12	신원, 정체성	
13	의향, 의지, 목적	
14	상호 작용	
15	초청하다, 권유하다	
16	길이	
17	수평, 수준	
18	자유	

C. Listen, write the word and meaning. Track 42

	Word	Meaning		Word	Meaning
01			10		
02			11		
03			12		
04			13		
05			14		
06			15		
07			16		
08			17		
09			18		

Review 7

A. Read and fill in the word and meaning.

word	definition	meaning
	showing care and effort in your duties	
	a measurement in space	
	to produce a change in somebody / something	
	a problem; a situation that causes problems	
	the state that somebody is in	
	disagreeing with somebody / something	
	a very small piece of food, especially of bread	
	to go somewhere very quickly	
	a business which provides a service	
	a place where pedestrians can cross a street	
	to send out programmes on television or radio	
	a person who stands in front of an orchestra	
	the glass part that fits into an electric lamp, etc.	
	a scientist who studies biology	
	either side of the face below the eyes	
	1000000000; a thousand million	
	connected with sports	
	the period of somebody's life when they are children	

Hint
difficulty   conductor   broadcast   cheek   billion   affect   crosswalk   athletic   bulb
condition   dimension   agency   crumb   dash   biologist   childhood   diligent   against

B. Read and fill in the word and meaning.

word	definition	meaning
	a position or rank in a scale of importance	
	a type of hard hat that protects the head	
	a change that is caused by something	
	to give somebody a job by paying him / her	
	the freedom to live your life in the way that you want	
	all the people in a family or country who were born at about the same time	
	the time that will come after the present	
	who or what a person or a thing is	
	the joint between the upper and lower parts of the arm	
	what you plan to do; your aim	
	people in general	
	using many small parts that control a small electric current	
	approval or support for somebody / something	
	that involves people having an influence on each other	
	following a style that is popular at a particular time	
	the measurement of something from one end to the other	
	to ask somebody to come to a event	
	to fix or tie something to something	

Hint
future   intention   favor   interaction   identity   liberty   elbow   fasten   generation
effect   electronic   level   fashionable   folk   invite   hire   length   helmet

Unit 15

🎧 Listen and repeat. Track 43

01 mayor [méiəːr]
n 시장, 읍장 — the head of the government of a town or city
The **mayor** examined the report.
시장은 보고서를 검토했다.

02 measure [méʒəːr]
v 측정하다 / **n** 측정, 수단 — to find the size, quantity of something in standard units
They are **measuring** the distance around a tree.
그들은 나무주위의 거리를 측정하고 있다.

03 motion [móuʃən]
n 운동, 활동 — the act of moving or the way something moves
The **motion** of the ship made us all feel sick.
배의 움직임은 우리 모두를 멀미 나게 했다.

04 multiply [mʌ́ltəplài]
v 늘리다, 곱하다 — to make something increase very much in number or amount
Multiply four by zero and the result is nothing.
4에 0을 곱하면 그 답은 0이다.

05 native [néitiv]
a 출생지의, 타고난 — connected with the place where you born
I want to know your **native** country and language.
나는 당신이 태어난 나라와 언어를 알고 싶다.

06 nearby [níərbái]
a 가까운 / **ad** 가까이에 — not far away in distance
A new restaurant has opened **nearby**.
새로운 레스토랑이 가까이에 문을 열었다.

07 operation [àpəréiʃən]
n 작용, 운영, 수술 — the process of cutting open a patient's body to deal with the inside
After the **operation**, she had to rest in bed for two weeks.
그녀는 수술을 받은 후 2주 동안 침대에서 휴식을 취해야 했다.

08 organization [ɔ̀ːrɡənizéiʃən]
n 조직, 기구, 체제 — official group of people
She works for a voluntary **organization** helping homeless people.
그녀는 노숙자를 돕는 봉사 기구에서 일한다.

09 ounce [auns]
n (중량 단위의) 온스 — a unit for measuring weight equal to 28.35 grams
A pound contains 16 **ounces**.
1 파운드는 16온스다.

---

key words
examine **v** 검사하다 / distance **n** 거리, 간격 / voluntary **a** 자발적인, 자원한

🎧 Listen and repeat. (Track 44)

10 poet [póuit]
n 시인   a person who writes poems
He is a **poet** as well as a scholar.
그는 학자일 뿐만 아니라 시인이기도 하다.

11 policy [páləsi]
n 정책, 방침   a plan of chosen by a political party, a business, etc.
Our **policy** is complete readers' satisfaction.
저희의 방침은 독자 여러분을 만족시키는 것입니다.

12 popular [pápjələr]
a 대중적인, 인기 있는   liked by a large number of people
Collecting old coins is a **popular** hobby.
옛날 동전을 수집하는 것은 인기 있는 취미생활이다.

13 provide [prəváid]
v 제공하다, 준비하다   to give something to somebody
The club **provides** a wide variety of activities.
그 클럽은 다양한 활동을 제공한다.

14 public [páblik]
a 공중의, 공적인   connected with ordinary people in society in general
Public libraries are handy for finding information.
공공도서관은 정보를 찾는 데 편리하다.

15 publish [pábliʃ]
v 발표하다, 출판하다   to produce a book, etc. and sell it to the public
Has any of your work been **published**?
당신 연구물 중에 출판된 것이 있나요?

16 refuse [rifjú:z]
v 거절하다   to say firmly that you will not do something
His request for an interview was **refused**.
그의 인터뷰 신청은 거절되었다.

17 regard [rigá:rd]
v ~으로 여기다, 응시하다 / n 주목   to think someone to be something
I don't **regard** it as a misfortune.
나는 그것을 불행으로 여기지 않는다.

18 region [rí:dʒən]
n 지방, 지역   a large area of land without exact limits or borders
The southeast **region** is the playground of the rich and famous.
남동부 지역은 부유한 명사들의 휴양지입니다.

key words
scholar n 학자 / handy a 알맞은, 편리한 / firmly ad 단호하게 / interview n 인터뷰

Exercise

A. Complete the sentence.

1. A new restaurant has opened _____.
   새로운 레스토랑이 가까이에 문을 열었다.

2. The _____ of the ship made us all feel sick.
   배의 움직임은 우리 모두를 멀미 나게 했다.

3. Our _____ is complete readers' satisfaction.
   저희의 방침은 독자 여러분을 만족시키는 것입니다.

4. The _____ examined the report.
   시장은 보고서를 검토했다.

5. A pound contains 16 _____.
   1 파운드는 16온스다.

6. _____ four by zero and the result is nothing.
   4에 0을 곱하면 그 답은 0이다.

7. _____ libraries are handy for finding information.
   공공도서관은 정보를 찾는 데 편리하다.

8. His request for an interview was _____.
   그의 인터뷰 신청은 거절되었다.

9. I want to know your _____ country and language.
   나는 당신이 태어난 나라와 언어를 알고 싶다.

10. Collecting old coins is a _____ hobby.
    옛날 동전을 수집하는 것은 인기 있는 취미생활이다.

11. After the _____, she had to rest in bed for two weeks.
    그녀는 수술을 받은 후 2주 동안 침대에서 휴식을 취해야 했다.

12. I don't _____ it as a misfortune.
    나는 그것을 불행으로 여기지 않는다.

13. She works for a voluntary _____ helping homeless people.
    그녀는 노숙자를 돕는 봉사 기구에서 일한다.

14. He is a _____ as well as a scholar.
    그는 학자일 뿐만 아니라 시인이기도 하다.

15. They are _____ the distance around a tree.
    그들은 나무주위의 거리를 측정하고 있다.

16. The club _____ a wide variety of activities.
    그 클럽은 다양한 활동을 제공한다.

17. The southeast _____ is the playground of the rich and famous.
    남동부 지역은 부유한 명사들의 휴양지입니다.

18. Has any of your work been _____?
    당신 연구물 중에 출판된 것이 있나요?

Hint

| nearby | operation | mayor | publish | ounce | native | poet | motion | organization |
| popular | refuse | provide | region | multiply | public | measure | policy | regard |

Unit 15

Exercise

B. Fill in the word and meaning.

	Word	Meaning
01	motion	
02	poet	
03	regard	
04	mayor	
05	popular	
06	ounce	
07	policy	
08	measure	
09	region	
10	operation	
11	publish	
12	refuse	
13	multiply	
14	provide	
15	nearby	
16	public	
17	organization	
18	native	

	Meaning	Word
01	시장, 읍장	
02	측정하다, 측정, 수단	
03	운동, 활동	
04	늘리다, 곱하다	
05	출생지의, 타고난	
06	가까운, 가까이에	
07	작용, 운영, 수술	
08	조직, 기구, 체제	
09	(중량 단위의) 온스	
10	시인	
11	정책, 방침	
12	대중적인, 인기 있는	
13	제공하다, 준비하다	
14	공중의, 공적인	
15	발표하다, 출판하다	
16	거절하다	
17	~으로 여기다, 주목	
18	지방, 지역	

🎧 C. Listen, write the word and meaning. (Track 45)

	Word	Meaning		Word	Meaning
01			10		
02			11		
03			12		
04			13		
05			14		
06			15		
07			16		
08			17		
09			18		

Unit 16

🎧 **Listen and repeat.** Track 46

01 route [ruːt]
n 도로, 길 / v 순서를 정하다　a way from one place to another
More than 500,000 people lined the parade **route**.
5십만 명 넘는 사람들이 행렬이 지나가는 길에 늘어서 있었다.

02 rubble [rʌ́bəl]
n 벽돌조각　broken stones from a building or wall
Thousands of bodies are still buried under the **rubble**.
수천구의 시신이 벽돌조각 밑에 아직도 묻혀있다.

03 rude [ruːd]
a 버릇없는, 무례한　having a lack of respect for other people
Her **rude** manner annoyed me.
그녀의 무례한 태도가 나를 짜증나게 했다.

04 shelter [ʃéltəːr]
n 대피소, 은신처　a place which is made to protect people from danger
We took **shelter** in a nearby cabin.
우리는 근처 오두막을 피난처로 삼았다.

05 shock [ʃak]
n 충격, 쇼크　something suddenly happens which is unpleasant
The court's decision was a **shock** to everybody.
법원의 판결은 모든 사람들에게 충격이었다.

06 shuttle [ʃʌ́tl]
n 왕복 운행　a plane, bus or train that travels between two places
The New York to Washington, D.C. **shuttle** operates 12 times a day.
뉴욕과 워싱턴 D.C. 간의 정기 왕복항공기는 하루에 12번 운행된다.

07 standard [stǽndəːrd]
n 표준, 기준 / a 표준의, 일반적인　something that you use to judge the quality of something else
Is there a quality **standard** for these bolts?
이 나사못에 적용되는 품질 기준이 있나요?

08 statement [stéitmənt]
n 성명, 진술　something that you say or write that gives information
He demanded a strict **statement** of the facts.
그는 그 사실에 대한 정확한 진술을 요구했다.

09 statue [stǽtʃuː]
n 상, 조상　a figure of a person or an animal in stone, metal, etc.
Statues are located in an outdoor area.
몇몇 동상이 실외에 놓여 있다.

---

key words
parade n 행렬 / annoy v 괴롭히다 / court n 법정 / strict a 엄격한, 정확한

🎧 Listen and repeat. Track 47

| 10 | **suppose** | **v** 가정하다, 추측하다 | to think that something is true or possible |
| | [səpóuz] | | **Suppose** you are on a business trip in New York.
뉴욕에 출장을 갔다고 가정해 봅시다. |

| 11 | **survey** | **n** 관찰, 조사, 측량 | an investigation of the opinions, etc. of a particular group of people |
| | [sə:rvéi] | | When can they expect the results of the **survey**?
그들이 언제쯤 조사 결과를 알 수 있을까요? |

| 12 | **tax** | **n** 세금, 조세 | money that you have to pay to the government |
| | [tæks] | | How much will that be, including **tax**?
그것은 세금 포함해서 얼마입니까? |

| 13 | **tremble** | **v** 떨다, 흔들리다 | to shake in a way that you cannot control |
| | [trémbəl] | | My hand **trembled** so much that I could not write.
손이 와들와들 떨려서 글을 쓸 수가 없었다. |

| 14 | **trick** | **n** 묘기, 재주, 기술 | a clever action that somebody performs as a way of entertaining people |
| | [trik] | | The magician performed a **trick** in which he made a rabbit disappear.
마술사는 토끼를 사라지게 하는 재주를 보였다. |

| 15 | **unless** | **conj** ~하지 않으면 | if ~ not; except if |
| | [ənlés] | | **Unless** anyone has anything else to say, the meeting is closed.
누구도 하실 말씀이 없다면 모임을 마치겠습니다. |

| 16 | **wheat** | **n** 밀, 소맥 | a cereal crop grown for food which is used to make bread |
| | [hwi:t] | | Which country purchased the most **wheat** in 1990?
1990년도에 밀을 가장 많이 사들인 나라는 어디인가요? |

| 17 | **whole** | **a** 전부의, 모든 | full; complete |
| | [houl] | | The **whole** family was in agreement on what we should do.
모든 가족이 우리가 무엇을 해야 하는지에 관해 의견이 일치했다. |

| 18 | **wild** | **a** 야생의, 거친, 사나운 | without control or discipline; slightly crazy |
| | [waild] | | She behaved in a **wild** manner like a woman possessed.
그녀는 뭔가에 홀린 사람처럼 거칠게 행동했다. |

key words
opinion **n** 의견, 견해 / purchase **v** 사다 / possessed **a** 사로잡힌, 홀린

Exercise

A. Complete the sentence.

1. _____ anyone has anything else to say, the meeting is closed.
   누구도 하실 말씀이 없다면 모임을 마치겠습니다.

2. More than 500,000 people lined the parade _____.
   5십만 명 넘는 사람들이 행렬이 지나가는 길에 늘어서 있었다.

3. _____ are located in an outdoor area.
   몇몇 동상이 실외에 놓여 있다.

4. Thousands of bodies are still buried under the _____.
   수천구의 시신이 벽돌조각 밑에 아직도 묻혀있다.

5. How much will that be, including _____?
   그것은 세금 포함해서 얼마입니까?

6. We took _____ in a nearby cabin.
   우리는 근처 오두막을 피난처로 삼았다.

7. The New York to Washington, D.C. _____ operates 12 times a day.
   뉴욕과 워싱턴 D.C. 간의 정기 왕복항공기는 하루에 12번 운행된다.

8. Is there a quality _____ for these bolts?
   이 나사못에 적용되는 품질 기준이 있나요?

9. My hand _____ so much that I could not write.
   손이 와들와들 떨려서 글을 쓸 수가 없었다.

10. He demanded a strict _____ of the facts.
    그는 그 사실에 대한 정확한 진술을 요구했다.

11. When can they expect the results of the _____?
    그들이 언제쯤 조사 결과를 알 수 있을까요?

12. The magician performed a _____ in which he made a rabbit disappear.
    마술사는 토끼를 사라지게 하는 재주를 보였다.

13. Which country purchased the most _____ in 1990?
    1990년도에 밀을 가장 많이 사들인 나라는 어디인가요?

14. Her _____ manner annoyed me.
    그녀의 무례한 태도가 나를 짜증나게 했다.

15. The _____ family was in agreement on what we should do.
    모든 가족이 우리가 무엇을 해야 하는지에 관해 의견이 일치했다.

16. _____ you are on a business trip in New York.
    뉴욕에 출장을 갔다고 가정해 봅시다.

17. She behaved in a _____ manner like a woman possessed.
    그녀는 뭔가에 홀린 사람처럼 거칠게 행동했다.

18. The court's decision was a _____ to everybody.
    법원의 판결은 모든 사람들에게 충격이었다.

Hint

| statement | trick | rude | shelter | tremble | suppose | route | wild | shock |
| rubble | shuttle | unless | whole | standard | statue | tax | survey | wheat |

Exercise

B. Fill in the word and meaning.

	Word	Meaning
01	rude	
02	standard	
03	route	
04	suppose	
05	shuttle	
06	tax	
07	wheat	
08	statement	
09	tremble	
10	rubble	
11	unless	
12	statue	
13	wild	
14	shock	
15	whole	
16	trick	
17	shelter	
18	survey	

	Meaning	Word
01	도로, 길, 순서를 정하다	
02	벽돌조각	
03	버릇없는, 무례한	
04	대피소, 은신처	
05	충격, 쇼크	
06	왕복 운행	
07	표준, 기준, 표준의, 일반적인	
08	성명, 진술	
09	상, 조상	
10	가정하다, 추측하다	
11	관찰, 조사, 측량	
12	세금, 조세	
13	떨다, 흔들리다	
14	묘기, 재주, 기술	
15	~하지 않으면	
16	밀, 소맥	
17	전부의, 모든	
18	야생의, 거친, 사나운	

C. Listen, write the word and meaning. (Track 48)

	Word	Meaning		Word	Meaning
01			10		
02			11		
03			12		
04			13		
05			14		
06			15		
07			16		
08			17		
09			18		

Review 8

A. Read and fill in the word and meaning.

word	definition	meaning
	connected with the place where you born	
	a unit for measuring weight equal to 28.35 grams	
	to make something increase very much in number or amount	
	official group of people	
	the head of the government of a town or city	
	not far away in distance	
	the act of moving or the way something moves	
	connected with ordinary people in society in general	
	the process of cutting open a patient's body to deal with the inside	
	to find the size, quantity of something in standard units	
	to give something to somebody	
	to produce a book, etc. and sell it to the public	
	a plan of chosen by a political party, a business, etc.	
	a large area of land without exact limits or borders	
	liked by a large number of people	
	attention to or thought for somebody / something	
	a person who writes poems	
	to say firmly that you will not do something	

Hint

nearby   operation   mayor   publish   ounce   native   poet   motion   organization
popular   refuse   provide   region   multiply   public   measure   policy   regard

  Review 8

B. Read and fill in the word and meaning.

word	definition	meaning
	something that you say or write that gives information	
	a clever action that somebody performs as a way of entertaining people	
	something that you use to judge the quality of something else	
	a figure of a person or an animal in stone, metal, etc.	
	a way from one place to another	
	a plane, bus or train that travels between two places	
	having a lack of respect for other people	
	an investigation of the opinions, etc. of a particular group of people	
	broken stones from a building or wall	
	something suddenly happens which is unpleasant	
	a place which is made to protect people from danger	
	to shake in a way that you cannot control	
	if ~ not; except if	
	living in natural conditions	
	to think that something is true or possible	
	full; complete	
	money that you have to pay to the government	
	a cereal crop grown for food which is used to make bread	

Hint

statement　trick　rude　shelter　tremble　suppose　route　wild　shock
rubble　shuttle　unless　whole　standard　statue　tax　survey　wheat

Unit 17

🎧 Listen and repeat. Track 49

01 ambiguous [æmbígjuəs]
a 모호한, 다의의   having more than one possible meaning
He has the habit of saying or writing using **ambiguous** words.
그는 뜻이 모호한 단어를 이용하여 말하거나 글 쓰는 습관이 있다.

02 ancestor [ǽnsestər]
n 조상, 선조   a person in your family who lived a long time ago
The custom has come down to us from our **ancestors**.
그 풍습은 우리 선조로부터 전해 내려온 것이다.

03 atom [ǽtəm]
n 원자   the smallest part of a chemical element
About one hundred million **atoms** laid side by side are an inch long.
약 1억 개의 원자를 나란히 늘어놓으면 1인치의 길이가 된다.

04 attend [əténd]
v 출석하다   to be present at an event
Do you think you'll **attend** the seminar?
세미나에 참석할 거예요?

05 bitter [bítər]
a 쓴, 괴로운   having a strong taste making you feel very unhappy
He has tasted the sweet and **bitter** things of life.
그는 인생의 단맛 쓴맛을 다 맛본 사람이다.

06 blame [bleim]
v 비난하다   to say that somebody responsible for something bad
He **blamed** me for a little mistake at work.
그는 업무 상의 작은 실수를 가지고 나를 비난했다.

07 bud [bʌd]
n 싹, 봉오리   a small lump on a plant that develops into a flower
She was so happy to see that **buds** of the flowers are out.
그녀는 꽃의 싹이 튼 것을 보고 무척 기뻐했다.

08 career [kəríər]
n 경력, 직업   the series of jobs that somebody has in a particular area of work
Today she begins her **career** as a journalist.
그녀는 오늘 기자로서의 경력을 시작한다.

09 chore [tʃɔːr]
n 잡일, 허드렛일   an unpleasant or boring task
She is tied up with household **chores**.
그녀는 집안일에 얽매여 있다.

---

key words
responsible **a** 책임이 있는 / lump **n** 덩어리 / household **a** 가사의 / tie **v** 매다, 묶다

🎧 Listen and repeat. (Track 50)

10 clue [kluː]
n 실마리, 단서   a piece of evidence that helps the police solve a crime
The police were looking for **clues** to his disappearance.
경찰은 그의 실종에 관한 실마리를 찾고 있었다.

11 contact [kάntækt]
n 접촉, 교제 / **v** 접촉하다, 교제하다   meeting, talking to or writing to somebody else
They are trying to make **contact** with the kidnappers.
그들은 유괴범들과 접촉하려고 시도 중이다.

12 contain [kəntéin]
v 포함하다   to have something inside or as part of itself
The movie is for adults only, because it **contains** a lot of violence.
그 영화는 많은 폭력 장면을 포함하고 있어서 어른들만 관람할 수 있다.

13 debate [dibéit]
n 토론, 논쟁 / **v** 토론하다, 숙고하다   a formal discussion of an issue at a public meeting
The amendments were adopted after long **debate**.
그 수정 조항들은 오랜 논쟁 끝에 채택되었다.

14 deceive [disíːv]
v 속이다   to make somebody believe something that is not true
She **deceived** me with sweet words.
그녀는 달콤한 말로 나를 속였다.

15 decline [dikláin]
v 기울다, 사절하다   to refuse, usually politely
I decided to **decline** the offer of employment because the commute would have been too long.
나는 출퇴근거리가 너무 멀기 때문에 고용 제의를 거절하기로 결정했다.

16 disappear [dìsəpíər]
v 사라지다   to become impossible to see
The light flashed, and then **disappeared**.
빛이 번쩍이더니 사라졌다.

17 discover [diskʌ́vər]
v 발견하다   to find somebody / something that was hidden
She seemed to have **discovered** a new joy in life.
그녀는 인생에서 새로운 기쁨을 발견한 것 같았다.

18 disgusting [disgʌ́stiŋ]
a 구역질나는, 정말 싫은   extremely unpleasant
If you see or read anything **disgusting**, do you stop right away?
혐오스러운 것을 보거나 읽으면, 여러분은 보거나 읽는 것을 즉시 멈추나요?

---

key words
disappearance **n** 실종, 행방불명 / kidnapper **n** 유괴자
adult **n** 성인 / amendment **n** 개정, 변경 / commute **n** 통근

Exercise

A. Complete the sentence.

1. He has tasted the sweet and _____ things of life.
   그는 인생의 단맛 쓴맛을 다 맛본 사람이다.

2. He has the habit of saying or writing using _____ words.
   그는 뜻이 모호한 단어를 이용하여 말하거나 글 쓰는 습관이 있다.

3. The light flashed, and then _____.
   빛이 번쩍이더니 사라졌다.

4. Today she begins her _____ as a journalist.
   그녀는 오늘 기자로서의 경력을 시작한다.

5. She _____ me with sweet words.
   그녀는 달콤한 말로 나를 속였다.

6. The custom has come down to us from our _____.
   그 풍습은 우리 선조로부터 전해 내려온 것이다.

7. About one hundred million _____ laid side by side are an inch long.
   약 1억 개의 원자를 나란히 늘어놓으면 1인치의 길이가 된다.

8. He _____ me for a little mistake at work.
   그는 업무 상의 작은 실수를 가지고 나를 비난했다.

9. They are trying to make _____ with the kidnappers.
   그들은 유괴범들과 접촉하려고 시도 중이다.

10. The movie is for adults only, because it _____ a lot of violence.
    그 영화는 많은 폭력 장면을 포함하고 있어서 어른들만 관람할 수 있다.

11. The amendments were adopted after long _____.
    그 수정 조항들은 오랜 논쟁 끝에 채택되었다.

12. I decided to _____ the offer of employment because the commute would have been too long.
    나는 출퇴근거리가 너무 멀기 때문에 고용 제의를 거절하기로 결정했다.

13. She is tied up with household _____.
    그녀는 집안일에 얽매여 있다.

14. Do you think you'll _____ the seminar?
    세미나에 참석할 거예요?

15. She seemed to have _____ a new joy in life.
    그녀는 인생에서 새로운 기쁨을 발견한 것 같았다.

16. She was so happy to see that _____ of the flowers are out.
    그녀는 꽃의 싹이 튼 것을 보고 무척 기뻐했다.

17. If you see or read anything _____, do you stop right away?
    혐오스러운 것을 보거나 읽으면, 여러분은 보거나 읽는 것을 즉시 멈추나요?

18. The police were looking for _____ to his disappearance.
    경찰은 그의 실종에 관한 실마리를 찾고 있었다.

Hint

| bud | deceive | ambiguous | clue | attend | ancestor | career | blame | chore |
| debate | contain | disgusting | atom | contact | disappear | discover | bitter | decline |

Exercise

B. Fill in the word and meaning.

	Word	Meaning
01	bitter	
02	ambiguous	
03	bud	
04	debate	
05	career	
06	disappear	
07	contain	
08	decline	
09	ancestor	
10	disgusting	
11	chore	
12	discover	
13	atom	
14	deceive	
15	clue	
16	blame	
17	contact	
18	attend	

	Meaning	Word
01	모호한, 다의의	
02	조상, 선조	
03	원자	
04	출석하다	
05	쓴, 괴로운	
06	비난하다	
07	싹, 봉오리	
08	경력, 직업	
09	잡일, 허드렛일	
10	실마리, 단서	
11	접촉, 교제, 접촉하다, 교제하다	
12	포함하다	
13	토론, 논쟁, 토론하다, 숙고하다	
14	속이다	
15	기울다, 사절하다	
16	사라지다	
17	발견하다	
18	구역질나는, 정말 싫은	

C. Listen, write the word and meaning. (Track 51)

	Word	Meaning		Word	Meaning
01			10		
02			11		
03			12		
04			13		
05			14		
06			15		
07			16		
08			17		
09			18		

Unit 18

🎧 Listen and repeat. Track 52

01 emperor [émpərər]
n 황제, 제왕   the ruler of an empire
For how long was **emperor** Nero in power?
네로 황제는 얼마 동안 권좌에 있었습니까?

02 endangered [endéindʒərd]
a 멸종위기에 처한   to put something in a situation where they might be destroyed completely
I want you to write an essay on **endangered** species.
나는 네가 멸종 위기에 처한 종에 관하여 에세이를 썼으면 해.

03 entrance [éntrəns]
n 입구, 입장   a door, gate, etc. used for entering a place
The building's **entrance** is at the top of the steps.
건물 출입구는 계단 맨 위에 있다.

04 fellowship [félouʃip]
n 단체, 학회 회원   an organized group of people who share an aim
I have wanted to join the Art History **Fellowship** for a long time.
나는 오랫동안 미술사학회에 가입하기를 원해왔다.

05 figure [fígjər]
n 숫자, 모양, 인물   a number representing a particular amount
I just need to check some of the **figures**.
나는 몇 가지 수치만 확인해 보면 된다.

06 flavor [fléivər]
n 맛, 조미료 / v ~에 맛을 내다   the taste of food
The company is famous for making unusual **flavors** of candy.
그 회사는 색다른 맛의 사탕을 만드는 것으로 유명하다.

07 garbage [gáːrbidʒ]
n 쓰레기   waste food, paper, etc. that you throw away
The **garbage** truck will be filled soon.
쓰레기차가 곧 가득 찰 것이다.

08 genius [dʒíːnjəs]
n 천재   who has unusually great intelligence or artistic ability
I didn't know that computer **genius** had a talent for music, too.
컴퓨터 천재가 음악에도 재능이 있는 줄은 몰랐어요.

09 grateful [gréitfəl]
a 감사하고 있는   feeling or showing thanks
I would be **grateful** if you could send me details of your hotel.
당신의 호텔에 대한 상세한 정보를 보내주시면 감사하겠습니다.

key words
empire n 제국 / species n 종, 종류 / aim n 목적 / intelligence n 지능 / detail n 세부, 항목

🎧 Listen and repeat. Track 53

10 horror [hɔ́:rər]
n 공포, 혐오   a feeling of great fear or disgust
They watched in **horror** as the building collapsed.
그들은 건물이 붕괴되는 것을 공포에 사로잡힌 채 지켜보았다.

11 huge [hju:dʒ]
a 거대한, 무한한   extremely large in size or amount
But you already have a **huge** workload.
하지만 당신은 이미 산더미 같은 업무량을 갖고 있잖아요.

12 hunt [hʌnt]
v 사냥하다, 추적하다   to chase wild animals or birds in order to catch or kill
Are tigers still **hunted** in India?
인도에서는 여전히 호랑이를 사냥합니까?

13 issue [íʃu:]
n 발행, 논쟁 / v 발행하다   to make something known formally
How often is the 'World Report' **issued**?
월드 리포트는 얼마나 자주 발행됩니까?

14 jury [dʒúəri]
n 배심, 심사원   a group of people in a court who decide if somebody is guilty or not
The court leaves the decision to the **jury**.
법정은 배심원에게 판단을 맡기고 있다.

15 kindness [káindnis]
n 친절, 호의, 친절한 행위   a kind act
He has tried to return **kindness** from other people.
그는 다른 사람들의 친절에 보답하기 위해 노력해 왔다.

16 lifetime [láiftàim]
n 일생 / a 생애의   the length of time that somebody lives
She is eager to be a great pianist in her **lifetime**.
그녀는 일생 동안 훌륭한 피아니스트가 되기를 열망했다.

17 lift [lift]
v 들어 올리다, 향상시키다   to be raised to a higher position or level
The teacher **lifted** up the box and saw that it was leaking.
선생님은 그 상자를 들어 올려보고 그것이 새고 있는 것을 알았다.

18 likely [láikli]
a 있음직한, 할 것 같은   something will probably happen in a particular situation
Where is this advertisement most **likely** to be seen?
이 광고가 가장 잘 보일 것 같은 곳은 어디일까요?

---

key words
collapse v 붕괴하다 / chase v 추적하다 / guilty a 유죄의 / eager a 갈망하는 / leak n 새다

Unit 18

Exercise

A. Complete the sentence.

1. I just need to check some of the _____.
   나는 몇 가지 수치만 확인해 보면 된다.

2. I want you to write an essay on _____ species.
   나는 네가 멸종 위기에 처한 종에 관하여 에세이를 썼으면 해.

3. She is eager to be a great pianist in her _____.
   녀는 일생 동안 훌륭한 피아니스트가 되기를 열망했다.

4. I have wanted to join the Art History _____ for a long time.
   나는 오랫동안 미술사학회에 가입하기를 원해왔다.

5. The company is famous for making unusual _____ of candy.
   그 회사는 색다른 맛의 사탕을 만드는 것으로 유명하다.

6. The court leaves the decision to the _____.
   법정은 배심원에게 판단을 맡기고 있다.

7. I didn't know that computer _____ had a talent for music, too.
   컴퓨터 천재가 음악에도 재능이 있는 줄은 몰랐어요.

8. For how long was _____ Nero in power?
   네로 황제는 얼마 동안 권좌에 있었습니까?

9. I would be _____ if you could send me details of your hotel.
   당신의 호텔에 대한 상세한 정보를 보내주시면 감사하겠습니다.

10. They watched in _____ as the building collapsed.
    그들은 건물이 붕괴되는 것을 공포에 사로잡힌 채 지켜보았다.

11. But you already have a _____ workload.
    하지만 당신은 이미 산더미 같은 업무량을 갖고 있잖아요.

12. Are tigers still _____ in India?
    인도에서는 여전히 호랑이를 사냥합니까?

13. How often is the 'World Report' _____?
    월드 리포트는 얼마나 자주 발행됩니까?

14. The building's _____ is at the top of the steps.
    건물 출입구는 계단 맨 위에 있다.

15. He has tried to return _____ from other people.
    그는 다른 사람들의 친절에 보답하기 위해 노력해 왔다.

16. The teacher _____ up the box and saw that it was leaking.
    선생님은 그 상자를 들어 올려보고 그것이 새고 있는 것을 알았다.

17. The _____ truck will be filled soon.
    쓰레기차가 곧 가득 찰 것이다.

18. Where is this advertisement most _____ to be seen?
    이 광고가 가장 잘 보일 것 같은 곳은 어디일까요?

Hint

| garbage | lift | flavor | genius | figure | emperor | grateful | hunt | kindness |
| entrance | jury | likely | lifetime | huge | fellowship | horror | issue | endangered |

Exercise

B. Fill in the word and meaning.

	Word	Meaning
01	fellowship	
02	emperor	
03	garbage	
04	lifetime	
05	endangered	
06	grateful	
07	kindness	
08	issue	
09	entrance	
10	likely	
11	horror	
12	lift	
13	hunt	
14	flavor	
15	jury	
16	genius	
17	huge	
18	figure	

	Meaning	Word
01	황제, 제왕	
02	멸종위기에 처한	
03	입구, 입장	
04	단체, 학회 회원	
05	숫자, 모양, 인물	
06	맛, 조미료, ~에 맛을 내다	
07	쓰레기	
08	천재	
09	감사하고 있는	
10	공포, 혐오	
11	거대한, 무한한	
12	사냥하다, 추적하다	
13	발행, 논쟁, 발행하다	
14	배심, 심사원	
15	친절, 호의, 친절한 행위	
16	일생, 생애의	
17	들어올리다, 향상시키다	
18	있음직한, 할 것 같은	

C. Listen, write the word and meaning. (Track 54)

	Word	Meaning		Word	Meaning
01			10		
02			11		
03			12		
04			13		
05			14		
06			15		
07			16		
08			17		
09			18		

Review 9

A. Read and fill in the word and meaning.

word	definition	meaning
	a piece of evidence that helps the police solve a crime	
	a formal discussion of an issue at a public meeting	
	meeting, talking to or writing to somebody else	
	having more than one possible meaning	
	to have something inside or as part of itself	
	a person in your family who lived a long time ago	
	an unpleasant or boring task	
	to make somebody believe something that is not true	
	the series of jobs that somebody has in a particular area of work	
	a continuous decrease in the value, etc. of something	
	to find somebody / something that was hidden	
	the smallest part of a chemical element	
	a small lump on a plant that develops into a flower	
	to become impossible to see	
	having a strong taste making you feel very unhappy	
	extremely unpleasant	
	to be present at an event	
	to say that somebody responsible for something bad	

Hint
bud   deceive   ambiguous   clue   attend   ancestor   career   blame   chore
debate   contain   disgusting   atom   contact   disappear   discover   bitter   decline

B. Read and fill in the word and meaning.

word	definition	meaning
	who has unusually great intelligence or artistic ability	
	the ruler of an empire	
	waste food, paper, etc. that you throw away	
	something will probably happen in a particular situation	
	the taste of food	
	to put something in a situation where they might be destroyed completely	
	a feeling of great fear or disgust	
	feeling or showing thanks	
	to be raised to a higher position or level	
	a door, gate, etc. used for entering a place	
	the length of time that somebody lives	
	extremely large in size or amount	
	an organized group of people who share an aim	
	to chase wild animals or birds in order to catch or kill	
	to make something known formally	
	a kind act	
	a number representing a particular amount	
	a group of people in a court who decide if somebody is guilty or not	

Hint

garbage   lift   flavor   genius   figure   emperor   grateful   hunt   kindness
entrance   jury   likely   lifetime   huge   fellowship   horror   issue   endangered

Unit 19

🎧 Listen and repeat. (Track 55)

01 medium
[míːdiəm]
n 중간, 매개물 / a 중간의   a means you can use to express or communicate something
Radio would be the best advertising **medium** for your Internet Web site.
라디오는 당신의 인터넷 웹사이트를 위한 가장 효과적인 광고 매개체입니다.

02 merry
[méri]
a 명랑한, 축제 기분의   happy and cheerful
I was in no mood to make **merry**.
나는 유쾌하게 떠들고 놀 기분이 나지 않았다.

03 mess
[mes]
n 혼란, 어수선함, 불결   a dirty or untidy state
Please tell them to clean up their **mess** after they finish.
일을 끝내면 어질러 놓은 것들을 치우고 가라고 하세요.

04 neither
[níːðər]
a 어느 쪽도 ~아니다   not one nor the other of two things or people
Neither of us know how to operate this machine.
우리는 둘 다 이 기계를 작동하는 법을 모른다.

05 nickname
[níknèim]
n 별명   an informal name that is connected with real name
According to the advertisement, what is the **nickname** of Chicago?
광고에 따르면, 시카고의 애칭은 무엇입니까?

06 nonsense
[nánsens]
a 무의미한 말, 허튼 소리   silly or unacceptable saying
The teacher won't stand for any **nonsense**.
선생님은 어떤 허튼 소리도 참지 않으실 거예요.

07 package
[pǽkidʒ]
n 포장, 꾸러미   a bag, box, etc. in which things are wrapped
The **package** was returned to its sender.
그 소포는 발신인에게 반송되었다.

08 pardon
[páːrdn]
n 용서 / v 용서하다   the action of forgiving somebody for something
You will **pardon** the personal reference.
개인적인 문제에 대해 언급하는 것을 용서해 주세요.

09 passenger
[pǽsəndʒər]
n 승객, 여객   a person who is travelling in a car, plane or ship
The airline **passengers** are having their bags screened.
비행기 승객들이 가방 검사를 받고 있다.

---

key words
wrap v 싸다, 포장하다 / reference n 언급 / screen v (소지품 등을)검사하다

🎧 Listen and repeat. Track 56

10 possible
[pásəbəl]
a 가능한   that can be done or achieved
We look forward to doing business with you as soon as **possible**.
가능하면 빨리 거래를 시작할 수 있기를 바랍니다.

11 praise
[preiz]
n 칭찬 / **v** 칭찬하다   what you say when you are expressing admiration
The new movie received a lot of **praise** from the critics.
새 영화는 비평가들로부터 많은 찬사를 받았다.

12 pray
[prei]
v 기도하다, 빌다   to speak to God
He had almost never **prayed** in his life, but at that moment, he **prayed** from the bottom of his heart.
그는 일생 동안 기도를 한 적이 거의 없지만, 그 순간에는 마음에서 우러나오는 기도를 드렸다.

13 race
[reis]
n 인종, 종족   a group of people who have the same language, customs, history, etc
People of different **races** have tended to dislike one another.
다른 인종의 사람들은 서로 싫어하는 경향이 있다.

14 raise
[reiz]
v 올리다, 일으키다, 기르다   to move something to a higher level, to care for a child or young animal
It's illegal for them to **raise** your rent like that.
그들이 집세를 그렇게 마구 올리는 것은 위법이다.

15 rapid
[rǽpid]
a 빠른, 신속한   done very quickly
The industry is currently undergoing **rapid** change.
그 산업은 현재 급속한 변화를 겪고 있는 중이다.

16 relax
[rilǽks]
v 늦추다, 긴장을 풀다   to rest while you are doing something
In a second his brow **relaxes**, and his eyes brighten.
잠시 후, 그의 눈썹에선 긴장이 풀리고 그의 눈은 총총해진다.

17 religious
[rilídʒəs]
a 종교(상)의, 신앙의   connected with religion
Most children fear ghosts, especially children from **religious** homes.
대부분의 아이들, 특히 종교적 가정 출신의 아이들은 유령을 두려워한다.

18 republic
[ripʌ́blik]
n 공화국   a country that is governed by a president
Our country is an independent **republic**.
우리 나라는 독립 공화국이다.

---

key words
critic **n** 비평가 / illegal **a** 위법의 / brighten **v** 밝아지다

Unit 19

Exercise

A. Complete the sentence.

1. In a second his brow _____, and his eyes brighten.
   잠시 후, 그의 눈썹에선 긴장이 풀리고 그의 눈은 총총해진다.

2. Radio would be the best advertising _____ for your Internet Web site.
   라디오는 당신의 인터넷 웹사이트를 위한 가장 효과적인 광고 매개체입니다.

3. The _____ was returned to its sender.
   그 소포는 발신인에게 반송되었다.

4. We look forward to doing business with you as soon as _____.
   가능하면 빨리 거래를 시작할 수 있기를 바랍니다.

5. Please tell them to clean up their _____ after they finish.
   일을 끝내면 어질러 놓은 것들을 치우고 가라고 하세요.

6. _____ of us know how to operate this machine.
   우리는 둘 다 이 기계를 작동하는 법을 모른다.

7. According to the advertisement, what is the _____ of Chicago?
   광고에 따르면, 시카고의 애칭은 무엇입니까?

8. People of different _____ have tended to dislike one another.
   다른 인종의 사람들은 서로 싫어하는 경향이 있다.

9. The teacher won't stand for any _____.
   선생님은 어떤 허튼 소리도 참지 않으실 거예요.

10. The airline _____ are having their bags screened.
    비행기 승객들이 가방 검사를 받고 있다.

11. I was in no mood to make _____.
    나는 유쾌하게 떠들고 놀 기분이 나지 않았다.

12. The new movie received a lot of _____ from the critics.
    새 영화는 비평가들로부터 많은 찬사를 받았다.

13. Our country is an independent _____.
    우리 나라는 독립 공화국이다.

14. He had almost never _____ in his life, but at that moment, he _____ from the bottom of his heart.
    그는 일생 동안 기도를 한 적이 거의 없지만, 그 순간에는 마음에서 우러나오는 기도를 드렸다.

15. It's illegal for them to _____ your rent like that.
    그들이 집세를 그렇게 마구 올리는 것은 위법이다.

16. You will _____ the personal reference.
    개인적인 문제에 대해 언급하는 것을 용서해 주세요.

17. The industry is currently undergoing _____ change.
    그 산업은 현재 급속한 변화를 겪고 있는 중이다.

18. Most children fear ghosts, especially children from _____ homes.
    대부분의 아이들, 특히 종교적 가정 출신의 아이들은 유령을 두려워한다.

Hint

| passenger | neither | possible | rapid | republic | pray | pardon | merry | praise |
| nickname | religious | medium | raise | nonsense | race | mess | package | relax |

Exercise

B. Fill in the word and meaning.

	Word	Meaning
01	neither	
02	pardon	
03	race	
04	merry	
05	pray	
06	passenger	
07	raise	
08	mess	
09	praise	
10	nickname	
11	religious	
12	possible	
13	republic	
14	nonsense	
15	rapid	
16	package	
17	relax	
18	medium	

	Meaning	Word
01	중간, 매개물, 중간의	
02	명랑한, 축제 기분의	
03	혼란, 어수선함, 불결	
04	어느 쪽도 ~아니다	
05	별명	
06	무의미한 말, 허튼 소리	
07	포장, 꾸러미	
08	용서, 용서하다	
09	승객, 여객	
10	가능한	
11	칭찬, 칭찬하다	
12	기도하다, 빌다	
13	인종, 종족	
14	올리다, 일으키다, 기르다	
15	빠른, 신속한	
16	늦추다, 긴장을 풀다	
17	종교(상)의, 신앙의	
18	공화국	

C. Listen, write the word and meaning. (Track 57)

	Word	Meaning		Word	Meaning
01			10		
02			11		
03			12		
04			13		
05			14		
06			15		
07			16		
08			17		
09			18		

Unit 19

Unit 20

🎧 Listen and repeat. Track 58

01 ruin [rúːin]
v 파괴하다, 망쳐놓다 / n 파괴, 몰락   to damage something so badly
Rush-hour traffic can **ruin** the day before it even starts.
출퇴근 교통 혼잡은 하루를 시작도 하기 전에 망쳐 놓아요.

02 rule [ruːl]
n 규칙, 통례 / v 다스리다, 규정하다   a statement of what must or must not be done in a particular situation
As from next week this **rule** will come into effect.
다음 주 후부터 이 규칙이 효력이 있다.

03 saint [seint]
n 성인   a very good, kind or patient person
He is some kind of Satan and **saint** combined.
그는 악마와 성인을 합쳐 놓은 듯 한 사람이다.

04 sightsee [sáitsìː]
v 유람하다, 관광하다   to visit interesting places as a tourist
By the way, is this a business trip or are you just **sightseeing**?
그런데 출장 중이신가요 아니면 관광 중 이신가요?

05 slave [sleiv]
n 노예   a person who is legally owned by another person
The king issued a command for the **slave** to be set free.
왕은 노예를 석방하라는 어명을 내렸다.

06 smart [smaːrt]
a 영리한, 세련된   clever; intelligent
It was very **smart** of him not to miss the chance.
그는 영리하게도 그 기회는 놓치지 않았다.

07 steal [stiːl]
v 훔치다   to take something from a person without permission
I hadn't the slightest intention to **steal** it.
그것을 훔칠 생각은 추호도 없었다.

08 steel [stiːl]
n 강철   a strong hard metal that is made of a mixture of iron and carbon
From the graph, what can be said of **steel** imports from Asia?
그래프를 보고 아시아에서 수입된 철강에 대해 말할 수 있는 것은 무엇인가?

09 storage [stɔ́ːridʒ]
n 저장, 창고   the place where things are kept
This room is being used for **storage**.
이 방은 지금 창고로 쓰이고 있어요.

---

key words
permission n 허락 / slight a 약간의, 적은 / carbon n 탄소 / import v 수입하다

🎧 Listen and repeat. (Track 59)

10 technique [tekníːk]
n 기술, 수법 — a particular way of doing something
The new **technique** will lower the cost of production.
그 신기술은 생산 원가를 낮출 것이다.

11 temperature [témpərətʃuəːr]
n 온도, 기온 — the measurement in degrees of how hot or cold
Today's high **temperatures** will be in the mid 80's.
오늘의 최고 기온은 84-6도 정도 되겠습니다.

12 terrific [tərífik]
a 대단한, 아주 좋은 — excellent; wonderful
It's a **terrific** shape in a great location, and the asking price is very reasonable.
집 상태도 좋고 위치도 최상인데다 제시한 가격도 꽤 적당하네요.

13 truth [truːθ]
n 진실, 사실 — the true facts about something
The **truth** will be out someday.
언젠가는 진실이 밝혀질 것이다.

14 tumble [tʌ́mbəl]
v 넘어지다, 폭락하다 / **n** 넘어짐, 폭락 — to fall downwards, a sudden fall
She lost her balance and **tumbled** over.
그녀는 중심을 잃고 넘어졌다.

15 turkey [tə́ːrki]
n 칠면조 — a large bird that is kept on a farm for its meat
Eat more chicken, **turkey**, and fish in place of red meat.
붉은색 육류 대신 닭고기나 칠면조, 생선을 드세요.

16 wisdom [wízdəm]
n 지혜, 슬기로움 — the ability to make sensible decisions
He is here with us today to share his expertise and **wisdom**.
그는 오늘 이 자리에서 그의 전문지식과 지혜를 들려주실 거야.

17 worth [wəːθ]
a 가치가 있는 / **n** 가치 — having a particular value
His academic achievement has undeniable **worth**.
그의 학문적인 업적은 부정할 수 없는 가치를 가지고 있다.

18 zoologist [zouálədʒist]
n 동물학자 — a scientist who studies zoology
He studied the zoology in a college and finally became a renowned **zoologist**.
그는 대학에서 동물학을 공부하고 마침내 유명한 동물학자가 되었다.

key words
expertise **n** 전문 지식 / undeniable **a** 부정할 수 없는 / renowned **a** 유명한

Unit 20 101

Exercise

A. Complete the sentence.

1. The _____ will be out someday.
   언젠가는 진상이 밝혀질 것이다.

2. His academic achievement has undeniable _____.
   그의 학문적인 업적은 부정할 수 없는 가치를 가지고 있다.

3. Rush-hour traffic can _____ the day before it even starts.
   출퇴근 교통 혼잡은 하루를 시작도 하기 전에 망쳐 놓아요.

4. He is some kind of Satan and _____ combined.
   그는 악마와 성자를 합쳐 놓은 듯 한 사람이다.

5. By the way, is this a business trip or are you just _____?
   그런데 출장 중이신가요 아니면 관광 중 이신가요?

6. She lost her balance and _____ over.
   그녀는 중심을 잃고 넘어졌다.

7. The king issued a command for the _____ to be set free.
   왕은 노예를 석방하라는 어명을 내렸다.

8. I hadn't the slightest intention to _____ it.
   그것을 훔칠 생각은 추호도 없었다.

9. From the graph, what can be said of _____ imports from Asia?
   그래프를 보고 아시아에서 수입된 철강에 대해 말할 수 있는 것은 무엇인가?

10. The new _____ will lower the cost of production.
    그 신기술은 생산 원가를 낮출 것이다.

11. He studied the zoology in a college and finally became a renowned _____.
    그는 대학에서 동물학을 공부하고 마침내 유명한 동물학자가 되었다.

12. Today's high _____ will be in the mid 80's.
    오늘의 최고 기온은 84-6도 정도 되겠습니다.

13. It's a _____ shape in a great location, and the asking price is very reasonable.
    집 상태도 좋고 위치도 최상인데다 제시한 가격도 꽤 적당하네요.

14. As from next week this _____ will come into effect.
    다음 주 후부터 이 규칙이 효력이 있다.

15. Eat more chicken, _____, and fish in place of red meat.
    붉은색 육류 대신 닭고기나 칠면조, 생선을 드세요.

16. It was very _____ of him not to miss the chance.
    그는 약빠르게도 그 기회를 놓치지 않았다.

17. This room is being used for _____.
    이 방은 지금 창고로 쓰이고 있어요.

18. He is here with us today to share his expertise and _____.
    그는 오늘 이 자리에서 그의 전문지식과 지혜를 들려주실 거야.

Hint

| storage | technique | steel | slave | saint | ruin | turkey | steal | temperature |
| wisdom | zoologist | tumble | sightsee | worth | truth | smart | terrific | rule |

Exercise

B. Fill in the word and meaning.

	Word	Meaning
01	sightsee	
02	technique	
03	ruin	
04	wisdom	
05	smart	
06	truth	
07	steal	
08	turkey	
09	rule	
10	tumble	
11	zoologist	
12	steel	
13	terrific	
14	worth	
15	slave	
16	temperature	
17	storage	
18	saint	

	Meaning	Word
01	파괴하다, 망쳐놓다, 파괴, 몰락	
02	규칙, 통례, 다스리다, 규정하다	
03	성인	
04	유람하다, 관광하다	
05	노예	
06	영리한, 세련된	
07	훔치다	
08	강철	
09	저장, 창고	
10	기술, 수법	
11	온도, 기온	
12	대단한, 아주 좋은	
13	진실, 사실	
14	넘어지다, 폭락하다, 넘어짐, 폭락	
15	칠면조	
16	지혜, 슬기로움	
17	가치가 있는, 가치	
18	동물학자	

C. Listen, write the word and meaning. Track 60

	Word	Meaning		Word	Meaning
01			10		
02			11		
03			12		
04			13		
05			14		
06			15		
07			16		
08			17		
09			18		

Review 10

A. Read and fill in the word and meaning.

word	definition	meaning
	happy and cheerful	
	an informal name that is connected with real name	
	what you say when you are expressing admiration	
	not one nor the other of two things or people	
	a country that is governed by a president	
	to speak to God	
	a dirty or untidy state	
	a group of people who have the same language, customs, history, etc	
	a means you can use to express or communicate something	
	connected with religion	
	a person who is travelling in a car, plane or ship	
	to move something to a higher level, to care for a child or young animal	
	a bag, box, etc. in which things are wrapped	
	silly or unacceptable saying	
	done very quickly	
	that can be done or achieved	
	the action of forgiving somebody for something	
	to rest while you are doing something	

Hint

passenger neither possible rapid republic pray pardon merry praise
nickname religious medium raise nonsense race mess package relax

B. Read and fill in the word and meaning.

word	definition	meaning
	a strong hard metal that is made of a mixture of iron and carbon	
	a particular way of doing something	
	the place where things are kept	
	to damage something so badly	
	the measurement in degrees of how hot or cold	
	a statement of what must or must not be done in a particular situation	
	excellent; wonderful	
	having a particular value	
	a very good, kind or patient person	
	the true facts about something	
	to take something from a person without permission	
	to fall downwards, a sudden fall	
	to visit interesting places as a tourist	
	a large bird that is kept on a farm for its meat	
	clever; intelligent	
	the ability to make sensible decisions	
	a person who is legally owned by another person	
	a scientist who studies zoology	

Hint

storage   technique   steel   slave   saint   ruin   turkey   steal   temperature
wisdom   zoologist   tumble   sightsee   worth   truth   smart   terrific   rule

Review 10

Unit 21

🎧 Listen and repeat. Track 61

01 absolute **a** 완전한, 절대의, 순수한   complete; total
[ǽbsəlù:t]
The whole trip was an **absolute** disaster.
여행 전부가 완전한 재난이었다.

02 achieve **v** 이루다, 성취하다   to complete something by hard work and skill
[ətʃí:v]
He did everything within his power to **achieve** the goal.
그는 목표를 달성하기 위해 자기가 할 수 있는 모든 일을 다 했다.

03 adolescent **a** 사춘기의, 미숙한   being no longer a child and not yet an adult
[ӕdəlésənt]
Her **adolescent** daughter wants to be prettier.
그녀의 사춘기 딸은 더 예뻐지고 싶어해.

04 advanced **a** 앞으로 나온, 진보한, 상급의   of a high level, highly developed
[ӕdvǽnst]
I registered for the **advanced** Spanish class.
나는 스페인어 상급반에 등록했어.

05 arctic **n** 북극지방 / **a** 북극의, 북극 지방의   connected with the region around the North Pole
[á:rktik]
Migrants return to the **Arctic** from far and wide.
아주 멀리, 다양한 지역에서 철새들이 북극으로 돌아옵니다.

06 area **n** 지역, 지방, 구역   a part of a town or a country
[έəriə]
Traffic will be directed around **areas** affected by the accident.
그 사고에 영향 받은 지역 주변 교통이 통제될 것이다.

07 argument **n** 논의, 토론, 요지   a discussion between people who disagree with each other
[á:rgjəmənt]
He accepted the decision without **argument**.
그는 논의 없이 그 결정을 받아들였다.

08 border **n** 테두리, 국경 / **v** 접하다, 인접하다   a line that divides two countries, etc
[bɔ́:rdər]
We'll be safe once we've escaped across the **border**.
일단 국경선을 탈출하면 안전할 것이다.

09 bundle **n** 꾸러미, 묶음   a number of things tied or folded together
[bʌ́ndl]
There was a **bundle** of letters with an elastic band round them on the table.
탁자 위에 고무줄로 묶여진 편지 꾸러미가 있었다.

key words
disaster **n** 재해, 재앙 / register **v** 등록하다 / region **n** 지방, 지역 / North Pole 북극
migrant **n** 철새 / affected **a** 영향 받은, 침범된 / escape **v** 탈출하다

🎧 Listen and repeat. `Track 62`

10 carton [káːrtən]
n 용기, 상자   a small container made of cardboard or plastic
You can recycle the **cartons** of milk.
우유 용기는 재활용이 가능해요.

11 ceremony [sérəmòuni]
n 의식, 의례, 예의   a formal public or religious event
The master is conducting the wedding **ceremony**.
사회자가 결혼 의례를 진행하고 있습니다.

12 charge [tʃaːrdʒ]
v 청구하다, 고발하다, 책임지다   to ask somebody to pay a particular amount of money
Will my bill automatically be **charged** to my card?
모든 결제는 자동적으로 제 카드로 청구되나요?

13 chase [tʃeis]
v 쫓다 / n 추적, 추구   to run after somebody/something to catch
A bunch of bats **chased** me down the street.
박쥐 떼가 길을 따라가며 날 쫓아 왔습니다.

14 conduct [kəndʌ́kt]
v 수행하다, 인도하다, 지도하다   to organize and do something, especially research
Nowadays, virtually every kind of organization throughout the world **conducts** business with computers.
요즈음 전세계에 걸쳐서 사실상 모든 종류의 기관이 컴퓨터로 일을 수행한다.

15 confuse [kənfjúːz]
v 혼동하다, 혼란시키다   to make somebody unable to think clearly
You must be **confusing** me with someone else.
저를 다른 누군가와 혼동하고 계시군요.

16 connection [kənékʃən]
n 연결, 결합, 관계   an association between people
Is there any **connection** between the two organizations?
그 두 조직 사이에 어떤 관계가 있습니까?

17 cushion [kúʃən]
v (충격을)흡수하다, 무마하다 / n 쿠션   a bag filled with soft material to make it more comfortable
The company produces sleeping mats and **cushions**.
그 회사는 취침용 매트와 쿠션을 생산한다.

18 daily [déili]
a 매일의 / ad 매일   done, made or happening every day
The six hours' overtime pay is much more than his **daily** wage.
6시간 초과근무 수당이 그의 일당보다 훨씬 많다.

key words
caffeine n 카페인 / formal a 의례상의, 공식의 / religious a 종교적인 automatically ad 자동적으로 / bunch n 다발, 떼 / virtually ad 사실상, 실질적으로 association a 관련, 결합 / overtime n 초과근무 / wage n 임금

Unit 21 107

Exercise

A. Complete the sentence.

1. He accepted the decision without _____.
   그는 논의 없이 그 결정을 받아들였다.
2. The company produces sleeping mats and _____.
   그 회사는 취침용 매트와 쿠션을 생산한다.
3. He did everything within his power to _____ the goal.
   그는 목표를 달성하기 위해 자기가 할 수 있는 모든 일을 다 했다.
4. I registered for the _____ Spanish class.
   나는 스페인어 상급반에 등록했어.
5. Migrants return to the _____ from far and wide.
   아주 멀리, 다양한 지역에서 철새들이 북극으로 돌아옵니다.
6. Is there any _____ between the two organizations?
   그 두 조직 사이에 어떤 관계가 있습니까?
7. We'll be safe once we've escaped across the _____.
   일단 국경선을 탈출하면 안전할 것이다.
8. The whole trip was an _____ disaster.
   여행 전부가 완전한 재난이었다.
9. There was a _____ of letters with an elastic band round them on the table.
   탁자 위에 고무줄로 묶여진 편지 꾸러미가 있었다.
10. Will my bill automatically be _____ to my card?
    모든 결제는 자동적으로 제 카드로 청구되나요?
11. A bunch of bats _____ me down the street.
    박쥐 떼가 길을 따라가며 날 쫓아 왔습니다.
12. Nowadays, virtually every kind of organization throughout the world _____ business with computers.
    요즈음 전세계에 걸쳐서 사실상 모든 종류의 기관이 컴퓨터로 일을 수행한다.
13. Traffic will be directed around _____ affected by the accident.
    그 사고에 영향 받은 지역 주변 교통이 통제될 것이다.
14. Her _____ daughter wants to be prettier.
    그녀의 사춘기 딸은 더 예뻐지고 싶어해.
15. You must be _____ me with someone else.
    저를 다른 누군가와 혼동하고 계시군요.
16. The six hours' overtime pay is much more than his _____ wage.
    6시간 초과근무 수당이 그의 일당보다 훨씬 많다.
17. You can recycle the _____ of milk.
    우유 용기는 재활용이 가능해요.
18. The master is conducting the wedding _____.
    사회자가 결혼 의례를 진행하고 있습니다.

Hint
carton   bundle   argument   connection   achieve   ceremony   border   area   cushion
daily   conduct advanced   absolute   confuse   adolescent chase   arctic charge

Exercise

B. Fill in the word and meaning.

	Word	Meaning
01	area	
02	ceremony	
03	absolute	
04	charge	
05	border	
06	achieve	
07	conduct	
08	argument	
09	cushion	
10	confuse	
11	advanced	
12	connection	
13	bundle	
14	chase	
15	arctic	
16	daily	
17	carton	
18	adolescent	

	Meaning	Word
01	완전한, 절대의, 순수한	
02	이루다, 성취하다	
03	사춘기의, 미숙한	
04	앞으로 나온, 진보한, 상급의	
05	북극의, 북극 지방	
06	지역, 지방, 구역	
07	논의, 토론, 요지	
08	테두리, 국경, 접하다	
09	꾸러미, 묶음	
10	용기, 상자	
11	의식, 의례, 예의	
12	청구하다, 고발하다, 책임지다	
13	쫓다, 추적, 추구	
14	수행하다, 인도하다, 지도하다	
15	혼동하다, 혼란시키다	
16	연결, 결합, 관계	
17	(충격을)흡수하다, 쿠션	
18	매일의, 매일	

C. Listen, write the word and meaning. (Track 63)

	Word	Meaning		Word	Meaning
01			10		
02			11		
03			12		
04			13		
05			14		
06			15		
07			16		
08			17		
09			18		

Unit 21

Unit 22

🎧 Listen and repeat. Track 64

01 decent [díːsənt]
a 상당한, 제대로 된, 점잖은   being of an acceptable standard; satisfactory
Is there a **decent** dry cleaner around here?
이 근처에 괜찮은 세탁소 있어요?

02 dig [dig]
v 파다, 파헤치다, 발굴하다   to move earth and make a hole in the ground
The children in the playground are busy **digging** in the sand.
운동장에 있는 아이들은 모래를 파헤치느라 정신이 없다.

03 define [difáin]
n 규정하다, 정의를 내리다   to say exactly what a word or idea means
Before we study the latest research, let's **define** a few terms.
최근의 연구를 공부하기 전에, 몇 가지 용어의 뜻을 규정합시다.

04 disappointed [dìsəpɔ́intid]
a 실망한, 낙담한   sad because something was not as good as you had hoped
I was a little **disappointed** about the play, because it wasn't as funny as I thought it would be.
난 그 연극에 약간 실망했는데, 내가 예상했던 것만큼 재미가 없었기 때문이었다.

05 effort [éfərt]
n 노력, 수고   the physical or mental strength or energy
All my **efforts** turned out to be in vain.
나의 모든 노력이 수포로 돌아갔다.

06 element [éləmənt]
n 요소, 성분, 원소   one important part of something
Letters are the **elements** out of which all our words are formed.
문자는 모든 말을 구성하는 요소이다.

07 emergency [imə́ːrdʒənsi]
n 비상사태, 위급   a serious event that needs immediate action
Emergency funds are kept in a separate account.
비상금은 별도의 계좌에 넣어 둔다.

08 extra [ékstrə]
a 여분의, 임시의   more than is usual, expected or than exist already
She needs an **extra** room to store her luggage.
그녀는 짐을 놓기 위한 여분의 방이 필요하다.

09 factor [fǽktər]
n 요인, 인자, 요소   one of the things that influences a decision, situation, etc
A key **factor** is fear and stress and the way we handle it.
핵심적인 요인은 두려움과 스트레스 그리고 우리가 그것들을 다루는 방식입니다.

---

key words
satisfactory a 만족한 / term n 용어 / vain a 헛된, 보람없는
store v 창고에 보관하다 / luggage n 수화물 / influenc v 영향을 주다

🎧 Listen and repeat. Track 65

10 fail [feil]
v 실패하다, 못하다, 부족하다   not to be successful in something
It is said that the first love is likely to **fail**.
첫 사랑은 실패하기 쉽다고 한다.

11 familiar [fəmíljər]
a 친밀한, 잘 알고 있는   well-known to you
We understand that you're somewhat **familiar** with the church.
우리는 당신이 교회에 대해 어느 정도 알고 계신 것으로 알고 있습니다.

12 faithful [féiθfəl]
a 충실한, 정확한   always staying with and supporting a person, organization or belief
He is **faithful** in the performance of his duties.
그는 그의 의무를 이행하는 일에 충실하다.

13 freeze [fri:z]
v 얼다 / n 동결   to become hard because of extreme cold
When water **freezes** solid, it is called ice.
물이 단단하게 얼면, 그것은 얼음이라 불린다.

14 guard [ga:rd]
n 경계, 경호인 / v 지키다   a person who protects a place or people
Most of celebrities have private **guards** around them.
대부분의 유명 인사들은 그들 주위에 개인 경호원들을 두고 있다.

15 harmoniously [ha:rmóuniəsli]
ad 사이 좋게, 화목하게   peacefully without any disagreement
It is not common interests alone that create relationships **harmoniously**.
공동 관심사만이 조화로운 인간관계를 맺게 해주는 것은 아니다.

16 hoop [hu:p]
n 테, 후프 / v 테를 두르다   a large ring made of wood, metal, or plastic
The girl student is playing for the hula **hoop** on the playground.
여학생은 운동장에서 훌라 후프를 돌리고 있다.

17 imitate [ímitèit]
v 모방하다, 흉내 내다   to copy the behavior of somebody / something
Our ancestors produced fine handicrafts using skills that are difficult to **imitate** today.
우리의 조상들은 오늘날 모방하기 힘든 기술을 사용해서 훌륭한 수공품들을 제작했다.

18 impact [ímpækt]
n 영향(력), 충돌   an effect or impression
The **impact** of the new policy was not immediately clear.
새 정책의 영향력을 즉각적으로 알 수는 없었다.

key words
celebrity n 유명인 / disagreement n 불화, 안 맞음 / handicraft n 수공예(품)

Unit 22

Exercise

A. Complete the sentence.

1. Is there a _____ dry cleaner around here?
   이 근처에 괜찮은 세탁소 있어요?

2. It is said that the first love is likely to _____.
   첫 사랑은 실패하기 쉽다고 한다.

3. She needs an _____ room to store her luggage.
   그녀는 짐을 놓기 위한 여분의 방이 필요하다.

4. We understand that you're somewhat _____ with the church.
   우리는 당신이 교회에 대해 어느 정도 알고 계신 것으로 알고 있습니다.

5. Most of celebrities have private _____ around them.
   대부분의 유명 인사들은 그들 주위에 개인 경호원들을 두고 있다.

6. It is not common interests alone that create relationships _____.
   공동 관심사만이 조화로운 인간관계를 맺게 해주는 것은 아니다.

7. The girl student is playing for the hula _____ on the playground.
   여학생은 운동장에서 훌라 후프를 돌리고 있다.

8. Our ancestors produced fine handicrafts using skills that are difficult to _____ today.
   우리의 조상들은 오늘날 모방하기 힘든 기술을 사용해서 훌륭한 수공품들을 제작했다.

9. The children in the playground are busy _____ in the sand.
   운동장에 있는 아이들은 모래를 파헤치느라 정신이 없다.

10. He is _____ in the performance of his duties.
    그는 그의 의무를 이행하는 일에 충실하다.

11. Before we study the latest research, let's _____ a few terms.
    최근의 연구를 공부하기 전에, 몇 가지 용어의 뜻을 규정합시다.

12. All my _____ turned out to be in vain.
    나의 모든 노력이 수포로 돌아갔다.

13. When water _____ solid, it is called ice.
    물이 단단하게 얼면, 그것은 얼음이라 불린다.

14. The _____ of the new policy was not immediately clear.
    새 정책의 효과를 즉각적으로 알 수는 없었다.

15. Letters are the _____ out of which all our words are formed.
    문자는 모든 말을 구성하는 요소이다.

16. _____ funds are kept in a separate account.
    비상금은 별도의 계좌에 넣어 둔다.

17. I was a little _____ about the play, because it wasn't as funny as I thought it would be.
    난 그 연극에 약간 실망했는데, 내가 예상했던 것만큼 재미가 없었기 때문이었다.

18. A key _____ is fear and stress and the way we handle it.
    핵심적인 요인은 두려움과 스트레스 그리고 우리가 그것들을 다루는 방식입니다.

Hint

define   extra   faithful   decent   harmoniously   hoop   fail   guard   impact
familiar   freeze   effort   imitate   disappointed   element   dig   factor   emergency

Exercise

B. Fill in the word and meaning.

	Word	Meaning
01	effort	
02	factor	
03	decent	
04	guard	
05	extra	
06	fail	
07	element	
08	imitate	
09	freeze	
10	dig	
11	impact	
12	harmoniously	
13	emergency	
14	hoop	
15	faithful	
16	disappointed	
17	familiar	
18	define	

	Meaning	Word
01	상당한, 제대로 된, 점잖은	
02	파다, 파헤치다, 발굴하다	
03	규정하다, 정의를 내리다	
04	실망한, 낙담한	
05	노력, 수고	
06	요소, 성분, 원소	
07	비상사태, 위급	
08	여분의, 임시의, 특별한	
09	요인, 인자, 요소	
10	실패하다, 못하다, 부족하다	
11	친밀한, 잘 알고 있는	
12	충실한, 정확한	
13	얼다, 동결	
14	경계, 경호인, 지키다	
15	사이 좋게, 화목하게	
16	테, 후프, 테를 두르다	
17	모방하다, 흉내 내다	
18	영향(력), 충돌	

🎧 **C. Listen, write the word and meaning.** (Track 66)

	Word	Meaning		Word	Meaning
01			10		
02			11		
03			12		
04			13		
05			14		
06			15		
07			16		
08			17		
09			18		

Review 11

A. Read and fill in the word and meaning.

word	definition	meaning
	to make somebody unable to think clearly	
	complete; total	
	to organize and do something, especially research	
	done, made or happening every day	
	an association between people	
	to complete something by hard work and skill	
	a bag filled with soft material to make it more comfortable	
	to run after somebody/something to catch	
	a number of things tied or folded together	
	being no longer a child and not yet an adult	
	a line that divides two countries, etc	
	connected with the region around the North Pole	
	the reason that you give to support your opinion	
	to ask somebody to pay a particular amount of money	
	of a high level, highly developed	
	a formal public or religious event	
	a part of a town or a country	
	a small container made of cardboard or plastic	

Hint

carton bundle argument connection achieve ceremony border area cushion
daily conduct advanced absolute confuse adolescent chase arctic charge

B. Read and fill in the word and meaning.

word	definition	meaning
	to move earth and make a hole in the ground	
	a serious event that needs immediate action	
	one of the things that influences a decision, situation, etc	
	a large ring made of wood, metal, or plastic	
	more than is usual, expected or than exist already	
	being of an acceptable standard; satisfactory	
	one important part of something	
	not to be successful in something	
	to say exactly what a word or idea means	
	the physical or mental strength or energy	
	well-known to you	
	sad because something was not as good as you had hoped	
	to copy the behavior of somebody / something	
	to become hard because of extreme cold	
	a person who protects a place or people	
	always staying with and supporting a person, organization or belief	
	an effect or impression	
	peacefully without any disagreement	

Hint

define   extra   faithful   decent   harmoniously   hoop   fail   guard   impact
familiar   freeze   effort   imitate   disappointed   element   dig   factor   emergency

Review 11

Unit 23

🎧 Listen and repeat. Track 67

01	**impossible**	**a** 불가능한, ~할 수 없는 not able to be done
	[impásəbəl]	His handwriting is **impossible** to read. 그의 필체는 읽을 수가 없다.

02	**impress**	**a** 감동시키다, ~에게 감명을 주다 to make somebody feel admiration and respecte
	[imprés]	I was particularly **impressed** by the graphic presentation of the storm. 나는 태풍을 사실적으로 표현한 것에 대해 깊은 감명을 받았다.

03	**interpret**	**v** 해석하다, 통역하다 to explain the meaning of something or to translate
	[intə́:rprit]	It can be **interpreted** in various ways. 그것은 여러 가지로 해석될 수 있다.

04	**jaw**	**n** 턱 either or the two bones in your face that contain your teeth
	[dʒɔː]	If you are lying on your back, your tongue and **jaw** slide backward a little. 등을 바닥에 대고 누우면, 혀와 턱이 뒤쪽으로 약간 흘러내린다.

05	**join**	**v** 가입하다, 결합하다 to become a member of a club
	[dʒɔin]	Did you **join** any of the extracurricular activities? 당신은 어느 과외 활동에 가입하셨습니까?

06	**lumberjack**	**n** 재목 벌채인 a person whose job is to cut down trees
	[lʌ́mbərdʒæk]	**Lumberjacks** often worked twelve hours a day and faced incredible dangers on the job. 벌목꾼들은 하루에 12시간 일하며 믿을 수 없을 만큼 위험한 일에 직면했다.

07	**luxury**	**n** 사치(품) / **a** 사치스러운, 고급의 the enjoyment of expensive and beautiful things
	[lʌ́kʃəri]	He despises her because she lives in **luxury**. 그는 그녀가 사치스럽게 생활하기 때문에 그녀를 경멸한다.

08	**machine**	**n** 기계, 기구 / **a** 기계의 a piece of equipment with moving parts
	[məʃíːn]	The **machine** is good value for the money. 그 기계는 값어치를 한다.

09	**mechanic**	**n** 정비사, 수리공 someone whose job is to repair and maintain machines and engines
	[məkǽnik]	Can you recommend a good **mechanic**? 괜찮은 정비사를 추천해 주시겠어요?

key words
handwriting **n** 필적 / translate **v** 번역하다 / tongue **n** 혀 / maintain **v** 간수하다

🎧 Listen and repeat. (Track 68)

10 moment [móumənt]
n 순간, 단시간, 중요성 — a very short period of time
The error of one **moment** becomes the sorrow of a lifetime.
한 순간의 실수가 일생의 슬픔이 된다.

11 moral [mɔ́(ː)rəl]
a 도덕적인, 윤리적인 / n 교훈 — concerned with what is right and wrong
This **moral** law is still in full force.
이 도덕률은 아직도 엄연히 존재하고 있다.

12 movable [múːvəbəl]
a 움직일 수 있는 — that can be moved
He decided to buy a doll with **movable** arms and legs for his daughter.
그는 딸아이를 위하여 팔다리가 움직이는 인형을 사주기로 결심했다.

13 official [əfíʃəl]
a 공무상의, 공식의 / n 공무원 — a person who has a position of authority
Due to fires and hot lava, **officials** cannot enter the city to check the damage.
화염과 뜨거운 용암 때문에 공무원들이 피해 정도를 알아보기 위해 도시에 들어갈 수도 없다.

14 omit [oumít]
v 빼다, 빠뜨리다, 게을리 하다 — not to include something
A few names had been **omitted** from the list.
몇몇 이름이 명단에서 빠져 있었습니다.

15 oppose [əpóuz]
v 반대하다, 대항하다, 대비시키다 — to disagree with somebody's beliefs or plans
He did not dare **oppose** me.
그는 감히 나를 반대하지 않았다.

16 permission [pərmíʃən]
n 허가, 면허 — the act of allowing to do something
I wonder who we have to talk to get **permission** to toss this junk.
이 물건들을 버리려면 누구의 허락을 받아야 하는지 모르겠어요.

17 personality [pə̀ːrsənǽləti]
n 성격, 개성, 인물 — the different qualities of a person's character
Birth rank effects **personality**.
출생순위가 성격에 영향을 미친다.

18 physically [fízikəli]
ad 육체적으로, 물질적으로 — connected with your body rather than your mind
These exercises will help you keep **physically** fit this winter.
이런 운동들이 이번 겨울에 여러분들을 신체적으로 건강하게 지켜줄 것입니다.

key words
lava n 용암 / toss v 던지다, 버리다 / junk n 쓰레기, 폐물

Exercise

A. Complete the sentence.

1. The error of one _____ becomes the sorrow of a lifetime.
   한 순간의 실수가 일생의 슬픔이 된다.

2. I was particularly _____ by the graphic presentation of the storm.
   나는 태풍을 사실적으로 표현한 것에 대해 깊은 감명을 받았다.

3. Can you recommend a good _____?
   괜찮은 정비사를 추천해 주시겠어요?

4. If you are lying on your back, your tongue and _____ slide backward a little.
   등을 바닥에 대고 누우면, 혀와 턱이 뒤쪽으로 약간 흘러내린다.

5. _____ often worked twelve hours a day and faced incredible dangers on the job.
   벌목꾼들은 하루에 12시간 일하며 믿을 수 없을 만큼 위험한 일에 직면했다.

6. He despises her because she lives in _____.
   그는 그녀가 사치스럽게 생활하기 때문에 그녀를 경멸한다.

7. He did not dare _____ me.
   그는 감히 나를 반대하지 않았다.

8. The _____ is good value for the money.
   그 기계는 값어치를 한다.

9. I wonder who we have to talk to get _____ to toss this junk.
   이 물건들을 버리려면 누구의 허락을 받아야 하는지 모르겠어요.

10. This _____ law is still in full force.
    이 도덕률은 아직도 엄연히 존재하고 있다.

11. He decided to buy a doll with _____ arms and legs for his daughter.
    그는 딸아이를 위하여 팔다리가 움직이는 인형을 사주기로 결심했다.

12. His handwriting is _____ to read.
    그의 필체는 읽을 수가 없다.

13. Due to fires and hot lava, _____ cannot enter the city to check the damage.
    화염과 뜨거운 용암 때문에 공무원들이 피해 정도를 알아보기 위해 도시에 들어갈 수도 없다.

14. Birth rank effects _____.
    출생순위가 성격에 영향을 미친다.

15. Did you _____ any of the extracurricular activities?
    당신은 어느 과외 활동에 가입하셨습니까?

16. It can be _____ in various ways.
    그것은 여러 가지로 해석될 수 있다.

17. A few names had been _____ from the list.
    몇몇 이름이 명단에서 빠져 있었습니다.

18. These exercises will help you keep _____ fit this winter.
    이런 운동들이 이번 겨울에 여러분들을 신체적으로 건강하게 지켜줄 것입니다.

Hint

permission   mechanic   oppose   impossible   official   luxury   join   physically   jaw
lumberjack   moment   impress   personality   machine   movable   moral   interpret   omit

Exercise

B. Fill in the word and meaning.

	Word	Meaning
01	impress	
02	lumberjack	
03	moment	
04	impossible	
05	mechanic	
06	omit	
07	luxury	
08	official	
09	permission	
10	interpret	
11	physically	
12	machine	
13	personality	
14	join	
15	movable	
16	oppose	
17	moral	
18	jaw	

	Meaning	Word
01	불가능한, ~할 수 없는	
02	감동시키다, ~에게 감명을 주다	
03	해석하다, 통역하다	
04	턱	
05	가입하다, 결합하다	
06	재목 벌채인	
07	사치(품), 사치스러운, 고급의	
08	기계, 기구, 기계의	
09	정비사, 수리공	
10	순간, 단시간, 중요성	
11	도덕적인, 윤리적인, 교훈	
12	움직일 수 있는	
13	공무상의, 공식의, 공무원	
14	빼다, 빠뜨리다, 게을리하다	
15	반대하다, 대항하다, 대비시키다	
16	허가, 면허	
17	성격, 개성, 인물	
18	육체적으로, 물질적으로	

🎧 C. Listen, write the word and meaning. (Track 69)

	Word	Meaning		Word	Meaning
01			10		
02			11		
03			12		
04			13		
05			14		
06			15		
07			16		
08			17		
09			18		

Unit 24

🎧 Listen and repeat. (Track 70)

01 pressure [préʃər]
n 압박, 압력, 곤란   the force that is produced when you press on something
Apply **pressure** to the source of the bleeding.
출혈이 일어나는 곳에 압박을 가하세요.

02 production [prədʌ́kʃən]
n 생산, 제작, 생산량   the making or growing of something
We're supposed to halve **production** for the next six weeks.
앞으로 6주 동안 생산량을 절반으로 줄여야 한다.

03 promise [prámis]
n 약속, 계약 / v 약속하다   a written or spoken statement or agreement
Don't make **promises** you can't keep, though.
그렇다고 지킬 수 없는 약속은 하지 마십시오.

04 register [rédʒəstər]
v 등록하다, 기록하다   to put a name on an official list
You must **register** for campsites in accordance with the instructions.
지시사항에 따라 야영장에 등록해야 합니다.

05 regret [rigrét]
v 후회하다, 슬퍼하다 / n 유감   to feel sorry that you did or didn't do something
Although he was excited about buying the new car, he now **regrets** it.
그는 새 차를 샀을 때 굉장히 좋아했지만, 지금은 그것을 후회한다.

06 repair [ripéər]
v 수리하다, 회복하다   to put something damaged back into good condition
The restaurant will be closed for three weeks to **repair**.
그 레스토랑은 수리를 하기 위해 3주 동안 휴업할 것이다.

07 search [səːrtʃ]
v 찾다, 탐색하다   to look for or to examine something
I can **search** for information, shop on the Internet.
나는 인터넷으로 정보를 찾고 쇼핑을 할 수 있다.

08 seldom [séldəm]
a 좀처럼 ~않는, 드물게   not often; rarely
He very **seldom** eats breakfast.
그는 아침 식사를 좀처럼 하지 않는다.

09 selfish [sélfiʃ]
a 이기적인, 자기 본위의   thinking only about your own needs or wishes
The **selfish** man was despised by his companions.
그 이기적인 남자는 동료들에게 멸시받았다.

---

key words
halve v 반감하다 / in accordance with ~에 따라 / despise v 경멸하다, 얕보다

🎧 Listen and repeat. Track 71

10 specific [spisífik]
a 특수한, 특정한, 명확한   particular; not general
But beyond that there's nothing **specific** that you need to do.
그 외에 당신이 해야 할 특정한 일은 없어요.

11 split [split]
v 쪼개다, 분리하다 / n 분리   to divide or share something
Green wood **splits** more easily than dry.
마른 나무보다 생나무가 잘 쪼개진다.

12 stage [steidʒ]
n 무대, 단계 / v 상연하다   one part of the progress or development
I cannot say yes at the present **stage**.
현 단계에서는 긍정적인 답을 드릴 수 없습니다.

13 therefore [ðéərfɔ̀:r]
ad 그런 까닭에, 그 결과   for that reason
Therefore, you should learn how to use a computer.
그러므로 여러분은 컴퓨터를 사용하는 방법을 배워야 합니다.

14 thorough [θə́:rou]
a 철저한, 완벽주의자인   doing things in a very careful way
He is a **thorough** vegetarian.
그는 철저한 채식주의자이다.

15 thought [θɔ:t]
n 생각, 사색, 사상   the power or process of thinking
He was lost in **thought**.
그는 사색에 잠겨 있었다.

16 vehicle [ví:ikəl]
n 수송 수단, 탈것   something which transports people or things from place to place
Car manufactures ought to produce more secure **vehicles**.
자동차 제조업자들은 좀 더 안전한 수송 수단을 생산해야 한다.

17 vitamin [váitəmin]
n 비타민   one of several substances that are important for health
Orange juice contains a lot of **vitamin** C.
오렌지 주스는 비타민 C가 많이 들어 있다.

18 watercolor [wɔ́:tərkʌ̀lər]
n 그림물감, 수채화   a picture that has been painted with watercolors
People are reviewing the **watercolors**.
사람들이 수채화를 살펴보고 있다.

key words
progress n 진행, 진전 / vegetarian r n 채식주의자 / ought to v ~해야만 한다

Exercise

A. Complete the sentence.

1. He was lost in _____.
   그는 사색에 잠겨 있었다.

2. We're supposed to halve _____ for the next six weeks.
   앞으로 6주 동안 생산량을 절반으로 줄여야 한다.

3. You must _____ for campsites in accordance with the instructions.
   지시사항에 따라 야영장에 등록해야 합니다.

4. The _____ man was despised by his companions.
   그 이기적인 남자는 동료들에게 멸시받았다.

5. Don't make _____ you can't keep, though.
   그렇다고 지킬 수 없는 약속은 하지 마십시오.

6. But beyond that there's nothing _____ that you need to do.
   그 외에 당신이 해야 할 특정한 일은 없어요.

7. Although he was excited about buying the new car, he now _____ it.
   그는 새 차를 샀을 때 굉장히 좋아했지만, 지금은 그것을 후회한다.

8. Car manufactures ought to produce more secure _____.
   자동차 제조업자들은 좀 더 안전한 수송 수단을 생산해야 한다.

9. The restaurant will be closed for three weeks to _____.
   그 레스토랑은 수리를 하기 위해 3주 동안 휴업할 것이다.

10. I can _____ for information, shop on the Internet.
    나는 인터넷으로 정보를 찾고 쇼핑을 할 수 있다.

11. Green wood _____ more easily than dry.
    마른 나무보다 생나무가 잘 쪼개진다.

12. I cannot say yes at the present _____.
    현 단계에서는 긍정적인 답을 드릴 수 없습니다.

13. Apply _____ to the source of the bleeding.
    출혈이 일어나는 곳에 압박을 가하세요.

14. _____, you should learn how to use a computer.
    그러므로 여러분은 컴퓨터를 사용하는 방법을 배워야 합니다.

15. Orange juice contains a lot of _____ C.
    오렌지 주스는 비타민 C가 많이 들어 있다.

16. He very _____ eats breakfast.
    그는 아침 식사를 좀처럼 하지 않는다.

17. He is a _____ vegetarian.
    그는 철저한 채식주의자이다.

18. People are reviewing the _____.
    사람들이 수채화를 살펴보고 있다.

Hint

| selfish | repair | stage | vehicle | promise | regret | seldom | pressure | thought |
| specific | production | vitamin | register | split | | thorough | search | watercolor | therefore |

Exercise

B. Fill in the word and meaning.

	Word	Meaning
01	register	
02	pressure	
03	specific	
04	therefore	
05	repair	
06	stage	
07	thought	
08	search	
09	vitamin	
10	selfish	
11	watercolor	
12	production	
13	vehicle	
14	seldom	
15	thorough	
16	split	
17	regret	
18	promise	

	Meaning	Word
01	압박, 압력, 곤란	
02	생산, 제작, 생산량	
03	약속, 계약, 약속하다	
04	등록하다, 기록하다	
05	후회하다, 슬퍼하다, 유감	
06	수리하다, 회복하다	
07	찾다, 탐색하다	
08	좀처럼 ~않는, 드물게	
09	이기적인, 자기 본위의	
10	특수한, 특정한, 명확한	
11	쪼개다, 분리하다, 분리	
12	무대, 단계, 상연하다	
13	그런 까닭에, 그 결과	
14	철저한, 완벽주의자인	
15	생각, 사색, 사상	
16	수송 수단, 탈것	
17	비타민	
18	그림물감, 수채화	

🎧 **C. Listen, write the word and meaning.** (Track 72)

	Word	Meaning		Word	Meaning
01			10		
02			11		
03			12		
04			13		
05			14		
06			15		
07			16		
08			17		
09			18		

Review 12

A. Read and fill in the word and meaning.

word	definition	meaning
	a very short period of time	
	to become a member of a club	
	connected with your body rather than your mind	
	not able to be done	
	either or the two bones in your face that contain your teeth	
	to explain the meaning of something or to translate	
	concerned with what is right and wrong	
	the different qualities of a person's character	
	to make somebody feel admiration and respect	
	someone whose job is to repair and maintain machines and engines	
	not to include something	
	a piece of equipment with moving parts	
	a person who has a position of authority	
	the act of allowing to do something	
	that can be moved	
	a person whose job is to cut down trees	
	to disagree with somebody's beliefs or plans	
	the enjoyment of expensive and beautiful things	

Hint

permission   mechanic   oppose   impossible   official   luxury   join   physically   jaw
lumberjack   moment   impress   personality   machine   movable   moral   interpret   omit

B. Read and fill in the word and meaning.

word	definition	meaning
	a written or spoken statement or agreement	
	one part of the progress or development	
	the force that is produced when you press on something	
	the making or growing of something	
	something which transports people or things from place to place	
	to divide or share something	
	one of several substances that are important for health	
	for that reason	
	particular; not general	
	a picture that has been painted with watercolors	
	to put a name on an official list	
	the power or process of thinking	
	to put something damaged back into good condition	
	thinking only about your own needs or wishes	
	doing things in a very careful way	
	to look for or to examine something	
	not often; rarely	
	to feel sorry that you did or didn't do something	

Hint

selfish   repair   stage   vehicle   promise   regret   seldom   pressure   thought
specific production   vitamin   register split   thorough search   watercolor therefore

Review 12

Unit 25

🎧 Listen and repeat. Track 73

01 academic
[ækədémik]
a 학구적인, 대학의   connected with education, especially in school and universities
Universities waste far too much attention on sports activities, often doing harm to **academic** programs.
대학들은 학구적인 활동에 해를 끼치면서까지 스포츠 활동에 지나친 관심을 쓰고 있다.

02 adventure
[ædvéntʃər]
n 모험(심) / **v** 위험을 무릅쓰다   an experience that is very unusual, exciting or dangerous
Mark Twain wrote the book **Adventures** of Huckleberry Finn more than one hundred years ago.
마크 트웨인이 "허클베리 핀의 모험"을 쓴 지 100년이 넘었다.

03 aerobics
[ɛəróubiks]
n 에어로빅스   physical exercises that people do to music
She does **aerobics** every day to improve her figure.
그녀는 몸매를 위해 매일 에어로빅스를 한다.

04 alarming
[əláːrmiŋ]
a 심각한, 불안하게 만드는   that makes you frightened or worried
Nowadays accidents and crimes augment in an **alarming** way.
요즘 사고와 범죄가 심각하게 증가하고 있다.

05 article
[áːrtikl]
n 기사, 물건, 조항   a piece of writing in a newspaper or magazine
I had to read more than 10 **articles** before writing the paper.
그 보고서를 쓰기 위해 10개 이상의 기사를 읽어야 했다.

06 assure
[əʃúər]
v 보증하다, 안심 시키다   to promise somebody that something will certainly happen
I **assure** you that it is perfectly safe.
나는 그것이 더할 나위 없이 안전하다는 것을 보증한다.

07 astronaut
[æstrənɔ̀ːt]
n 우주비행사   a person who travels in a spacecraft
The **astronauts** were greeted with enthusiastic applause.
우주 비행사들은 열광적인 갈채로 환영받았다.

08 brief
[briːf]
a 짧은, 간단한 / **v** 간단히 알리다   short or quick
The typhoon will hit the island for only a **brief** time.
태풍은 짧은 시간 동안 섬을 습격할 것이다.

09 bronze
[branz]
n 청동(제품) / **a** 청동(색)의   a reddish-brown metal
The school bell is made of **bronze**.
학교의 종은 청동으로 만들어졌다.

---

key words
frighten **v** 두려워하게 하다 / augment **v** 증대하다, 늘다 / enthusiastic **a** 열광적인 / applause **n** 박수갈채

🎧 Listen and repeat. Track 74

10 brow [brau]
n 이마   forehead
We must live by the sweat of our **brow**.
우리들은 이마에 땀 흘려 일하며 살아야 한다.

11 chief [tʃi:f]
a 최고의, 주요한 / n 장   most important, of the highest level
The **chief** foods eaten in any country depend largely on what grows best in its climate.
어떤 나라에서 소비되는 주요 음식들은 주로 그 나라의 기후에서 무엇이 가장 잘 자라는가에 달려있다.

12 chip [tʃip]
n 얇은 조각, 토막 / v 잘게 썰다   to break into a small piece
They **chipped** the carrots to cook stew.
그들은 스튜를 만들기 위해 당근을 잘게 썰었다.

13 civil [sívəl]
a 시민의, 민간인의   connected with the people who live in a country
He insists that it is the time to show **civil** spirit.
그는 지금이 시민 정신을 발휘해야 할 때라고 주장한다.

14 climate [kláimit]
n 기후, 풍토   the normal weather conditions of a particular region
In some areas of the United States, bad **climate** and soil make farming an impossible task.
미국의 어떤 지역에서는, 나쁜 기후와 토양이 농사를 불가능한 일로 만든다.

15 consider [kənsídər]
v 고려하다, 숙고하다   to think about something carefully
It is not possible for us to **consider** your proposal.
당신의 제안을 고려하는 것이 불가능합니다.

16 consumer [kənsú:mər]
n 소비자, 수요자   a person who buys things or uses services
What do tests show about **consumer** preferences?
소비자의 선호도 조사는 무엇을 보여주고 있나요?

17 decrease [dí:kri:s]
v 감소하다 / n 감소   to become or to make something smaller or less
The number of persons sitting in the waiting room has **decreased**.
대기실에 앉아있던 사람들의 수가 점점 줄어들었다.

18 demand [dimǽnd]
v 요구하다, 묻다 / n 요구, 수요   to ask a strong request, desire or need
He **demanded** a strict statement of the accident.
그는 그 사고에 대한 정확한 진술을 요구했다.

key words
proposal **n** 신청, 제안 / preference **n** 더 좋아함

Unit 25

Exercise

A. Complete the sentence.

1. Universities waste far too much attention on sports activities, often doing harm to _____ programs.
   대학들은 학구적인 활동에 해를 끼치면서까지 스포츠 활동에 지나친 관심을 쓰고 있다.

2. They _____ the carrots to cook stew.
   그들은 스튜를 만들기 위해 당근을 잘게 썰었다.

3. She does _____ every day to improve her figure.
   그녀는 몸매를 위해 매일 에어로빅스를 한다.

4. I had to read more than 10 _____ before writing the paper.
   그 보고서를 쓰기 위해 10개 이상의 기사를 읽어야 했다.

5. What do tests show about _____ preferences?
   소비자의 선호도 조사는 무엇을 보여주고 있나요?

6. He _____ a strict statement of the accident.
   그는 그 사고에 대한 정확한 진술을 요구했다.

7. I _____ you that it is perfectly safe.
   나는 그것이 더할 나위 없이 안전하다는 것을 보증한다.

8. The typhoon will hit the island for only a _____ time.
   태풍은 짧은 시간 동안 섬을 습격할 것이다.

9. The _____ were greeted with enthusiastic applause.
   우주 비행사들은 열광적인 갈채로 환영받았다.

10. The school bell is made of _____.
    학교의 종은 청동으로 만들어졌다.

11. The _____ foods eaten in any country depend largely on what grows best in its climate.
    어떤 나라에서 소비되는 주요 음식들은 주로 그 나라의 기후에서 무엇이 가장 잘 자라는가에 달려있다.

12. Mark Twain wrote the book _____ of Huckleberry Finn more than one hundred years ago.
    마크 트웨인이 "허클베리 핀의 모험"을 쓴 지 100년이 넘었다.

13. He insists that it is the time to show _____ spirit.
    그는 지금이 시민 정신을 발휘해야 할 때라고 주장한다.

14. We must live by the sweat of our _____.
    우리들은 이마에 땀 흘려 일하며 살아야 한다.

15. In some areas of the United States, bad _____ and soil make farming an impossible task.
    미국의 어떤 지역에서는, 나쁜 기후와 토양이 농사를 불가능한 일로 만든다.

16. It is not possible for us to _____ your proposal.
    당신의 제안을 고려하는 것이 불가능합니다.

17. The number of persons sitting in the waiting room has _____.
    대기실에 앉아있던 사람들의 수가 점점 줄어들었다.

18. Nowadays accidents and crimes augment in an _____ way.
    요즘 사고와 범죄가 심각하게 증가하고 있다.

Hint

astronaut alarming consumer chip demand brief chief article bronze
consider adventure decrease brow academic aerobics climate civil assure

Exercise

B. Fill in the word and meaning.

	Word	Meaning
01	brief	
02	academic	
03	brow	
04	adventure	
05	civil	
06	astronaut	
07	consumer	
08	assure	
09	decrease	
10	chip	
11	demand	
12	article	
13	consider	
14	bronze	
15	climate	
16	alarming	
17	chief	
18	aerobics	

	Meaning	Word
01	학구적인, 대학의	
02	모험(심), 위험을 무릅쓰다	
03	에어로빅스	
04	심각한, 불안하게 만드는	
05	기사, 물건, 조항	
06	보증하다, 안심 시키다	
07	우주비행사	
08	짧은, 간단한, 간단히 알리다	
09	청동(제품), 청동(색)의	
10	이마	
11	최고의, 주요한, 장	
12	얇은 조각, 토막, 잘게 썰다	
13	시민의, 민간인의	
14	기후, 풍토	
15	고려하다, 숙고하다	
16	소비자, 수요자	
17	감소하다, 감소	
18	요구하다, 묻다, 요구, 수요	

C. Listen, write the word and meaning. (Track 75)

	Word	Meaning
01		
02		
03		
04		
05		
06		
07		
08		
09		
10		
11		
12		
13		
14		
15		
16		
17		
18		

Unit 26

🎧 Listen and repeat. (Track 76)

01 democracy [dimákrəsi]
n 민주주의, 민주정치 — a system in which the government of a country is elected by the people
The road to **democracy** is never smooth.
민주주의로 가는 길은 결코 평탄하지 않다.

02 disaster [dizǽstər]
n 재해, 재난 — an event that causes a lot of harm or damage
The immediate cause of the tragic accident is, of course, a natural **disaster**.
이 비극적인 사고의 직접 원인은 물론 자연 재난이다.

03 discourage [diskə́:ridʒ]
v 용기를 잃게 하다, 실망시키다 — to make somebody realize that it would not be successful
She was **discouraged** by losing so many of her tennis matches.
그녀는 테니스 시합에서 그토록 많이 져서 실망했다.

04 display [displéi]
v 보이다, 전시하다 — to put something in a place where people will see it
The New Stone Age tools are **displayed** in the museum.
신석기 시대의 도구들이 그 박물관에 전시되어 있다.

05 emphasis [émfəsis]
n 강조, 중점 — special importance or attention
My English teacher puts great **emphasis** on grammar.
우리 영어 선생님은 문법을 크게 강조하신다.

06 epidemic [èpədémik]
n 유행(병) / a 유행성의 — a large number of people suffering from the same disease
The **epidemic** has swept through the town for two weeks.
유행병이 2주간 한 마을을 휩쓸었다.

07 essence [ésəns]
n 본질, 진수 — the basic or most important quality of something
The **essence** of the problem is that there is not enough money available.
문제의 본질은 사용 가능한 돈이 충분하지 않다는데 있다.

08 fan [fæn]
n 부채, 선풍기 / v 부채로 부치다 — a machine with parts that turn around quickly to create a cool air
Excuse me. I'd like to return this **fan**.
실례합니다만 이 선풍기를 환불하고 싶은데요.

09 fear [fiər]
n 공포, 두려움 / v 두려워하다 — to be afraid of somebody / something
She **fears** losing her lover, and with good reason.
그녀가 애인을 잃을 까봐 두려워하는 것에는 충분한 근거가 있다.

---

key words
tragic a 비극적인 / realize v 실현하다, 실감하다 / New Stone Age 신석기 시대 / available a 쓸 수 있는

🎧 Listen and repeat. Track 77

10 feed [fi:d]
v 먹을 것을 주다, 부양하다 — to give food to a person or an animal
Trained attendants will **feed** the animals.
전속 훈련사들만이 동물들에게 먹이를 줄 수 있습니다.

11 fright [frait]
n 두려움, 공포 — a sudden feeling of fear or shock
When the rescue team reached him, he was shaking with **fright**.
구조대가 그에게 다가갔을 때, 그는 공포에 떨고 있었다.

12 fund [fʌnd]
n 자금, 기금 / v 투자하다 — a sum of money that is collected for a particular purpose
The hospital set up a special **fund** to buy new equipment.
그 병원은 새 장비를 구입할 특별 자금을 마련했다.

13 funeral [fjú:nərəl]
n 장례(식) / a 장례식의, 장례식용의 — a ceremony for burying a dead person
The **funeral** passed like some awful dream.
그 장례식은 무시무시한 꿈처럼 지나갔다.

14 harvest [há:rvist]
n 수확, 추수 / v 수확하다 — the act of collecting the grain, fruit, etc
The **harvest** is dependent upon the weather.
수확은 날씨에 의해 좌우됩니다.

15 heaven [hévən]
n 천국, 하늘 — the place that God lives and good people go when they die
Heaven helps those who help themselves.
하늘은 스스로 돕는 자를 돕는다.

16 height [hait]
n 높이, 고도, 절정 — the measurement from the bottom to the top of a person or thing
The chair seems a little too low, how do I adjust the **height**?
의자가 너무 낮은 것 같은데, 높이를 어떻게 조정하죠?

17 improve [imprú:v]
v 개선하다, 향상시키다 — to become or to make something better
The office's work was to **improve** consumer service.
그 영업소의 업무는 고객 서비스를 개선하는 일이었다.

18 impulse [ímpʌls]
n 충격, 충동 — a sudden desire to do without thinking about the results
He bought the car on **impulse** for a lot of money.
그는 많은 돈을 들여 충동적으로 그 차를 샀다.

---

key words
rescue n 구조 / awful a 두려운 / dependent a 의지하고 있는

Exercise

A. Complete the sentence.

1. The immediate cause of the tragic accident is, of course, a natural _____.
   이 비극적인 사고의 직접 원인은 물론 자연 재난이다.

2. The _____ is dependent upon the weather.
   수확은 날씨에 의해 좌우됩니다.

3. She was _____ by losing so many of her tennis matches.
   그녀는 테니스 시합에서 그토록 많이 져서 실망했다.

4. The hospital set up a special _____ to buy new equipment.
   그 병원은 새 장비를 구입할 특별 자금을 마련했다.

5. My English teacher puts great _____ on grammar.
   우리 영어 선생님은 문법을 크게 강조하신다.

6. The _____ has swept through the town for two weeks.
   유행병이 2주간 한 마을을 휩쓸었다.

7. The office's work was to _____ consumer service.
   그 영업소의 업무는 고객 서비스를 개선하는 일이었다.

8. The _____ of the problem is that there is not enough money available.
   문제의 본질은 사용 가능한 돈이 충분하지 않다는데 있다.

9. Excuse me. I'd like to return this _____.
   실례합니다만 이 선풍기를 환불하고 싶은데요.

10. The road to _____ is never smooth.
    민주주의로 가는 길은 결코 평탄하지 않다.

11. When the rescue team reached him, he was shaking with _____.
    구조대가 그에게 다가갔을 때, 그는 공포에 떨고 있었다.

12. The _____ passed like some awful dream.
    그 장례식은 무시무시한 꿈처럼 지나갔다.

13. _____ helps those who help themselves.
    하늘은 스스로 돕는 자를 돕는다.

14. Trained attendants will _____ the animals.
    전속 훈련사들만이 동물들에게 먹이를 줄 수 있습니다.

15. She _____ losing her lover, and with good reason.
    그녀가 애인을 잃을 까봐 두려워하는 것에는 충분한 근거가 있다.

16. The chair seems a little too low, how do I adjust the _____?
    의자가 너무 낮은 것 같은데, 높이를 어떻게 조정하죠?

17. The New Stone Age tools are _____ in the museum.
    신석기 시대의 도구들이 그 박물관에 전시되어 있다.

18. He bought the car on _____ for a lot of money.
    그는 많은 돈을 들여 충동적으로 그 차를 샀다.

Hint

essence   discourage   disaster   height   heaven   fear   display   fan   funeral
democracy   emphasis   harvest   feed   epidemic   fund   impulse   fright   improve

Unit 26

Exercise

B. Fill in the word and meaning.

	Word	Meaning
01	fan	
02	democracy	
03	feed	
04	harvest	
05	display	
06	fear	
07	impulse	
08	disaster	
09	improve	
10	emphasis	
11	fund	
12	height	
13	essence	
14	fright	
15	heaven	
16	epidemic	
17	funeral	
18	discourage	

	Meaning	Word
01	민주주의, 민주정치	
02	재해, 재난	
03	용기를 잃게 하다, 실망시키다	
04	보이다, 전시하다	
05	강조, 중점	
06	유행(병), 유행성의	
07	본질, 진수	
08	부채, 선풍기, 부채로 부치다	
09	공포, 두려움, 두려워하다	
10	먹을 것을 주다, 부양하다	
11	두려움, 공포	
12	자금, 기금, 투자하다	
13	장례(식), 장례식의, 장례식용의	
14	수확, 추수, 수확하다	
15	천국, 하늘	
16	높이, 고도, 절정	
17	개선하다, 향상시키다	
18	충격, 충동	

🎧 C. Listen, write the word and meaning. (Track 78)

	Word	Meaning		Word	Meaning
01			10		
02			11		
03			12		
04			13		
05			14		
06			15		
07			16		
08			17		
09			18		

Review 13

A. Read and fill in the word and meaning.

word	definition	meaning
assure	to promise somebody that something will certainly happen	
brief	short or quick	
astronaut	a person who travels in a spacecraft	
consumer	a person who buys things or uses services	
academic	connected with education, especially in school and universities	
bronze	a reddish-brown metal	
chief	most important, of the highest level	
brow	forehead	
adventure	an experience that is very unusual, exciting or dangerous	
decrease	to become or to make something smaller or less	
chip	a small piece of stone, glass, wood etc	
demand	to ask a strong request, desire or need	
civil	connected with the people who live in a country	
aerobics	physical exercises that people do to music	
climate	the normal weather conditions of a particular region	
article	a piece of writing in a newspaper or magazine	
consider	to think about something carefully	
alarming	that makes you frightened or worried	

Hint

astronaut   alarming   consumer   chip   demand   brief   chief   article   bronze
consider   adventure   decrease   brow   academic   aerobics   climate   civil   assure

B. Read and fill in the word and meaning.

word	definition	meaning
	an event that causes a lot of harm or damage	
	a machine with parts that turn around quickly to create a cool air	
	a system in which the government of a country is elected by the people	
	a sudden desire to do without thinking about the results	
	to make somebody realize that it would not be successful	
	to be afraid of somebody / something	
	special importance or attention	
	to become or to make something better	
	to give food to a person or an animal	
	to put something in a place where people will see it	
	a sudden feeling of fear or shock	
	the basic or most important quality of something	
	the measurement from the bottom to the top of a person or thing	
	a sum of money that is collected for a particular purpose	
	a large number of people suffering from the same disease	
	the act of collecting the grain, fruit, etc	
	a ceremony for burying a dead person	
	the place that God lives and good people go when they die	

Hint

essence   discourage   disaster   height   heaven   fear   display   fan   funeral
democracy   emphasis   harvest   feed   epidemic   fund   impulse   fright   improve

Unit 27

🎧 Listen and repeat. (Track 79)

01 increase [inkríːs]
v 늘리다, 증대하다 / n 증가 — to make something larger in number or amount
I work out every day to **increase** muscle and develop endurance.
나는 근육을 늘리고 지구력을 키우기 위해 운동을 매일 한다.

02 incredible [inkrédəbəl]
a 믿을 수 없는 — impossible or very difficult to believe
Witnesses said the force of the explosion was **incredible**.
목격자들은 폭발력이 믿을 수 없을 만한 것이었다고 말했다.

03 journalism [dʒə́ːrnəlìzəm]
n 저널리즘, 신문 잡지업계 — the profession of writing about news or talking about it on the TV or radio
In America, the President reigns for four years, and **journalism** governs forever.
미국에서 대통령은 4년간 통치하지만 저널리즘은 영구히 지배한다.

04 kneel [niːl]
v 무릎을 꿇다 — to rest on one or both knees
It looks really hard for the Buddhist believers to **kneel** and bow so many times before the Buddha.
불교 신자들이 무릎을 꿇고 불상 앞에서 여러 번 절하는 건 정말 힘들어 보여.

05 lean [liːn]
v 기대다, 의지하다 — to rest against something that it gives support
The old man turned off the tape recorder and **leaned** back in his chair.
노인은 녹음기를 끄고, 의자에 몸을 기댔다.

06 maintain [meintéin]
v 유지하다, 지속하다 — to make something continue at the same level
The body requires proper nutrition in order to **maintain** it.
신체는 그것을 유지하는데 필요한 알맞은 영양소를 요구한다.

07 mammal [mǽməl]
n 포유동물 — an animal of the type that gives birth to live babies
Mammals have a larger, more well-developed brain than do other animals.
포유동물은 다른 동물들보다 더 크고 더 잘 발달된 두뇌를 가지고 있다.

08 manage [mǽnidʒ]
v 해내다, 경영하다, 다루다 — to succeed in doing something difficult
I finally **managed** to find what I was looking for.
난 마침내 내가 찾던 것을 가까스로 발견해냈다.

09 melt [melt]
v 녹다, 녹이다 — to make something change from a solid to a liquid
Warmer temperatures create more water by **melting** glaciers.
더 따뜻해진 기온은 빙산을 녹게 함으로써 더 많은 물이 생기게 한다.

---

key words
endurance n 인내, 지구력 / witness n 목격자, 증인 / explosion n 폭발
nutrition n 영양 / glacier n 빙하

🎧 Listen and repeat. Track 80

10 merely [míərli]
ad 단지, 전혀   only; just
I am **merely** making an inquiry.
저는 단지 문의를 해보려고 합니다.

11 naked [néikid]
a 벌거벗은, 꾸밈 없는   not wearing any clothes
The little maiden walked on with her tiny **naked** feet, that were quite red and blue from cold.
그 어린 소녀는 그녀의 작고 벌거벗은 발이 추위로 파래질 때까지 계속 걸어야 했다.

12 national [nǽʃənəl]
a 국민의, 국가의   connected with all of a country
Successful economists must be able to understand the effect of world events on **national** economies.
성공적인 경제학자들은 국가경제에 끼치는 세계적 사건들의 영향을 이해해야만 한다.

13 origin [ɔ́:rədʒin]
n 기원, 출생, 유래   the point from which something starts
Its exact **origins** are not known but it seems to have been prevalent during the mid eighteenth century.
그것의 정확한 기원은 알려져 있지 않지만 18세기 중반의 성행을 했었던 것 같다.

14 orphanage [ɔ́:rfənidʒ]
n 고아원   a home for children whose parents are dead
I do volunteer work at the **orphanage** every Sunday.
저는 매주 일요일 고아원에서 자원 봉사를 합니다.

15 otherwise [ʌ́ðərwàiz]
ad 그렇지 않으면   if you do not do something or something does not happen
Please make sure you dry this inside out, **otherwise** the color can easily fade.
이 옷은 꼭 뒤집어서 말려야 하는데, 안 그러면 색이 쉽게 바래니까요.

16 pace [peis]
n (일, 걸음)속도, 걸음   the speed at which you walk, run, etc
My grandparents walk at a steady **pace** every day.
나의 조부모님은 매일마다 일정한 속도로 산보를 하신다.

17 plain [plein]
a 쉬운, 명백한, 단순한   easy to understand; clear
The document is written in **plain** language, not in legal jargon.
그 서류는 법률 용어가 아니고 쉬운 언어로 쓰여 있다.

18 palm [pa:m]
n 손바닥   the flat, inner surface of your hand
She held the coins tightly in the **palm** of her hand.
그녀는 손바닥으로 동전들을 꽉 쥐었다.

key words
maiden n 소녀 / prevalent a 널리 보급된 / fade v (색이) 바래다 / steady a 한결 같은 / jargon n 특수 용어

Unit 27 137

Exercise

A. Complete the sentence.

1. I finally _____ to find what I was looking for.
   난 마침내 내가 찾던 것을 가까스로 발견해냈다.
2. The old man turned off the tape recorder and _____ back in his chair.
   노인은 녹음기를 끄고, 의자에 몸을 기댔다.
3. Witnesses said the force of the explosion was _____.
   목격자들은 폭발력이 믿을 수 없을 만한 것이었다고 말했다.
4. The little maiden walked on with her tiny _____ feet, that were quite red and blue from cold.
   그 어린 소녀는 그녀의 작고 벌거벗은 발이 추위로 파래질 때까지 계속 걸어야 했다.
5. In America, the President reigns for four years, and _____ governs forever.
   미국에서 대통령은 4년간 통치하지만 저널리즘은 영구히 지배한다.
6. It looks really hard for the Buddhist believers to _____ and bow so many times before the Buddha.
   불교 신자들이 무릎을 꿇고 불상 앞에서 여러 번 절하는 건 정말 힘들어 보여.
7. I work out every day to _____ muscle and develop endurance.
   나는 근육을 늘리고 지구력을 키우기 위해 운동을 매일 한다.
8. Warmer temperatures create more water by _____ glaciers.
   더 따뜻해진 기온은 빙산을 녹게 함으로써 더 많은 물이 생기게 한다.
9. Successful economists must be able to understand the effect of world events on _____ economies.
   성공적인 경제학자들은 국가경제에 끼치는 세계적 사건들의 영향을 이해해야만 한다.
10. Its exact _____ are not known but it seems to have been prevalent during the mid eighteenth century.
    그것의 정확한 기원은 알려져 있지 않지만 18세기 중반의 성행을 했었던 것 같다.
11. My grandparents walk at a steady _____ every day.
    나의 조부모님은 매일마다 일정한 속도로 산보를 하신다.
12. I am _____ making an inquiry.
    저는 단지 문의를 해보려고 합니다.
13. I do volunteer work at the _____ every Sunday.
    저는 매주 일요일 고아원에서 자원 봉사를 합니다.
14. _____ have a larger, more well-developed brain than do other animals.
    포유동물은 다른 동물들보다 더 크고 더 잘 발달된 두뇌를 가지고 있다.
15. The document is written in _____ language, not in legal jargon.
    그 서류는 법률 용어가 아니고 쉬운 언어로 쓰여 있다.
16. Please make sure you dry this inside out _____ the color can easily fade.
    이 옷은 꼭 뒤집어서 말려야 하는데, 안 그러면 색이 쉽게 바래니까요.
17. The body requires proper nutrition in order to _____ it.
    신체는 그것을 유지하는데 필요한 알맞은 영양소를 요구한다.
18. She held the coins tightly in the _____ of her hand.
    그녀는 손바닥으로 동전들을 꽉 쥐었다.

Hint

| increase | orphanage | mammal | melt | kneel | merely | lean | incredible | palm |
| manage | journalism | otherwise | naked | plain | national | origin | maintain | pace |

Exercise

B. Fill in the word and meaning.

	Word	Meaning
01	lean	
02	increase	
03	national	
04	kneel	
05	melt	
06	orphanage	
07	maintain	
08	otherwise	
09	plain	
10	mammal	
11	pace	
12	journalism	
13	merely	
14	palm	
15	manage	
16	origin	
17	naked	
18	incredible	

	Meaning	Word
01	늘리다, 증대하다, 증가	
02	믿을 수 없는	
03	저널리즘, 신문 잡지업계	
04	무릎을 꿇다	
05	기대다, 의지하다	
06	유지하다, 지속하다	
07	포유 동물	
08	해내다, 경영하다, 다루다	
09	녹다, 녹이다	
10	단지, 전혀	
11	벌거벗은, 꾸밈 없는	
12	국민의, 국가의	
13	기원, 출생, 유래	
14	고아원	
15	그렇지 않으면	
16	(일, 걸음)속도, 걸음	
17	쉬운, 명백한, 단순한	
18	손바닥	

🎧 C. Listen, write the word and meaning. (Track 81)

	Word	Meaning		Word	Meaning
01			10		
02			11		
03			12		
04			13		
05			14		
06			15		
07			16		
08			17		
09			18		

Unit 27

Unit 28

🎧 Listen and repeat. Track 82

01 promote　　v 증진하다, 촉진하다　　to encourage something
[prəmóut]　　Proper exercise **promotes** health.
적절한 운동은 건강을 증진시킨다.

02 proper　　a 적당한, 타당한, 고유의　　right, suitable or correct
[prápər]　　It's dangerous to neglect to have **proper** treatment.
적당한 치료를 등한시하면 위험하다.

03 protein　　n 단백질 / a 단백질의　　a substance found in food such as meat or beans
[próuti:in]　　This **protein**'s structure is particularly complex.
이 단백질 구조는 특히 복잡하다.

04 replace　　v 대신하다, 대체하다　　to use somebody in place of another person
[ripléis]　　During the twentieth century, many synthetic products have **replaced** the natural products.
20세기 동안 많은 합성물이 천연물을 대체해 왔다.

05 reply　　v 대답하다, 응답하다　　to say, write or do something as an answer
[riplái]　　I have been so busy with my homework that I couldn't **reply**.
나는 숙제로 너무 바빠서 응답하지 못했다.

06 respect　　v 존경하다 / n 존경, 주의　　to admire or have a high opinion of somebody
[rispékt]　　I always **respect** my parents because they brought us up well.
부모님이 우리를 잘 키워 주셔서 나는 부모님을 항상 존경한다.

07 secret　　a 비밀의 / n 비밀　　something that is not or must not be known by other people
[sí:krit]　　The **secret** that we share must never become public.
우리 사이의 비밀이 절대로 알려지면 안됩니다.

08 sensible　　a 분별 있는, 현명한　　able to make good judgements based on reason
[sénsəbəl]　　To work merely to earn more money than they need is not **sensible**.
필요 이상의 돈을 벌기 위해서만 일하는 것은 현명하지 못한 일이다.

09 shelf　　n 선반　　a long flat piece of wood or glass used for putting things on
[ʃelf]　　Those up on the **shelf** over here are all of excellent quality.
이쪽 선반 위에 있는 것들이 모두 품질이 우수합니다.

key words
neglect v 게을리 하다, 경시하다 / synthetic a 합성의, 종합적인 / merely ad 단지

🎧 Listen and repeat. (Track 83)

10 steadily [stédili]
ad 착실히, 확실하게, 꾸준히   developing or happening gradually, firmly
Nutritionists say that vitamin supplements are not necessary for a child who is **steadily** gaining height and weight.
영양학자들은 비타민 보충제들이 착실하게 키와 몸무게가 느는 아이들에게는 필요하지 않다고 말한다.

11 steward [stjúːərd]
v ~의 일을 보다 / **v** 집사   a man whose job is to look after somebody
After a considerable amount to drink, he asked the **steward** directions to the men's room.
꽤 많은 양을 마신 후, 이 남자는 집사에게 화장실이 어딘지 물었다.

12 stroke [strouk]
n 한번 치기, 타격   a sudden successful action
An oak is not felled with one **stroke**.
참나무는 한 번 쳐서 쓰러지지 않는다.

13 throughout [θruːáut]
prep ~동안, ~에 걸쳐서   from the beginning to the end of something
A passenger seated very close to me coughed continually **throughout** the flight.
나와 가까이 앉은 한 승객이 비행기를 타고 가는 동안 내내 기침을 한다.

14 tide [taid]
n 조류, 흥망 / **v** 조류를 타다   the regular change in the level of the sea
The **tides** are a response of the waters of the ocean to the pull of the moon and the sun.
조류는 달과 태양의 인력에 대한 바닷물의 반응이다.

15 tightly [taitli]
ad 단단히, 꽉   firmly, strongly
She kept her eyes **tightly** closed.
그녀는 두 눈을 꼭 감았다.

16 vocabulary [voukǽbjəlèri]
n 어휘, 단어집   all the words that somebody knows
English will continue to grow and change as countries everywhere add new **vocabulary** and expressions.
영어는 도처의 나라들이 새로운 어휘와 표현을 추가함에 따라 계속 성장하고 변화할 것이다.

17 volunteer [vàləntíər]
n 지원자 / **v** 지원하다, 자생하다   a person who offers to do something without being forced
Volunteers collected donations for the benefit of the handicapped.
자원 봉사자들이 장애자들을 위한 기부금을 모았다.

18 wage [weidʒ]
n 임금, 보상   the regular amount of money that you earn
As the **wages** were low, there were few applicants for the job.
임금이 낮아서 그 일자리에는 지원자가 거의 없었다.

---

key words
nutritionist **n** 영양학자 / considerable **a** 상당한 / donation **n** 기부금 / applicant **n** 지원자

Exercise

A. Complete the sentence.

1. An oak is not felled with one _____.
   참나무는 한 번 쳐서 쓰러지지 않는다.
2. A passenger seated very close to me coughed continually _____ the flight.
   나와 가까이 앉은 한 승객이 비행기를 타고 가는 동안 내내 기침을 한다.
3. I have been so busy with my homework that I couldn't _____.
   나는 숙제로 너무 바빠서 응답하지 못했다.
4. Nutritionists say that vitamin supplements are not necessary for a child who is _____ gaining height and weight.
   영양학자들은 비타민 보충제들이 착실하게 키와 몸무게가 느는 아이들에게는 필요하지 않다고 말한다.
5. Proper exercise _____ health.
   적절한 운동은 건강을 증진시킨다.
6. _____ collected donations for the benefit of the handicapped.
   자원 봉사자들이 장애자들을 위한 기부금을 모았다.
7. The _____ are a response of the waters of the ocean to the pull of the moon and the sun.
   조류는 달과 태양의 인력에 대한 바닷물의 반응이다.
8. English will continue to grow and change as countries everywhere add new _____ and expressions.
   영어는 도처의 나라들이 새로운 어휘와 표현을 추가함에 따라 계속 성장하고 변화할 것이다.
9. Those up on the _____ over here are all of excellent quality.
   이쪽 선반 위에 있는 것들이 모두 품질이 우수합니다.
10. The _____ that we share must never become public.
    우리 사이의 비밀이 절대로 알려지면 안됩니다.
11. As the _____ were low, there were few applicants for the job.
    임금이 낮아서 그 일자리에는 지원자가 거의 없었다.
12. I always _____ my parents because they brought us up well.
    부모님이 우리를 잘 키워 주셔서 나는 부모님을 항상 존경한다.
13. After a considerable amount to drink, he asked the _____ directions to the men's room.
    꽤 많은 양을 마신 후, 이 남자는 집사에게 화장실이 어딘지 물었다.
14. It's dangerous to neglect to have _____ treatment.
    적당한 치료를 등한시하면 위험하다.
15. She kept her eyes _____ closed.
    그녀는 두 눈을 꼭 감았다.
16. This _____'s structure is particularly complex.
    이 단백질 구조는 특히 복잡하다.
17. During the twentieth century, many synthetic products have _____ the natural products.
    20세기 동안 많은 합성물이 천연물을 대체해 왔다.
18. To work merely to earn more money than they need is not _____.
    필요 이상의 돈을 벌기 위해서만 일하는 것은 현명하지 못한 일이다.

Hint

| promote | reply | vocabulary | steward | replace | wage | secret | steadily | volunteer |
| stroke | shelf | throughout | protein | proper | tide | tightly | respect | sensible |

Exercise

B. Fill in the word and meaning.

	Word	Meaning
01	replace	
02	steward	
03	reply	
04	promote	
05	vocabulary	
06	secret	
07	wage	
08	proper	
09	tightly	
10	sensible	
11	volunteer	
12	stroke	
13	protein	
14	tide	
15	steadily	
16	throughout	
17	respect	
18	shelf	

	Meaning	Word
01	증진하다, 촉진하다	
02	적당한, 타당한, 고유의	
03	단백질, 단백질의	
04	대신하다, 대체하다	
05	대답하다, 응답하다	
06	존경하다, 존경, 주의	
07	비밀의, 비밀	
08	분별 있는, 현명한	
09	선반	
10	착실히, 확실하게, 꾸준히	
11	~의 일을 보다, 집사	
12	한번 치기, 타격	
13	~동안, ~에 걸쳐서	
14	조류, 흥망, 조류를 타다	
15	단단히, 꽉	
16	어휘, 단어집	
17	지원자, 지원하다, 자생하다	
18	임금, 보상	

C. Listen, write the word and meaning. (Track 84)

	Word	Meaning		Word	Meaning
01			10		
02			11		
03			12		
04			13		
05			14		
06			15		
07			16		
08			17		
09			18		

Review 14

A. Read and fill in the word and meaning.

word	definition	meaning
	the point from which something starts	
	the flat, inner surface of your hand	
	to make something larger in number or amount	
	connected with all of a country	
	a home for children whose parents are dead	
	impossible or very difficult to believe	
	not wearing any clothes	
	if you do not do something or something does not happen	
	the profession of writing about news or talking about it on the TV or radio	
	to succeed in doing something difficult	
	to make something change from a solid to a liquid	
	to rest on one or both knees	
	only; just	
	an animal of the type that gives birth to live babies	
	to rest against something that it gives support	
	the speed at which you walk, run, etc	
	to make something continue at the same level	
	easy to understand; clear	

Hint

increase orphanage mammal melt kneel merely lean incredible palm
manage journalism otherwise naked plain national origin maintain pace

B. Read and fill in the word and meaning.

word	definition	meaning
	the regular change in the level of the sea	
	all the words that somebody knows	
	firmly, strongly	
	to encourage something	
	from the beginning to the end of something	
	a person who offers to do something without being forced	
	a substance found in food such as meat or beans	
	a sudden successful action	
	right, suitable or correct	
	the regular amount of money that you earn	
	a long flat piece of wood or glass used for putting things on	
	developing or happening gradually, firmly	
	to use somebody in place of another person	
	a man whose job is to look after somebody	
	to admire or have a high opinion of somebody	
	something that is not or must not be known by other people	
	to say, write or do something as an answer	
	able to make good judgements based on reason	

Hint

promote   reply   vocabulary   steward   replace   wage   secret   steadily   volunteer
stroke   shelf   throughout   protein   proper   tide   tightly   respect   sensible

Review 14

Unit 29

🎧 Listen and repeat. (Track 85)

01 acceptable
[ækséptəbəl]
a 받아들일 수 있는   that can be allowed
One or two mistakes are **acceptable** but no more than that.
한 두번의 실수는 받아들일 수 있지만 그 이상은 안됩니다.

02 accidental
[æksidéntl]
a 우연한, 비본질적인   happening by chance, not planned
Police do not know if the explosion was **accidental** or not.
경찰은 그 폭발이 우연한 것이었는지 아닌지를 모르고 있다.

03 although
[ɔːlðóu]
conj 비록 ~일지라도   in spite of the fact that
Although apples do not grow during the cold season, apple trees must have such a season in order to flourish.
비록 사과는 추운 계절 동안에는 자라지 않지만, 사과나무들이 번성하기 위해서는 추운 계절이 있어야만 한다.

04 amuse
[əmjúːz]
v 즐겁게 하다   to make time pass pleasantly for somebody
Toddlers don't need expensive toys to **amuse** themselves.
걸음마를 시작한 아이들을 즐겁게 하기 위해서 비싼 장난감은 필요 없다.

05 attitude
[ǽtitjùːd]
n 태도, 마음가짐, 자세   the way that you think, feel or behave
He has a very negative **attitude** about his work.
그는 자기 일에 아주 소극적인 태도를 갖고 있다.

06 awkward
[ɔ́ːkwərd]
a 어색한, 서투른   not convenient, difficult
This puts me in an **awkward** position because when I don't attend these functions, I hurt my family.
내가 이 행사들에 참석하지 않으면 가족들에게 상처를 주기 때문에 이 일은 나로 하여금 어색한 위치에 있게 한다.

07 balanced
[bǽlənst]
a 균형이 잡힌   keeping a balance so that different things exist in equal
It's best to have a well **balanced** diet.
제대로 균형 잡힌 식사를 하는 것이 가장 좋다.

08 burst
[bəːrst]
v 폭발하다, 터지다 / **n** 폭발   to break open suddenly and violently
My water heater just **burst**, and it's going to cost me $600 to get a new one.
보일러가 터져서 새로 사려면 600달러가 듭니다.

09 bury
[béri]
v 묻다   to put something in a hole in the ground
The house was **buried** under ten feet of snow.
그 집은 10 피트의 눈 속에 묻혀 있었다.

---

key words
in spite of ~에도 불구하고 / flourish **v** 우거지다, 번영하다 / toddler **n** 걸음마하는 유아 / violently **ad** 세차게

🎧 Listen and repeat. Track 86

10 buzz
[bʌz]
v 윙윙거리다 to make the sound that bees, etc make when flying
The mosquitoes **buzzed** about my ears.
모기가 귓가에서 윙윙거렸다.

11 clay
[klei]
n 찰흙, 점토 heavy earth that is soft and sticky when it is wet
In the hands of the great sculptor, the lump of **clay** seemed to take on all the attributes of a living thing.
위대한 조각가의 손에 들어가면 진흙덩이도 생물의 모든 속성을 얻게 되는 것 같다.

12 client
[kláiənt]
n 소송 의뢰인, 고객 somebody who receives a service from a professional person for example a lawyer
The lawyer made the point that her **client** had been at the scene of the crime before the murder.
변호사는 그의 소송의뢰인이 살인사건 전에 범죄현장에 있었다는 점을 내세웠다.

13 combine
[kəmbáin]
v 결합시키다, 결합하다 to join or mix two or more things together
It is difficult to **combine** work with pleasure.
일과 오락을 결합시키기는 어렵다.

14 contemporary
[kəntémpərèri]
a 동시대의, 현대의 / n 동시대사람 belong to the same time as somebody / something else
The professor is familiar with **contemporary** literature.
그 교수는 현대 문학에 정통하다.

15 contrast
[kántræst]
n 대조, 대비 a clear difference between two things or people
In **contrast**, English is the native tongue of only 400 million people in twelve countries.
대조적으로 영어는 12개 나라에서 4억의 인구만이 모국어로 쓰고 있다.

16 convert
[kənvə́ːrt]
v 전환하다, 변화시키다 to change from one form, system or use to another
Try **converting** them to another file format before you send them.
파일을 보내기 전에 다른 파일 형식으로 전환해 보세요.

17 deny
[dinái]
v 부정하다, 거절하다 to refuse to admit or accept something
He **denied** that he was involved.
그는 자신이 연루되었음을 부인했다.

18 drug
[drʌg]
n 약, 약품 a chemical which is used as a medicine
Some **drugs** cause permanent brain damage.
어떤 약물들은 영구적인 두뇌 손상을 초래한다.

key words
mosquito n 모기 / sticky a 끈적한, 점착성의 / sculptor n 조각가
lump n 덩어리 / permanent a 영구한, 불변의

Unit 29 147

Exercise

A. Complete the sentence.

1. One or two mistakes are _____ but no more than that.
   한 두번의 실수는 받아들일 수 있지만 그 이상은 안됩니다.
2. It is difficult to _____ work with pleasure.
   일과 오락을 결합시키기는 어렵다.
3. It's best to have a well _____ diet.
   제대로 균형 잡힌 식사를 하는 것이 가장 좋다.
4. This puts me in an _____ position because when I don't attend these functions, I hurt my family.
   내가 이 행사들에 참석하지 않으면 가족들에게 상처를 주기 때문에 이 일은 나로 하여금 어색한 위치에 있게 한다.
5. Some _____ cause permanent brain damage.
   어떤 약물들은 영구적인 두뇌 손상을 초래한다.
6. Try _____ them to another file format before you send them.
   파일을 보내기 전에 다른 파일 형식으로 전환해 보세요.
7. The professor is familiar with _____ literature.
   그 교수는 현대 문학에 정통하다.
8. The house was _____ under ten feet of snow.
   그 집은 10 피트의 눈 속에 묻혀 있었다.
9. _____ apples do not grow during the cold season, apple trees must have such a season in order to flourish.
   비록 사과는 추운 계절 동안에는 자라지 않지만, 사과나무들이 번성하기 위해서는 추운 계절이 있어야만 한다.
10. He has a very negative _____ about his work.
    그는 자기 일에 아주 소극적인 태도를 갖고 있다.
11. In the hands of the great sculptor, the lump of _____ seemed to take on all the attributes of a living thing.
    위대한 조각가의 손에 들어가면 진흙덩이도 생물의 모든 속성을 얻게 되는 것 같다.
12. My water heater just _____, and it's going to cost me $600 to get a new one.
    보일러가 터져서 새로 사려면 600달러가 듭니다.
13. Toddlers don't need expensive toys to _____ themselves.
    걸음마를 시작한 아이들을 즐겁게 하기 위해서 비싼 장난감은 필요 없다.
14. The lawyer made the point that her _____ had been at the scene of the crime before the murder.
    변호사는 그의 소송의뢰인이 살인사건 전에 범죄현장에 있었다는 점을 내세웠다.
15. In _____, English is the native tongue of only 400 million people in twelve countries.
    대조적으로 영어는 12개 나라에서 4억의 인구만이 모국어로 쓰고 있다.
16. He _____ that he was involved.
    그는 자신이 연루되었음을 부인했다.
17. Police do not know if the explosion was _____ or not.
    경찰은 그 폭발이 우연한 것이었는지 아닌지를 모르고 있다.
18. The mosquitoes _____ about my ears.
    모기가 귓가에서 윙윙거렸다.

Hint

| balanced | buzz | deny | although | burst | convert | clay | attitude | accidental |
| awkward | drug | bury | contrast | amuse | acceptable | client | combine | contemporary |

Exercise

B. Fill in the word and meaning.

	Word	Meaning
01	balanced	
02	acceptable	
03	clay	
04	awkward	
05	combine	
06	accidental	
07	contrast	
08	bury	
09	deny	
10	attitude	
11	drug	
12	buzz	
13	contemporary	
14	although	
15	convert	
16	client	
17	burst	
18	amuse	

	Meaning	Word
01	받아들일 수 있는	
02	우연한, 비본질적인	
03	비록 ~일지라도	
04	즐겁게 하다	
05	태도, 마음가짐, 자세	
06	어색한, 서투른	
07	균형이 잡힌	
08	폭발하다, 터지다, 폭발	
09	묻다	
10	윙윙거리다	
11	찰흙, 점토	
12	소송 의뢰인, 고객	
13	결합시키다, 결합하다	
14	동시대의, 현대의, 동시대사람	
15	대조, 대비	
16	전환하다, 변화시키다	
17	부정하다, 거절하다	
18	약, 약품	

🎧 C. Listen, write the word and meaning. (Track 87)

	Word	Meaning		Word	Meaning
01			10		
02			11		
03			12		
04			13		
05			14		
06			15		
07			16		
08			17		
09			18		

Unit 30

🎧 Listen and repeat. Track 88

01 describe
[diskráib]
v 묘사하다, 기술하다   to say what somebody / something is like
War is **described** as a crime against humanity.
전쟁은 인류에 대한 범죄로 묘사된다.

02 domestic
[douméstik]
a 국내의, 가정의   connected with the home or family
The growing problem of modern society is **domestic** violence.
현대 사회에서 증가되고 있는 문제로는 가정 내 폭력이 있다.

03 drag
[dræg]
v 끌다, 질질 끌다   to move partly touching the ground
Why are they **dragging** their feet?
왜 그들은 그렇게 발을 질질 끌고 가는 거지요?

04 else
[els]
ad 그 밖에, 그 외에   another, different person, thing or place
What **else** would you like to eat?
그 외에 먹고 싶은 것이 뭐가 있니?

05 evolution
[èvəlú:ʃən]
n 진화, 발달   the development of animals, etc over many thousands of years
The theory of **evolution** is beyond the reach of my imagination.
진화론은 내 상상의 범위를 초월한다.

06 exact
[igzǽkt]
a 정확한, 정밀한, 꼼꼼한   correct in every detail
The **exact** locations are being kept secret for reasons of security.
정확한 위치는 보안상의 이유로 비밀이다.

07 except
[iksépt]
v ~을 제외하다   to not include somebody / something
Only children under five are **excepted** from this survey.
5세 미만의 어린이만 이 조사에서 제외 됩니다.

08 female
[fí:meil]
a 여성의, 암컷의   being a woman or a girl
Female tigers have babies every 2 to 2.5 years.
암컷 호랑이는 2년에서 2.5년을 주기로 새끼를 갖는다.

09 fiber
[fáibər]
n 섬유, 섬유질식품   a thin thread of a natural or artificial substance
I will see if I can get a match from the crime scene **fibers**.
저는 범죄현장에서 나온 섬유와 일치하는지 알아볼 것입니다.

key words
theory n 학설, 이론 / imagination n 상상 / survey n 조사, 검사

🎧 Listen and repeat. (Track 89)

10 fist [fist] — **v** 주먹으로 치다 / **n** 주먹 — a hand when it is tightly closed with the fingers bent into the palm
Roll up your right sleeve and make a **fist**, please.
오른팔 소매를 걷으시고 주먹을 꼭 쥐세요.

11 gather [gǽðər] — **v** 모으다, 모이다 — to come together in one place to form a group
His friends **gathered** to condole him over his loss.
그의 친구들은 모여서 그의 피해에 대해 위로했다.

12 generosity [dʒènərásəti] — **n** 관대, 너그러움 — the fact of being generous
We were overwhelmed by her **generosity** and accepted the invitation at once.
우리는 그녀의 관대함에 압도되어 즉시 그 초대를 받아들였다.

13 globalization [glóubəlizéiʃən] — **n** 세계화, 국제화 — growth to a global or worldwide scale
The meetings drew thousands of anti-**globalization** demonstrators.
이번 회담장에는 수천명의 세계화 반대 시위자들이 몰려들었습니다.

14 herb [həːrb] — **n** 약용식물, 풀잎 — a plant whose leaves are used in cooking to add flavor to food, or as a medicine
My mom boiled down medicinal **herb** for me.
엄마가 나를 위해 약용식물을 달여 주셨다.

15 heroine [hérouin] — **n** 여걸, 여장부 — a woman who is admired for doing something brave
The novelist characterizes his **heroine** as passionate.
그 소설가는 여주인공의 성격을 열정적인 것으로 그리고 있다.

16 historical [histɔ́(ː)rikəl] — **a** 역사의, 역사적인 — connected with the study of history
I spent one week travelling all over the country and saw many **historical** places.
나는 전국 방방곡곡을 일주일 동안 여행하면서 수많은 역사적인 장소들을 구경했다.

17 idiom [ídiəm] — **n** 숙어, 관용구 — an expression whose meaning is different from the meanings of the individual words in it
Americans use a lot of slang and **idioms** whose meanings foreigners do not know.
미국인들은 외국인들이 알지 못하는 많은 속어나 관용구를 사용한다.

18 independence [indipéndəns] — **n** 독립, 자주 — freedom from political control by other countries
It's the 45th anniversary of our country's **independence**.
오늘은 마흔 다섯 번째 맞는 우리나라의 독립 기념일이다.

---

key words
palm **n** 손바닥 / sleeve **n** 소매 / condole **v** 위로하다 / overwhelm **v** 압도하다 / demonstrator **n** 시위운동자 / characterize **v** 성격묘사를 하다 / passionate **a** 열의에 찬 / slang **n** 속어

Exercise

A. Complete the sentence.

1. We were overwhelmed by her _____ and accepted the invitation at once.
   우리는 그녀의 관대함에 압도되어 즉시 그 초대를 받아들였다.

2. Why are they _____ their feet?
   왜 그들은 그렇게 발을 질질 끌고 가는 거지요?

3. My mom boiled down medicinal _____ for me.
   엄마가 나를 위해 약용식물을 달여 주셨다.

4. What _____ would you like to eat?
   그 외에 먹고 싶은 것이 뭐가 있니?

5. I will see if I can get a match from the crime scene _____.
   저는 범죄현장에서 나온 섬유와 일치하는지 알아볼 것입니다.

6. The theory of _____ is beyond the reach of my imagination.
   진화론은 내 상상의 범위를 초월한다.

7. Only children under five are _____ from this survey.
   5세 미만의 어린이만 이 조사에서 제외 됩니다.

8. _____ tigers have babies every 2 to 2.5 years.
   암컷 호랑이는 2년에서 2.5년을 주기로 새끼를 갖는다.

9. War is _____ as a crime against humanity.
   전쟁은 인류에 대한 범죄로 묘사된다.

10. Roll up your right sleeve and make a _____, please.
    오른팔 소매를 걷으시고 주먹을 꼭 쥐세요.

11. It's the 45th anniversary of our country's _____.
    오늘은 마흔 다섯 번째 맞는 우리나라의 독립 기념일이다.

12. His friends _____ to condole him over his loss.
    그의 친구들은 모여서 그의 피해에 대해 위로했다.

13. The growing problem of modern society is _____ violence.
    현대 사회에서 증가되고 있는 문제로는 가정 내 폭력이 있다.

14. The meetings drew thousands of anti-_____ demonstrators.
    이번 회담장에는 수천명의 세계화 반대 시위자들이 몰려들었습니다.

15. The novelist characterizes his _____ as passionate.
    그 소설가는 여주인공의 성격을 열정적인 것으로 그리고 있다.

16. The _____ locations are being kept secret for reasons of security.
    정확한 위치는 보안상의 이유로 비밀이다.

17. I spent one week travelling all over the country and saw many _____ places.
    나는 전국 방방곡곡을 일주일 동안 여행하면서 수많은 역사적인 장소들을 구경했다.

18. Americans use a lot of slang and _____ whose meanings foreigners do not know.
    미국인들은 외국인들이 알지 못하는 많은 속어나 관용구를 사용한다.

Hint

evolution　else　exact　heroine　idiom　fiber　domestic　except　globalization
describe　fist　female　historical　gather　drag　generosity　herb　independence

Exercise

B. Fill in the word and meaning.

	Word	Meaning
01	evolution	
02	describe	
03	generosity	
04	female	
05	globalization	
06	except	
07	historical	
08	else	
09	gather	
10	heroine	
11	fiber	
12	idiom	
13	fist	
14	independence	
15	domestic	
16	herb	
17	exact	
18	drag	

	Meaning	Word
01	묘사하다, 기술하다	
02	국내의, 가정의	
03	끌다, 질질 끌다	
04	그 밖에, 그 외에	
05	진화, 발달	
06	정확한, 정밀한, 꼼꼼한	
07	~을 제외하다	
08	여성의, 암컷의	
09	섬유, 섬유질식품	
10	주먹으로 치다, 주먹	
11	모으다, 모이다	
12	관대, 너그러움	
13	세계화, 국제화	
14	약용식물, 풀잎	
15	여걸, 여장부	
16	역사의, 역사적인	
17	숙어, 관용구	
18	독립, 자주	

C. Listen, write the word and meaning. Track 90

	Word	Meaning		Word	Meaning
01			10		
02			11		
03			12		
04			13		
05			14		
06			15		
07			16		
08			17		
09			18		

Unit 30

Review 15

A. Read and fill in the word and meaning.

word	definition	meaning
	to make the sound that bees, etc make when flying	
	happening by chance, not planned	
	a chemical which is used as a medicine	
	heavy earth that is soft and sticky when it is wet	
	in spite of the fact that	
	somebody who receives a service from a professional person for example a lawyer	
	that can be allowed	
	to refuse to admit or accept something	
	to join or mix two or more things together	
	to change from one form, system or use to another	
	to make time pass pleasantly for somebody	
	keeping a balance so that different things exist in equal	
	belong to the same time as somebody/something else	
	not convenient, difficult	
	to break open suddenly and violently	
	the way that you think, feel or behave	
	a clear difference between two things or people	
	to put something in a hole in the ground	

Hint

balanced buzz deny although burst convert clay attitude accidental
awkward drug bury contrast amuse acceptable client combine contemporary

B. Read and fill in the word and meaning.

word	definition	meaning
	a hand when it is tightly closed with the fingers bent into the palm	
	to say what somebody / something is like	
	to come together in one place to form a group	
	a thin thread of a natural or artificial substance	
	the fact of being generous	
	connected with the home or family	
	growth to a global or worldwide scale	
	being a woman or a girl	
	to move partly touching the ground	
	to not include somebody / something	
	a plant whose leaves are used in cooking to add flavor to food, or as a medicine	
	another, different person, thing or place	
	a woman who is admired for doing something brave	
	the gradual development of something	
	an expression whose meaning is different from the meanings of the individual words in it	
	connected with the study of history	
	correct in every detail	
	freedom from political control by other countries	

Hint

evolution   else   exact   heroine   idiom   fiber   domestic   except   globalization
describe   fist   female   historical   gather   drag   generosity   herb   independence

Review 15

Unit 31

🎧 Listen and repeat. Track 91

01 individual
[ìndəvídʒuəl]
a 개개의, 개인적인 / **n** 개인   considered separately rather than as part of a group
It is difficult for a teacher to give **individual** attention to children in a large class.
학생이 많은 교실에서는 교사가 아이들에게 개인적인 관심을 주기가 어렵다.

02 inflation
[infléiʃən]
n 팽창, 인플레이션   a general rise in prices
To control the **inflation**, we must have high interest rates.
인플레이션 현상을 막기 위해 우리는 고금리를 취해야한다.

03 leap
[li:p]
v 뛰어 오르다 / **n** 도약   to jump high or a long way
The hunters **leaped** their horses over all the obstacles.
사냥꾼은 말을 뛰게 하여 모든 장애물을 뛰어넘었다.

04 legal
[líːgəl]
a 법적인, 합법의   using or connected with the law, allowed by law
The lawyer recommended that his client take **legal** action.
변호사는 의뢰인에게 법적 행동을 취하도록 권했다.

05 leisure
[líːʒər]
n 틈, 여가 / **a** 한가한   the time when you do not have to work; spare time
Now I have a lot more time for **leisure** activities.
이제 난 여가 활동을 할 시간이 훨씬 더 많아졌어요.

06 marginal
[máːrdʒənəl]
a 가장자리의, 한계의   connected the area around the edge of something
You should leave a **marginal** space in the note.
노트에 가장자리의 여백을 남겨 두어야 한다.

07 martial
[máːrʃəl]
a 군인다운, 전쟁의   connected with war
The sound of **martial** music is always inspiring.
전쟁에서 들리는 음악 소리는 항상 자극적이다.

08 material
[mətíəriəl]
n 재료 / **a** 물질의, 구체적인   a substance that can be used for making something
This **material** is being provided free of charge.
이 재료는 무상으로 제공해 드리는 것입니다.

09 meal
[mi:l]
n 식사 / **v** 식사를 하다   the time when you eat
It's good to use dental floss after each **meal**.
식사 후에는 치실을 사용하는 것이 좋다.

key words
obstacle **n** 장애물 / lawyer **n** 변호사 / recommend **v** 권하다
inspiring **a** 분발케하는, 감격시키는 / floss **n** 치실

🎧 Listen and repeat. (Track 92)

10 navy [néivi] — **n** 해군, 군함 — the part of a country's armed forces that fights at sea
After high school, I joined the **navy** and served for three years.
저는 고등학교 졸업한 후 해군에 입대해서 3년 동안 근무했습니다.

11 negative [négətiv] — **a** 부정적인, 소극적인 — only thinking about the bad thing
Violent movies might have a **negative** impact on kids.
폭력적인 영화들은 아이들에게 부정적인 영향을 줄 수가 있어요.

12 neighborhood [néibərhùd] — **n** 이웃, 근처 — a particular part of a town and the people who live there
Did you notice any strangers in your **neighborhood** lately?
최근에 근처에서 이상한 사람을 본 적이 있습니까?

13 outline [áutlàin] — **n** 윤곽, 외형 / **v** 윤곽을 그리다 — a line that shows the shape or outside edge
When a child is trying to draw a rabbit, we can help by sketching in the **outline** of the body.
어린이들이 토끼를 그리려 할 때, 우리들은 그 몸의 윤곽을 그려주는 도움을 줄 수 있다.

14 outlook [áutlùk] — **n** 시각, 태도, 통찰 — your attitude to or feeling about life and the world
An event happened and changed the entire **outlook** for our project.
어떤 사건이 일어나서 우리 계획에 대한 전체 시각을 바꾸어 놓았다.

15 overcome [òuvərkʌ́m] — **v** 극복하다, 이기다 — to manage to control or defeat somebody / something
I think he'll **overcome** this sorrow quickly.
나는 그가 이 슬픔을 빨리 이겨 낼 수 있으리라 생각한다.

16 politics [pálitìks] — **n** 정치, 정치학 — the work and ideas that are connected with governing a country, etc
We should root out bad practices in **politics**.
우리는 정치에 있어서 나쁜 관행을 뿌리 뽑아야 한다.

17 pollution [pəlú:ʃən] — **n** 오염 — the action of making the air, water, etc dirty and dangerous
Unfortunately cars were neither safer nor did they stop **pollution**.
불행히도, 차량은 안전하지도 않았고 오염을 멈추지도 않았다.

18 population [pàpjəléʃən] — **n** 인구, 주민 — all the people who live in a particular place
The city's **population** expanded by 12 percent.
그 도시의 인구가 12 퍼센트 늘어났다.

---

key words
sketch **v** 대략 그리다 / defeat **v** 쳐부수다 / root **v** 근절하다

Unit 31

Exercise

A. Complete the sentence.

1. Violent movies might have a _____ impact on kids.
   폭력적인 영화들은 아이들에게 부정적인 영향을 줄 수가 있어요.

2. You should leave a _____ space in the note.
   노트에 가장자리의 여백을 남겨 두어야 한다.

3. The city's _____ expanded by 12 percent.
   그 도시의 인구가 12 퍼센트 늘어났다.

4. Did you notice any strangers in your _____ lately?
   최근에 근처에서 이상한 사람을 본 적이 있습니까?.

5. When a child is trying to draw a rabbit, we can help by sketching in the _____ of the body.
   어린이들이 토끼를 그리려 할 때, 우리들은 그 몸의 윤곽을 그려주는 도움을 줄 수 있다.

6. We should root out bad practices in _____.
   우리는 정치에 있어서 나쁜 관행을 뿌리 뽑아야 한다.

7. The lawyer recommended that his client take _____ action.
   변호사는 의뢰인에게 법적 행동을 취하도록 권했다.

8. Unfortunately cars were neither safer nor did they stop _____.
   불행히도, 차량은 안전하지도 않았고 오염을 멈추지도 않았다.

9. It is difficult for a teacher to _____ attention to children in a large class.
   학생이 많은 교실에서는 교사가 아이들에게 개인적인 관심을 주기가 어렵다.

10. I think he'll _____ this sorrow quickly.
    나는 그가 이 슬픔을 빨리 이겨 낼 수 있으리라 생각한다.

11. To control the _____, we must have high interest rates.
    인플레이션 현상을 막기 위해 우리는 고금리를 취해야 한다.

12. The sound of _____ music is always inspiring.
    전쟁에서 들리는 음악 소리는 항상 자극적이다.

13. After high school, I joined the _____ and served for three years.
    저는 고등학교 졸업한 후 해군에 입대해서 3년 동안 근무했습니다.

14. The hunters _____ their horses over all the obstacles.
    사냥꾼들은 말을 뛰게 하여 모든 장애물을 뛰어넘었다.

15. Now I have a lot more time for _____ activities.
    이제 난 여가 활동을 할 시간이 훨씬 더 많아졌어요.

16. This _____ is being provided free of charge.
    이 재료는 무상으로 제공해 드리는 것입니다.

17. An event happened and changed the entire _____ for our project.
    어떤 사건이 일어나서 우리 계획에 대한 전체 시각을 바꾸어 놓았다.

18. It's good to use dental floss after each _____.
    식사 후에는 치실을 사용하는 것이 좋다.

Hint

politics   meal   leisure   individual   legal   outline   pollution   material   neighborhood
outlook   leap   marginal   negative   navy   overcome   inflation   martial   population

Exercise

B. Fill in the word and meaning.

	Word	Meaning
01	inflation	
02	outline	
03	marginal	
04	navy	
05	politics	
06	individual	
07	meal	
08	outlook	
09	martial	
10	population	
11	leap	
12	pollution	
13	negative	
14	leisure	
15	overcome	
16	neighborhood	
17	material	
18	legal	

	Meaning	Word
01	개개의, 개인적인, 개인	
02	팽창, 인플레이션	
03	뛰어 오르다, 도약	
04	법적인, 합법의	
05	틈, 여가, 한가한	
06	가장자리의, 한계의	
07	군인다운, 전쟁의	
08	재료, 물질의, 구체적인	
09	식사, 식사를 하다	
10	해군, 군함	
11	부정적인, 소극적인	
12	이웃, 근처	
13	윤곽, 외형, 윤곽을 그리다	
14	시각, 태도, 통찰	
15	극복하다, 이기다	
16	정치, 정치학	
17	오염	
18	인구, 주민	

🎧 C. Listen, write the word and meaning. (Track 93)

	Word	Meaning		Word	Meaning
01			10		
02			11		
03			12		
04			13		
05			14		
06			15		
07			16		
08			17		
09			18		

Unit 32

🎧 Listen and repeat. Track 94

01 purchase
[pə́ːrtʃəs]
v 구입하다 / **n** 구입, 구입품   to buy something
I had to **purchase** a few household supplies.
나는 생활용품도 몇 가지 구입해야 했다.

02 quite
[kwait]
ad 아주, 완전히   completely; very
I have grown **quite** attached to you.
나는 그동안 당신과 정이 완전히 들었어요.

03 remind
[rimáind]
v 생각나게 하다   to cause somebody to remember
That smell **reminds** me of school.
저 냄새는 학교를 생각나게 한다.

04 responsibility
[rispànsəbíləti]
n 책임, 의무   a duty to deal with something so that it is your fault if something goes wrong
My shoulders are heavy with **responsibilities**.
책임감 때문에 어깨가 무겁습니다.

05 retire
[ritáiəːr]
v 퇴직하다, 물러가다   to leave your job and stop working
If you **retire** at 50, you won't get your full pension.
만약 50세에 당신이 퇴직하면 연금을 다 받지 못한다.

06 reunify
[riːjúːnəfài]
v 다시 통일시키다   to unify a country, republic, etc that has been divided again
Only after the nation is **reunified**, Koreans will celebrate complete liberation.
국가가 다시 통일이 되고 난 뒤에야, 한국인들은 완전한 광복을 경축하게 될 것이다.

07 scale
[skeil]
n 눈금, 비율   a series of marks on a tool that you use for measuring
Could you let me know the **scale** of the ruler?
자의 눈금 좀 알려주시겠어요?

08 shy
[ʃai]
a 수줍어하는   nervous and uncomfortable about meeting and speaking to people
According to my friends, I am a little quiet and **shy**.
친구 이야기에 따르면, 나는 좀 조용하고 수줍음을 잘 탄다고 한다.

09 sigh
[sai]
v 한숨 쉬다, 탄식하다 / **n** 한숨   a long, deep breath that shows you are tired, sad, etc
Informed of his safety, the manager breathed a **sigh** of relief.
그의 무사함을 알고 나서, 매니저는 안도의 한숨을 쉬었다.

---

key words
household **a** 가사의 / attached **a** 애착을 갖고 있는 / pension **n** 연금
nervous **a** 겁많은 / uncomfortable **a** 거북한 / relief **n** 안심, 위안

🎧 Listen and repeat. Track 95

10 suggestion [səgdʒéstʃən] **n** 제안, 제의, 암시   putting an idea into a person's mind
How did he react to your **suggestion**?
당신의 제안에 그는 어떤 반응을 보였습니까?

11 sunset [sʌ́nsèt] **n** 일몰, 해질녘   the time when the sun goes down in the evening
The **sunset** reddened the clouds.
일몰이 구름을 붉게 물들였다.

12 survive [sərváiv] **v** 살아남다, 생존하다   to continue to live or exist after a difficult
To **survive**, most birds must eat at least half their own weight in food every day.
생존하기 위해서 대부분의 새들은 매일 최소한 그들 몸무게의 반 정도 되는 무게의 음식을 먹어야한다.

13 transportation [trænspəːrtéiʃən] **n** 운송, 교통수단   any type of vehicle that you can travel in or carry goods in
I would appreciate it if you could make an arrangement for **transportation** to my hotel.
제 호텔까지의 교통편을 준비해주시면 대단히 감사하겠습니다.

14 tray [trei] **n** 쟁반, 음식 접시   a flat piece of wood, plastic, etc that you use for carrying food
You can just put the **tray** outside the door when you're finished.
다 드신 후 쟁반을 문 밖에다 그냥 내 놓으시면 됩니다.

15 treat [triːt] **n** 다루다, 대우하다, 치료하다   to act or behave towards somebody / something in a particular way
Their request has been unfairly **treated**.
그들의 요구는 부당하게 다루어졌다.

16 weapon [wépən] **n** 무기   an object which is used for fighting or for killing people
A sword is a short-handed, long-bladed **weapon**, similar to a dagger but larger.
검은 짧은 손잡이와 긴 날을 가진 무기인데, 단검과 비슷하지만 더 길다.

17 weight [weit] **n** 무게, 체중 / **v** ~에 무게를 가하다   how heavy something / somebody is
I am above average in height and **weight**.
나는 신장과 체중이 평균을 넘는다.

18 welfare [wélfɛ̀əːr] **n** 복지, 복지 사업   the help and care that is given people who have problems with health, money, etc
One cannot emphasize too much the importance of **welfare**.
복지의 중요성은 아무리 강조해도 지나치지 않다.

---

key words
react **v** 반응하다 / appreciate **v** 고맙게 여기다 / unfairly **ad** 부당하게 / dagger **n** 단도

Unit 32

Exercise

A. Complete the sentence.

1. My shoulders are heavy with _____.
   책임감 때문에 어깨가 무겁습니다.

2. I had to _____ a few household supplies.
   나는 생활용품도 몇 가지 구입해야 했다.

3. One cannot emphasize too much the importance of _____.
   복지의 중요성은 아무리 강조해도 지나치지 않다.

4. Only after the nation is _____, Koreans will celebrate complete liberation.
   국가가 다시 통일이 되고 난 뒤에야, 한국인들은 완전한 광복을 경축하게 될 것이다.

5. Could you let me know the _____ of the ruler?
   자의 눈금 좀 알려주시겠어요?

6. I have grown _____ attached to you.
   나는 그 동안 당신과 정이 완전히 들었어요.

7. According to my friends, I am a little quiet and _____.
   친구 이야기에 따르면, 나는 좀 조용하고 수줍음을 잘 탄다고 한다.

8. A sword is a short-handed, long-bladed _____, similar to a dagger but larger.
   검은 짧은 손잡이와 긴 날을 가진 무기인데, 단검과 비슷하지만 더 길다.

9. You can just put the _____ outside the door when you're finished.
   다 드신 후 쟁반을 문 밖에다 그냥 내 놓으시면 됩니다.

10. How did he react to your _____?
    당신의 제안에 그는 어떤 반응을 보였습니까?

11. If you _____ at 50, you won't get your full pension.
    만약 50세에 당신이 퇴직하면 연금을 다 받지 못한다.

12. The _____ reddened the clouds.
    일몰이 구름을 붉게 물들였다.

13. That smell _____ me of school.
    저 냄새는 학교를 생각나게 한다.

14. To _____, most birds must eat at least half their own weight in food every day.
    생존하기 위해서 대부분의 새들은 매일 최소한 그들 몸무게의 반 정도 되는 무게의 음식을 먹어야 한다.

15. I would appreciate it if you could make an arrangement for _____ to my hotel.
    제 호텔까지의 교통편을 준비해주시면 대단히 감사하겠습니다.

16. Informed of his safety, the manager breathed a _____ of relief.
    그의 무사함을 알고 나서, 매니저는 안도의 한숨을 쉬었다.

17. Their request has been unfairly _____.
    그들의 요구는 부당하게 다루어졌다.

18. I am above average in height and _____.
    나는 신장과 체중이 평균을 넘는다.

Hint

| welfare | scale | weight | quite | shy | retire | treat | purchase | responsibility |
| sunset | tray | survive | reunify | remind | weapon | sigh | suggestion | transportation |

Unit 32

Exercise

B. Fill in the word and meaning.

	Word	Meaning
01	responsibility	
02	sunset	
03	purchase	
04	shy	
05	transportation	
06	scale	
07	treat	
08	suggestion	
09	welfare	
10	remind	
11	survive	
12	reunify	
13	weapon	
14	sigh	
15	weight	
16	retire	
17	tray	
18	quite	

	Meaning	Word
01	구입하다, 구입, 구입품	
02	아주, 완전히	
03	생각나게 하다	
04	책임, 의무	
05	퇴직하다, 물러가다	
06	다시 통일시키다	
07	눈금, 비율	
08	수줍어하는	
09	한숨 쉬다, 탄식하다, 한숨	
10	제안, 제의, 암시	
11	일몰, 해질녘	
12	살아남다, 생존하다	
13	운송, 교통수단	
14	쟁반, 음식 접시	
15	다루다, 대우하다, 치료하다	
16	무기	
17	무게, 체중, ~에 무게를 가하다	
18	복지, 복지 사업	

C. Listen, write the word and meaning. (Track 96)

	Word	Meaning		Word	Meaning
01			10		
02			11		
03			12		
04			13		
05			14		
06			15		
07			16		
08			17		
09			18		

Unit 32

Review 16

A. Read and fill in the word and meaning.

word	definition	meaning
	the time when you eat	
	only thinking about the bad thing	
	considered separately rather than as part of a group	
	the part of a country's armed forces that fights at sea	
	a particular part of a town and the people who live there	
	a substance that can be used for making something	
	a general rise in prices	
	your attitude to or feeling about life and the world	
	a line that shows the shape or outside edge	
	all the people who live in a particular place	
	connected with war	
	to jump high or a long way	
	the action of making the air, water, etc dirty and dangerous	
	the work and ideas that are connected with governing a country, etc	
	using or connected with the law, allowed by law	
	to manage to control or defeat somebody / something	
	connected the area around the edge of something	
	the time when you do not have to work; spare time	

Hint

politics   meal   leisure   individual   legal   outline   pollution   material   neighborhood
outlook   leap   marginal   negative   navy   overcome   inflation   martial   population

B. Read and fill in the word and meaning.

word	definition	meaning
	an object which is used for fighting or for killing people	
	to buy something	
	to act or behave towards somebody/something in a particular way	
	to cause somebody to remember	
	a flat piece of wood, plastic, etc that you use for carrying food	
	completely; very	
	to continue to live or exist after a difficult	
	any type of vehicle that you can travel in or carry goods in	
	to leave your job and stop working	
	a long, deep breath that shows you are tired, sad, etc	
	a duty to deal with something so that it is your fault if something goes wrong	
	putting an idea into a person's mind	
	nervous and uncomfortable about meeting and speaking to people	
	how heavy something/somebody is	
	the time when the sun goes down in the evening	
	a series of marks on a tool that you use for measuring	
	to unify a country, republic, etc that has been divided again	
	the help and care that is given people who have problems with health, money, etc	

Hint

welfare scale weight quite shy retire treat purchase responsibility
sunset tray survive reunify remind weapon sigh suggestion transportation

Unit 33

🎧 Listen and repeat. Track 97

01 according [əkɔ́:rdiŋ]
ad ~에 따라서   in a way that matches, follows or depends on something
According to the weather forecast, the weather will improve soon.
일기 예보에 따르면, 날씨가 곧 좋아질 것이라고 한다.

02 appear [əpíər]
v 나타나다   to suddenly be seen; to come into sight
He had to **appear** before the committee to explain his behavior.
그는 자신의 행동을 설명하기 위해서 위원회에 모습을 나타냈다.

03 apply [əplái]
v 신청하다, 지원하다   to ask for something in writing
As soon as I graduated from school, I plan to **apply** for a job.
나는 학교를 졸업하자마자 취업에 지원할 계획이다.

04 appoint [əpɔ́int]
v 임명하다, 지정하다, 정하다   to choose somebody for a job or position
He became wealthy, gained the trust of the townspeople, and even was **appointed** a mayor.
그는 부자가 되었고, 마을 사람들의 신임을 얻었으며 시장으로 임명되기까지 하였다.

05 bead [bi:d]
n 구슬, 염주   a small round piece of wood, glass or plastic with a hole in the middle
When monks close their eyes and count their **beads**, they look very devout.
스님들이 눈을 감고 염주를 세는 모습은 참 경건해 보입니다.

06 bear [bɛər]
v 낳다   to give birth to children
She **bore** him four children, all sons.
그녀는 그에게 아들만 넷을 낳아 주었다.

07 benefit [bénəfit]
n 이익, 수당 / v 이득을 보다   an advantage or useful effect
The discovery of oil brought many **benefits** to the town.
석유의 발견이 그 마을 사람들에게 많은 이익을 가져다주었다.

08 careless [kɛ́ərlis]
a 부주의한, 무관심한   not thinking enough about what you are doing
The accident was caused by **careless** driving.
그 사고는 부주의한 운전으로 인해 일어났다.

09 cast [kæst]
v 던지다, 주조하다, 배역하다   to choose an actor for a particular role in a play, film, etc
She always seems to be **cast** in the same sort of role.
그녀에게는 항상 같은 종류의 배역만 주어지는 것 같다.

---

key words
graduate v 졸업하다 / mayor n 시장 / monk n 수사 / devout a 경건한, 독실한

🎧 Listen and repeat. Track 98

10 citizen [sítəzən] **n** 시민 a person who is legally accepted as a member of a particular country
She was born in Japan, but she became an American **citizen** in 1981.
그녀는 일본에서 태어났으나 1981년에 미국 시민이 되었다.

11 claim [kleim] **v** 주장하다, 요구하다, 고소하다 to say that something is true, without having any proof
He **claimed** that he found the money in the forest.
그는 그 돈을 숲 속에서 발견했다고 주장했다.

12 committee [kəmíti] **n** 위원회 a group of people who have been chosen to discuss something
We had a meeting to discuss the formation of a new **committee**.
우리는 새로운 위원회 구성을 논의하기 위한 모임을 가졌다.

13 communicate [kəmjú:nəkèit] **v** 전달하다, 통신하다 to share and exchange information or feelings with somebody
While people still have pen pals, these days **communicating** by e-mail has become more popular.
여전히 펜팔 친구가 있기는 하지만 요즘에는 이메일을 통해 통신하는 것이 더 인기가 있다.

14 competition [kàmpətíʃən] **n** 경쟁, 시합 an organized event in which people try to win something
Did you hear that at this outing we're going to have a talent show **competition** between departments?
이번 야유회 때 부서별 장기자랑 시합이 있다는 말을 들으셨나요?

15 copper [kápər] **n** 구리, 동전 / **a** 구리(빛)의 a common reddish-brown metal
My wife still has the **copper** ring that I gave her on our wedding day.
아내는 내가 결혼식 날 주었던 구리 반지를 여전히 가지고 있었다.

16 copyright [kápiràit] **n** 저작권, 판권 the legal right to be the only person who may do a piece of original work
The Geneva-based WIPO promotes the worldwide protection of intellectual property, including patents and **copyrights**.
제네바에 본부가 있는 WIPO는 특허권, 저작권 등 지적 재산권의 세계적인 보호를 장려한다.

17 description [diskrípʃən] **n** 묘사, 서술 a picture in words of somebody or something that happened
This book gives a good **description** of life on a farm.
이 책은 농장에서의 삶을 잘 묘사해 주고 있다.

18 destroy [distrɔ́i] **v** 파괴하다, 부수다 to damage something so badly that it can no longer be used
More than half the world's tropical forests have been **destroyed** in the past fifty years.
세계 열대 삼림의 반 이상이 지난 50년 동안에 파괴되었다.

---

key words
formation **n** 구성, 조직 / promote **v** 장려하다, 진전시키다
worldwide **a** 세계적인 / intellectual **a** 지적인 / patent **n** 특허권

Unit 33

Exercise

A. Complete the sentence.

1. She was born in Japan, but she became an American _____ in 1981.
   그녀는 일본에서 태어났으나 1981년에 미국 시민이 되었다.
2. She _____ him four children, all sons.
   그녀는 그에게 아들만 넷을 낳아 주었다.
3. We had a meeting to discuss the formation of a new _____.
   우리는 새로운 위원회 구성을 논의하기 위한 모임을 가졌다.
4. He had to _____ before the committee to explain his behavior.
   그는 자신의 행동을 설명하기 위해서 위원회에 모습을 나타냈다.
5. While people still have pen pals, these days _____ by e-mail has become more popular.
   여전히 펜팔 친구가 있기는 하지만 요즘에는 이메일을 통해 통신하는 것이 더 인기가 있다.
6. When monks close their eyes and count their _____, they look very devout.
   스님들이 눈을 감고 염주를 세는 모습은 참 경건해 보입니다.
7. Did you hear that at this outing we're going to have a talent show _____ between departments?
   이번 야유회 때 부서별 장기자랑 시합이 있다는 말을 들으셨나요?
8. My wife still has the _____ ring that I gave her on our wedding day.
   아내는 내가 결혼식 날 주었던 구리 반지를 여전히 가지고 있었다.
9. As soon as I graduated from school, I plan to _____ for a job.
   나는 학교를 졸업하자마자 취업에 지원할 계획이다.
10. The Geneva-based WIPO promotes the worldwide protection of intellectual property, including patents and _____.
    제네바에 본부가 있는 WIPO는 특허권, 저작권 등 지적 재산권의 세계적인 보호를 장려한다.
11. This book gives a good _____ of life on a farm.
    이 책은 농장에서의 삶을 잘 묘사해 주고 있다.
12. He _____ that he found the money in the forest.
    그는 그 돈을 숲 속에서 발견했다고 주장했다.
13. More than half the world's tropical forests have been _____ in the past fifty years.
    세계 열대 삼림의 반 이상이 지난 50년 동안에 파괴되었다.
14. _____ to the weather forecast, the weather will improve soon.
    일기 예보에 따르면, 날씨가 곧 좋아질 것이라고 한다.
15. He became wealthy, gained the trust of the townspeople, and even was _____ a mayor.
    그는 부자가 되었고, 마을 사람들의 신임을 얻었으며 시장으로 임명되기까지 하였다.
16. The accident was caused by _____ driving.
    그 사고는 부주의한 운전으로 인해 일어났다.
17. The discovery of oil brought many _____ to the town.
    석유의 발견이 그 마을 사람들에게 많은 이익을 가져다 주었다.
18. She always seems to be _____ in the same sort of role.
    그녀에게는 항상 같은 종류의 배역만 주어지는 것 같다.

Hint

competition   bear   citizen   description   destroy   apply   copper   appoint   benefit
according   cast   bead   committee   copyright   claim   appear   careless   communicate

Exercise

B. Fill in the word and meaning.

	Word	Meaning
01	benefit	
02	copyright	
03	careless	
04	apply	
05	competition	
06	according	
07	description	
08	cast	
09	destroy	
10	committee	
11	appoint	
12	claim	
13	copper	
14	bead	
15	citizen	
16	communicate	
17	appear	
18	bear	

	Meaning	Word
01	~에 따라서	
02	나타나다	
03	신청하다, 지원하다	
04	임명하다, 지정하다, 정하다	
05	구슬, 염주	
06	낳다	
07	이익, 수당, 이득을 보다	
08	부주의한, 무관심한	
09	던지다, 주조하다, 배역하다	
10	시민	
11	주장하다, 요구하다, 고소하다	
12	위원회	
13	전달하다, 통신하다	
14	경쟁, 시합	
15	구리, 동전, 구리(빛)의	
16	저작권, 판권	
17	묘사, 서술	
18	파괴하다, 부수다	

C. Listen, write the word and meaning. (Track 99)

	Word	Meaning		Word	Meaning
01			10		
02			11		
03			12		
04			13		
05			14		
06			15		
07			16		
08			17		
09			18		

Unit 34

🎧 Listen and repeat. (Track 100)

01 develop [divéləp]
v 개발하다, 발전시키다 — to grow slowly and usually become more advanced
Mammals have a larger, more well-**developed** brain than do other animals.
포유동물은 다른 동물들보다 더 크고 더 잘 발달된 두뇌를 가지고 있다.

02 dynamic [dainǽmik]
a 활기 있는, 동력의, 동적인 — full of energy and ideas; active
A **dynamic** government is necessary to meet the demands of a changing society.
변화하는 사회의 욕구에 부응하기 위해 활기 있는 정부가 필요하다.

03 earthquake [ə́:rθkwèik]
n 지진 — violent movement of the earth's surface
A severe **earthquake** took place in LA yesterday.
어제 로스앤젤레스에서 심각한 지진이 발생했다.

04 echo [ékou]
v 메아리 치다, 모방하다 / **n** 메아리 — a sound that is repeated as it is sent back
Nothing, except for an **echo**, was heard.
메아리 외에는 아무것도 들리지 않았다.

05 exhibition [èksəbíʃən]
n 전시, 전시회 — a collection of objects, for example works of art
There was an **exhibition** of illustrated poems at the school garden.
학교 정원에서는 시화전이 있었다.

06 expense [ikspéns]
n 지출, 비용, 경비 — money that is spent for a particular purpose
We would be happy to take care of any **expenses** involved.
관련된 비용은 저희가 기꺼이 부담하겠습니다.

07 experience [ikspíəriəns]
n 경험, 체험, 경력 — the things that you have done in your life
Traveling provides opportunities to **experience** other cultures.
여행은 다른 문화를 경험할 수 있는 많은 기회를 준다.

08 fix [fiks]
v 고치다, 붙이다, 응시하다 — to put something firmly in place; to repair something
Refer to the instructions to **fix** the refrigerator.
냉장고를 고치려면 사용 설명서를 참조해 주세요.

09 flame [fleim]
n 불꽃, 불길 / **v** 타오르다 — bright burning gas that comes from something that is on fire
The **flames** from the fireplace gave off a warm glow.
벽난로에서 나온 불꽃들은 따뜻한 빛을 발산했다.

---

key words
severe **a** 격심한 / illustrated **a** 삽화가 든 / involve **v** 수반하다 / glow **n** 백열, 빛

🎧 Listen and repeat. Track 101

10 flat [flæt]
a 평탄한, 편평한   smooth and level, with no parts that are higher than the rest
People once believed that the earth was **flat**.
한때는 세상 사람들이 지구가 편평하다고 믿었다.

11 government [gʌ́vərnmənt]
n 정부, 통치(권)   the group of people who rule or control a country
I got to study abroad at **government** expense.
나는 정부 지원금으로 유학을 하게 되었다.

12 gradually [grǽdʒuəli]
ad 서서히, 점차로   happening slowly, not suddenly
Gradually he learned of his wife's extravagance and dishonesty.
서서히 그는 아내의 사치와 정직하지 못한 면을 알게 되었다.

13 grant [grænt]
v 시인하다, 인정하다   to agree that something is true
The governor **granted** liberty to many prisoners.
그 통치자는 많은 죄수들의 석방을 인정했다.

14 honest [ánist]
a 정직한, 진실한   telling the truth
There are very few clean and **honest** politicians nowadays.
요즘에는 깨끗하고 정직한 정치인들이 많지 않다.

15 hopeless [hóuplis]
a 희망 없는, 가망 없는   giving no hope; doing things wrong
I find this **hopeless** situation very depressing.
이 희망 없는 상황이 정말 우울하게 느껴진다.

16 hum [hʌm]
v 콧노래를 부르다   to sing with your lips closed
She is **humming** in a low tone.
그녀는 낮은 소리로 콧노래를 부르고 있다.

17 initial [iníʃəl]
a 최초의, 초기의   happening at the beginning; first
Most famous scientists achieved **initial** recognition while still quite young.
대부분의 과학자들은 그들이 아직도 꽤 어릴 때 최초의 명성을 얻었다.

18 insistent [insístənt]
a 고집 세우는, 주장하는   saying strongly
He was **insistent** on paying the bill.
그는 자기가 돈을 내겠다고 고집을 부렸다.

---

key words
extravagance n 사치, 낭비 / governor n 통치자, 지배자 / recognition n 인식, 인정

Unit 34

Exercise

A. Complete the sentence.

1. There are very few clean and _____ politicians nowadays.
   요즘에는 깨끗하고 정직한 정치인들이 많지 않다.

2. People once believed that the earth was _____.
   한때는 세상 사람들이 지구가 편평하다고 믿었다.

3. _____ he learned of his wife's extravagance and dishonesty.
   서서히 그는 아내의 사치와 정직하지 못한 면을 알게 되었다.

4. Traveling provides opportunities to _____ other cultures.
   여행은 다른 문화를 경험할 수 있는 많은 기회를 준다.

5. The governor _____ liberty to many prisoners.
   그 통치자는 많은 죄수들의 석방을 인정했다.

6. She is _____ in a low tone.
   그녀는 낮은 소리로 콧노래를 부르고 있다.

7. Most famous scientists achieved _____ recognition while still quite young.
   대부분의 과학자들은 그들이 아직도 꽤 어릴 때 최초의 명성을 얻었다.

8. Mammals have a larger, more well-_____ brain than do other animals.
   포유동물은 다른 동물들보다 더 크고 더 잘 발달된 두뇌를 가지고 있다.

9. There was an _____ of illustrated poems at the school garden.
   학교 정원에서는 시화전이 있었다.

10. He was _____ on paying the bill.
    그는 자기가 돈을 내겠다고 고집을 부렸다.

11. A severe _____ took place in LA yesterday.
    어제 로스앤젤레스에서 심각한 지진이 발생했다.

12. Nothing, except for an _____, was heard.
    메아리 외에는 아무것도 들리지 않았다.

13. A _____ government is necessary to meet the demands of a changing society.
    변화하는 사회의 욕구에 부응하기 위해 활기 있는 정부가 필요하다.

14. We would be happy to take care of any _____ involved.
    관련된 비용은 저희가 기꺼이 부담하겠습니다.

15. Refer to the instructions to _____ the refrigerator.
    냉장고를 고치려면 사용 설명서를 참조해 주세요.

16. I find this _____ situation very depressing.
    이 희망 없는 상황이 정말 우울하게 느껴진다.

17. I got to study abroad at _____ expense.
    나는 정부 지원금으로 유학을 하게 되었다.

18. The _____ from the fireplace gave off a warm glow.
    벽난로에서 나온 불꽃들은 따뜻한 빛을 발산했다.

Hint

| grant | insistent | government | hopeless | flame | honest | echo | initial | exhibition |
| flat | develop | experience | gradually | hum | expense | fix | dynamic | earthquake |

Exercise

B. Fill in the word and meaning.

	Word	Meaning
01	dynamic	
02	flame	
03	government	
04	develop	
05	hopeless	
06	expense	
07	honest	
08	initial	
09	earthquake	
10	insistent	
11	grant	
12	experience	
13	flat	
14	hum	
15	exhibition	
16	gradually	
17	fix	
18	echo	

	Meaning	Word
01	개발하다, 발전시키다	
02	활기 있는, 동력의, 동적인	
03	지진	
04	메아리 치다, 모방하다, 메아리	
05	전시, 전시회	
06	지출, 비용, 경비	
07	경험, 체험, 경력	
08	고치다, 붙이다, 응시하다	
09	불꽃, 불길, 타오르다	
10	평탄한, 편평한	
11	정부, 통치(권)	
12	서서히, 점차로	
13	시인하다, 인정하다	
14	정직한, 진실한	
15	희망 없는, 가망 없는	
16	콧노래를 부르다	
17	최초의, 초기의	
18	고집 세우는, 주장하는	

C. Listen, write the word and meaning. (Track 102)

	Word	Meaning		Word	Meaning
01			10		
02			11		
03			12		
04			13		
05			14		
06			15		
07			16		
08			17		
09			18		

Unit 34

Review 17

A. Read and fill in the word and meaning.

word	definition	meaning
	a person who is legally accepted as a member of a particular country	
	the legal right to be the only person who may do a piece of original work	
	in a way that matches, follows or depends on something	
	not thinking enough about what you are doing	
	to receive an advantage from something	
	an organized event in which people try to win something	
	to choose an actor for a particular role in a play, film, etc	
	to suddenly be seen; to come into sight	
	to give birth to children	
	to choose somebody for a job or position	
	a small round piece of wood, glass or plastic with a hole in the middle	
	to say that something is true, without having any proof	
	to ask for something in writing	
	a picture in words of somebody or something that happened	
	a group of people who have been chosen to discuss something	
	to damage something so badly that it can no longer be used	
	to share and exchange information or feelings with somebody	
	a common reddish-brown metal	

Hint
competition   bear   citizen   description   destroy   apply   copper   appoint   benefit
according   cast   bead   committee   copyright   claim   appear   careless   communicate

B. Read and fill in the word and meaning.

word	definition	meaning
	telling the truth	
	to grow slowly and usually become more advanced	
	to agree that something is true	
	giving no hope; doing things wrong	
	saying strongly	
	a sound that is repeated as it is sent back	
	happening slowly, not suddenly	
	violent movement of the earth's surface	
	the group of people who rule or control a country	
	full of energy and ideas; active	
	smooth and level, with no parts that are higher than the rest	
	money that is spent for a particular purpose	
	bright burning gas that comes from something that is on fire	
	a collection of objects, for example works of art	
	to sing with your lips closed	
	happening at the beginning; first	
	to put something firmly in place; to repair something	
	the things that you have done in your life	

Hint

grant insistent government hopeless flame honest echo initial exhibition
flat   develop   experience   gradually hum   expense fix   dynamic earthquake

Unit 35

🎧 Listen and repeat. (Track 103)

01 instance [ínstəns]
n 실례, 사례 / v 예를 들다 — an example or case
For **instance**, keep food covered and refrigerated, and wash your hands often.
예를 들면 음식을 싸놓거나 냉동시키고 손을 자주 씻는 것이다.

02 instant [ínstənt]
a 즉석의, 즉시의 — happening suddenly or immediately
He gave up smoking and the effect on his health was **instant**.
그가 담배를 끊자 건강에 대한 효과가 즉시 나타났다.

03 laundry [lɔ́:ndri]
n 세탁물, 세탁소 — clothes, etc that need washing or that are being washed
It's always my responsibility to do the **laundry**.
빨래하는 것은 언제나 제 담당입니다.

04 lick [lik]
v 핥다 — to move your tongue across something
The puppy **licked** up the spilt milk.
강아지는 엎질러진 우유를 다 핥아 먹었다.

05 limit [límit]
v 제한하다 / n 한계, 경계 — the outside edge of a place or area
No fishing is allowed within a twenty-mile **limit**.
20마일의 경계 내에서는 어떤 낚시 행위도 허용되지 않는다.

06 mention [ménʃən]
v 언급하다 / n 기재, 표창 — to say or write something about
Don't **mention** my little problem when we have company.
함께 있을 때는 나의 자그마한 문제점에 대해 말하지 마세요.

07 merchant [mə́:rtʃənt]
n 상인, 무역상인 — a person whose job is to buy and sell goods
Most **merchants** reported a slowdown in sales for October.
대부분의 상인들은 10월의 판매가 감소되었다고 말했다.

08 merit [mérit]
n 장점, 공적 — an advantage or a good quality
Its **merits** cannot be uncertain unless it is put to practice.
실지로 운용해 보지 않고서는 그 장점을 확인할 수 없다.

09 method [méθəd]
n 방법, 순서 — a way of doing something
This **method** has the advantage of saving a lot of fuel.
이 방법은 많은 연료를 절약하는 이점이 있다.

---

key words
refrigerate v 냉장하다, 냉동하다 / spill v 엎지르다 / unless conj ~하지 않으면 / fuel n 연료

Listen and repeat. Track 104

10 nervous [nə́ːrvəs]
a 신경(성)의, 신경질적인, 불안한　worried or afraid
I was a bit **nervous** for a start, but I soon got used to it.
처음에는 약간 불안했지만, 난 곧 그것에 적응했다.

11 neutral [njúːtrəl]
a 중립의, 공평한　not supporting to either side in an argument, war, etc
He remained **neutral** in the furious controversy.
그는 격한 논쟁에서 중립을 지켰다.

12 notice [nóutis]
v 알아채다 / **n** 주의　to see and become conscious of something
We didn't **notice** him leaving.
우리는 그가 떠난 것을 알아 차리지 못했다.

13 partially [páːrʃəli]
ad 부분적으로, 불공평하게　not completely
There are many factories running only **partially** due to the economic recession.
경기침체로 공장을 일부만 가동하는 곳이 많습니다.

14 passage [pǽsidʒ]
n 통행, 통과, 경과　the process of passing
His painful memories faded with the **passage** of time.
시간이 경과함에 따라 그의 고통스러운 기억들은 희미해졌다.

15 patience [péiʃəns]
n 인내(력), 참을성　the quality of being able to stay calm and not get angry
She has **patience** and she never loses her temper.
그녀는 매우 참을성이 많아 결코 화를 내지 않는다.

16 portable [pɔ́ːrtəbəl]
a 휴대용의　that can be moved or carried easily
With the growing popularity of hiking, all kinds of **portable** camping equipment are being sold.
하이킹의 인기가 높아짐에 따라 각종 휴대용 캠핑장비가 팔리고 있다.

17 priest [priːst]
n 성직자, 목사　a person who performs religious ceremonies in some religions
Now **priests** began to plan their church services throughout the day.
이제 목사들은 그들의 하루 전체 예배 시간을 계획할 수 있게 되었다.

18 potential [pouténʃəl]
a 잠재적인 / **n** 잠재성　that may possibly become something or happen
Could you provide me with data on the **potential** demand for our products in your country?
당신의 나라에 있는 우리 제품에 대한 잠재적인 수요에 관한 데이터를 저에게 주실 수 있습니까?

key words
remain **v** 여전히 ~인 채로이다 / conscious **a** 알고 있는 / recession **n** 경기 후퇴 / temper **n** 성질, 기질

Unit 35

Exercise

A. Complete the sentence.

1. He gave up smoking and the effect on his health was _____.
   그가 담배를 끊자 건강에 대한 효과가 즉시 나타났다.

2. She has _____ and she never loses her temper.
   그녀는 매우 참을성이 많아 결코 화를 내지 않는다.

3. It's always my responsibility to do the _____.
   빨래하는 것은 언제나 제 담당입니다.

4. Don't _____ my little problem when we have company.
   함께 있을 때는 나의 자그마한 문제점에 대해 말하지 마세요.

5. For _____, keep food covered and refrigerated, and wash your hands often.
   예를 들면 음식을 싸놓거나 냉동시키고 손을 자주 씻는 것이다.

6. Its _____ cannot be uncertain unless it is put to practice.
   실지로 운용해 보지 않고서는 그 장점을 확인할 수 없다.

7. I was a bit _____ for a start, but I soon got used to it.
   처음에는 약간 불안했지만, 난 곧 그것에 적응했다.

8. The puppy _____ up the spilt milk.
   강아지는 엎질러진 우유를 다 핥아 먹었다.

9. We didn't _____ him leaving.
   우리는 그가 떠난 것을 알아 차리지 못했다.

10. There are many factories running only _____ due to the economic recession.
    경기침체로 공장을 일부만 가동하는 곳이 많습니다.

11. He remained _____ in the furious controversy.
    그는 격한 논쟁에서 중립을 지켰다.

12. His painful memories faded with the _____ of time.
    시간이 경과함에 따라 그의 고통스러운 기억들은 희미해졌다.

13. Most _____ reported a slowdown in sales for October.
    대부분의 상인들은 10월의 판매가 감소되었다고 말했다.

14. With the growing popularity of hiking, all kinds of _____ camping equipment are being sold.
    하이킹의 인기가 높아짐에 따라 각종의 휴대용 캠핑장비가 팔리고 있다.

15. No fishing is allowed within a twenty-mile _____.
    20마일의 경계 내에서는 어떤 낚시 행위도 허용되지 않는다.

16. Now _____ began to plan their church services throughout the day.
    이제 목사들은 그들의 하루 전체 예배 시간을 계획할 수 있게 되었다.

17. This _____ has the advantage of saving a lot of fuel.
    이 방법은 많은 연료를 절약하는 이점이 있다.

18. Could you provide me with data on the _____ demand for our products in your country?
    당신의 나라에 있는 우리 제품에 대한 잠재적인 수요에 관한 데이터를 저에게 주실 수 있습니까?

Hint

| priest | laundry | portable | nervous | passage | merit | instant | notice | merchant |
| lick | potential | method | patience | instance | limit | mention | neutral | partially |

Unit 35

Exercise

B. Fill in the word and meaning.

	Word	Meaning
01	mention	
02	instance	
03	partially	
04	method	
05	instant	
06	patience	
07	merchant	
08	priest	
09	passage	
10	limit	
11	nervous	
12	notice	
13	potential	
14	lick	
15	portable	
16	merit	
17	neutral	
18	laundry	

	Meaning	Word
01	실례, 사례, 예를 들다	
02	즉석의, 즉시의	
03	세탁물, 세탁소	
04	핥다	
05	제한하다, 한계, 경계	
06	언급하다, 기재, 표창	
07	상인, 무역 상인	
08	장점, 공적	
09	방법, 순서	
10	신경(성)의, 신경질적인, 불안한	
11	중립의, 공평한	
12	알아채다, 주의	
13	부분적으로, 불공평하게	
14	통행, 통과, 경과	
15	인내(력), 참을성	
16	휴대용의	
17	성직자, 목사	
18	잠재적인, 잠재성	

🎧 C. Listen, write the word and meaning. (Track 105)

	Word	Meaning		Word	Meaning
01			10		
02			11		
03			12		
04			13		
05			14		
06			15		
07			16		
08			17		
09			18		

Unit 36

🎧 Listen and repeat. Track 106

01 realistic
[rìːəlístik]
a 현실주의의, 사실주의의   sensible and understanding what it is possible to achieve in a particular situation
The styles used in cartoon animation range from **realistic** representations of every day life to the most impossible fantasy.
만화영화에서 사용되는 스타일들은, 일상생활의 사실적인 반영으로부터 가장 불가능한 환상에 이르는 범위에 걸친다.

02 recent
[ríːsənt]
a 근래의, 최근의, 새로운   that happened or began only a short time ago
The **recent** changes in the Earth's climate are beginning to worry some scientists.
최근 지구 기후의 변화를 몇몇 과학자들이 걱정하기 시작했다.

03 reject
[ridʒékt]
v 거절하다, 무시하다   to refuse to accept somebody / something
The chairman **rejected** his stupid proposal.
의장은 그의 어리석은 제안을 거절했다.

04 review
[rivjúː]
v 재검토하다, 복습하다   to look at or think about something again to make sure that you understand it
All I did was to **review** what was covered in class every day.
제가 한 일은 매일 수업 시간에 다루어졌던 것을 복습하는 것이 전부였습니다.

05 role
[roul]
n 역할, 배역   the position or function of somebody / something
Religion has played an important **role** in society.
종교는 사회에서 중요한 역할을 해 오고 있다.

06 routine
[ruːtíːn]
a 일상의, 판에 박힌   normal and regular; not unusual or special
I'd like to escape from my **routine** of daily life.
나는 판에 박힌 매일의 삶에서 탈피하고 싶어요.

07 similar
[símələːr]
a 유사한, 닮은   like somebody / something but not exactly the same
Of all living things, the chimpanzee has a genetic make-up that is most **similar** to that of humans.
모든 생물들 중에서 침팬지는 인간과 가장 비슷한 유전적인 구성을 가진다.

08 situation
[sìtʃuéiʃən]
n 상태, 사정, 입장   the things that are happening in a particular place or time
Rather, we would suggest waiting for a more favorable **situation**.
차라리 더 나은 상태를 기다리는 것이 좋겠습니다.

09 skip
[skip]
v 빠뜨리다, 가볍게 뛰다, 거르다   to not do something that you usually do or should do
He **skipped** his daily walk to the town cafe where he had coffee with his friends.
그는 매일 친구들과 커피를 마시는 마을 카페까지의 산책을 빼먹었다.

key words
representation **n** 표현, 묘사력 / chairman **n** 의장 / genetic **a** 유전적인

🎧 Listen and repeat. (Track 107)

10 sweat [swet]
n 땀 / **v** 땀을 흘리다 — the salty colourless liquid which comes through your skin when you are hot, ill, or afraid
DNA can be taken from hair, **sweat** or saliva.
DNA는 머리카락, 땀 또는 침에서 채취할 수 있다.

11 taboo [təbúː]
n 금기 / **a** 금기의 — something that you must not say or do
Smoking used to be **taboo** for women in most Asian countries.
대부분의 아시아 국가에서 여성들에게 흡연은 금기였다.

12 tangle [tǽŋɡəl]
v 엉키게 하다, 혼란에 빠지다 — to confuse things that cannot easily be separated from each other
You smell like ashes and your hair is all **tangled**.
너에게서는 탄 냄새가 나고 너의 머리는 온통 헝클어져 있어.

13 trial [tráiəl]
n 공판, 시도, 시련 — the process in a court of law, an act of testing
There was a simultaneous broadcast of the **trial** on radio and TV.
라디오와 TV에서 그 공판을 동시에 방영했다.

14 typhoon [taifúːn]
n 태풍 — a violent tropical storm with very strong winds
According to the weather forecast the **typhoon** is likely to approach the coast.
일기 예보에 의하면 태풍은 연안으로 접근할 것 같다.

15 unfortunately [ʌnfɔ́ːrtʃənitli]
ad 불행하게 — not luckily
Unfortunately the restaurant he recommended fell far short of our expectations.
불행히도 그가 추천한 식당은 우리 기대에 훨씬 못 미쳤다.

16 whether [hwéðəːr]
conj ~인지 어떤지, ~이든지(아니든지) — used for expressing a choice or doubt between two or more possibilities
At the same time, please indicate **whether** you desire air or sea shipment.
항공편과 배편 중 어느 쪽을 원하시는지도 함께 알려주시길 바랍니다.

17 widow [wídou]
n 미망인, 과부 — a woman whose husband has died and who has not married again
She has been a **widow** for only six months.
그 여자는 미망인이 된지 반년 정도 되었다.

18 yield [jiːld]
v 생기게 하다, 산출하다 / **n** 산출, 수확 — to produce or provide crops, profits or results
An experienced farmer can estimate the annual **yield** of his acres with surprising accuracy.
경험이 많은 농부는 그의 토지의 연간 산출을 놀라울 만큼 정확하게 가늠할 수 있다.

---

key words
saliva **n** 침 / ash **n** 재 / court **n** 법정 / simultaneous **a** 동시의 / tropical **a** 열대의
expectation **n** 기대 / doubt **n** 의심, 불신 / profit **n** 이익, 수익 / acre **n** 에이커, 토지 / accuracy **n** 정확

Unit 36 181

Exercise

A. Complete the sentence.

1. The styles used in cartoon animation range from _____ representations of every day life to the most impossible fantasy.
   만화영화에서 사용되는 스타일들은, 일상생활의 사실적인 반영으로부터 가장 불가능한 환상에 이르는 범위에 걸친다.

2. The _____ changes in the Earth's climate are beginning to worry some scientists.
   최근 지구 기후의 변화를 몇몇 과학자들이 걱정하기 시작했다.

3. She has been a _____ for only six months.
   그 여자는 미망인이 된지 반년 정도 되었다.

4. I'd like to escape from my _____ of daily life.
   나는 판에 박힌 매일의 삶에서 탈피하고 싶어요.

5. Smoking used to be _____ for women in most Asian countries.
   대부분의 아시아 국가에서 여성들에게 흡연은 금기였었다.

6. Of all living things, the chimpanzee has a genetic make-up that is most _____ to that of humans.
   모든 생물들 중에서 침팬지는 인간과 가장 비슷한 유전적인 구성을 가진다.

7. All I did was to _____ what was covered in class every day.
   제가 한 일은 매일 수업 시간에 다루어졌던 것을 복습하는 것이 전부였습니다.

8. He _____ his daily walk to the town cafe where he had coffee with his friends.
   그는 매일 친구들과 커피를 마시는 마을 카페까지의 산책을 빼먹었다.

9. Religion has played an important _____ in society.
   종교는 사회에서 중요한 역할을 해 오고 있다.

10. DNA can be taken from hair, _____ or saliva.
    DNA는 머리카락, 땀 또는 침에서 채취할 수 있다.

11. There was a simultaneous broadcast of the _____ on radio and TV.
    라디오와 TV에서 그 공판을 동시에 방영했다.

12. According to the weather forecast the _____ is likely to approach the coast.
    일기 예보에 의하면 태풍은 연안으로 접근할 것 같다.

13. _____ the restaurant he recommended fell far short of our expectations.
    불행히도 그가 추천한 식당은 우리 기대에 훨씬 못 미쳤다.

14. At the same time, please indicate _____ you desire air or sea shipment.
    항공편과 배편 중 어느 쪽을 원하시는지도 함께 알려주시길 바랍니다.

15. The chairman _____ his stupid proposal.
    의장은 그의 어리석은 제안을 거절했다.

16. You smell like ashes and your hair is all _____.
    너에게서는 탄 냄새가 나고 너의 머리는 온통 헝클어져 있어.

17. An experienced farmer can estimate the annual _____ of his acres with surprising accuracy.
    경험이 많은 농부는 그의 토지의 연간 산출을 놀라울 만큼 정확하게 가늠할 수 있다.

18. Rather, we would suggest waiting for a more favorable _____.
    차라리 더 나은 상태를 기다리는 것이 좋겠습니다.

Hint

| similar | routine | widow | taboo | review | sweat | recent | skip | tangle |
| realistic | yield | reject | role | typhoon | whether | situation | trial | unfortunately |

Exercise

B. Fill in the word and meaning.

	Word	Meaning
01	reject	
02	skip	
03	tangle	
04	routine	
05	taboo	
06	typhoon	
07	realistic	
08	whether	
09	similar	
10	yield	
11	recent	
12	widow	
13	unfortunately	
14	situation	
15	trial	
16	role	
17	sweat	
18	review	

	Meaning	Word
01	현실주의의, 사실주의의	
02	근래의, 최근의, 새로운	
03	거절하다, 무시하다	
04	재검토하다, 복습하다	
05	역할, 배역	
06	일상의, 판에 박힌	
07	유사한, 닮은	
08	상태, 사정, 입장	
09	빠뜨리다, 가볍게 뛰다, 거르다	
10	땀, 땀을 흘리다	
11	금기, 금기의	
12	엉키게 하다, 혼란에 빠지다	
13	공판, 시도, 시련	trial
14	태풍	
15	불행하게	
16	~인지 어떤지, ~이든지(아니든지)	
17	미망인, 과부	
18	생기게 하다, 산출하다, 산출	

C. Listen, write the word and meaning. (Track 108)

	Word	Meaning		Word	Meaning
01			10		
02			11		
03			12		
04			13		
05			14		
06			15		
07			16		
08			17		
09			18		

Review 18

A. Read and fill in the word and meaning.

word	definition	meaning
	a way of doing something	
	not supporting to either side in an argument, war, etc	
	the process of passing	
	worried or afraid	
	clothes, etc that need washing or that are being washed	
	not completely	
	to see and become conscious of something	
	an example or case	
	an advantage or a good quality	
	the quality of being able to stay calm and not get angry	
	happening suddenly or immediately	
	that may possibly become something or happen	
	that can be moved or carried easily	
	to move your tongue across something	
	to say or write something about	
	a person who performs religious ceremonies in some religions	
	the outside edge of a place or area	
	a person whose job is to buy and sell goods	

Hint

priest   laundry   portable   nervous   passage   merit   instant   notice   merchant
lick   potential   method   patience   instance   limit   mention   neutral   partially

B. Read and fill in the word and meaning.

word	definition	meaning
	the salty colourless liquid which comes through your skin when you are hot, ill, or afraid	
	something that you must not say or do	
	sensible and understanding what it is possible to achieve in a particular situation	
	not luckily	
	to confuse things that cannot easily be separated from each other	
	to refuse to accept somebody/something	
	the process in a court of law, an act of testing	
	that happened or began only a short time ago	
	a violent tropical storm with very strong winds	
	the position or function of somebody / something	
	used for expressing a choice or doubt between two or more possibilities	
	to look at or think about something again to make sure that you understand it	
	to not do something that you usually do or should do	
	the things that are happening in a particular place or time	
	to produce or provide crops, profits or results	
	normal and regular; not unusual or special	
	like somebody/something but not exactly the same	
	a woman whose husband has died and who has not married again	

Hint

similar   routine   widow   taboo   review   sweat   recent   skip   tangle
realistic   yield   reject   role   typhoon   whether   situation   trial   unfortunately

Review 18

Unit 37

🎧 Listen and repeat. Track 109

01 account [əkáunt]
n 고려, 계산 / v 설명하다, 책임지다   consideration about something
After then you can take things like ethics into **account**.
그런 후에야 당신은 비로소 윤리관 같은 것들을 고려대상에 넣을 수 있다.

02 appropriate [əpróuprièit]
v 충당하다, 사유하다 / a 적절한, 적당한   suitable or right for a particular situation, person, etc
This is the most respectful way and is **appropriate** only in formal situations.
이것은 가장 존경어린 표현법이어서 예의를 갖추는 상황에만 쓰는 것이 적당합니다.

03 arbor [á:rbər]
n 수목   a tree-like structure
He's the owner of the house with **arbores** on the shore of the lake.
그는 호숫가에 나무들이 있는 집의 주인이다.

04 architect [á:rkitèkt]
n 건축가, 설계사   a person whose job is to design buildings
Who was the **architect** of this cathedral?
이 성당을 지은 건축가는 누구입니까?

05 biological [baiáləʤikəl]
a 생물학적인, 생물학의   connected with the scientific study of animals, plants, and other living things
People with **biological** differences are known as different races.
생물학적인 차이가 있는 사람들은 다른 인종이라고 알려져 있다.

06 bite [bait]
n 물린 상처 / v 물다   a painful place on the skin made by an insect, dog, etc
Maggots can invade the body from the **bite** of mosquitos.
구더기는 모기에 물린 상처를 통해서 인체에 침입할 수 있다.

07 blossom [blásəm]
v 꽃을 피우다 / v 꽃, 개화   to produce flowers
Peach trees **blossom** in April.
복숭아나무는 4월에 꽃을 피운다.

08 cease [si:s]
v 중단하다, 멈추다   to stop or end
The enemy's attack **ceased** at dawn.
적군은 공격을 새벽녘에 중단했다.

09 celebration [sèləbréiʃən]
n 축하, 의식, 칭찬   the act of doing something enjoyable because it is a special day
We gave a party in **celebration** of my grandfather's birthday.
우리는 할아버지의 생신을 축하하는 파티를 열었다.

key words
ethics n 윤리학 / shore n (강)기슭 / cathedral n 대성당 / maggot n 구더기 / invade v 침입하다

🎧 Listen and repeat. (Track 110)

10 complain [kəmpléin]
v 불평하다, 하소연하다   to say that you are not satisfied with or happy about something
She **complained** that the questions were an invasion of privacy.
그녀는 그 질문들이 사생활을 침해하는 것이라고 불평했다.

11 compose [kəmpóuz]
v 작곡하다, 작문하다   to write music, to produce a piece of writing
The program can **compose** music itself by analyzing a database.
이 프로그램은 데이터베이스를 분석해 스스로 작곡을 할 수 있다.

12 concentrate [kánsəntrèit]
v 집중하다, 집결시키다   to give all your attention or effort to something
They also learn how to **concentrate** and keep a clear mind.
그들은 또한 집중하는 방법과 밝은 마음을 유지하는 방법을 배운다.

13 core [kɔːr]
n 핵심, 속   the central or most important part of something
What's the **core** issue here?
여기서 핵심 쟁점은 무엇입니까?

14 cabin [kǽbin]
n 객실, 오두막   a small wooden house; a hut
After sleeping in small roadside **cabins**, they found their hotel suite comfortable.
그들은 길가 작은 오두막에서 자고 나서 그들의 호텔방이 편안함을 알았다.

15 calculator [kǽlkjəlèitər]
n 계산기, 계산자   a small electronic machine used for calculating figures
We have moved on to better things only with the help of mechanical **calculators** and computers.
우리는 기계식 계산기와 컴퓨터의 도움을 받고서야 더 향상된 방향으로 나아가게 되었다.

16 cure [kjuər]
v 치료하다, 구원하다 / n 치료   to make somebody healthy again after an illness
Time is a herb that **cure**s all diseases.
시간은 모든 병을 치료하는 약초이다.

17 device [diváis]
n 장치, 도구, 책략   a tool or piece of equipment, a clever method
Put all your things in this basket and go through the inspection **device**.
소지품들은 이 바구니에 전부 담으시고 검사 장치를 통과하십시오.

18 devote [divóut]
v 바치다, 헌신하다   to give a lot of time, energy, etc
The nominee of our party is a man who has **devoted** his life to public service.
우리 정당의 지명을 받은 사람은 공공의 봉사에 평생을 바친 사람이다.

key words
invasion n 침해 / inspection n 검사, 조사 / nominee n 지명된 사람

Unit 37

Exercise

A. Complete the sentence.

1. After then you can take things like ethics into _____.
   그런 후에야 당신은 비로소 윤리관 같은 것들을 고려대상에 넣을 수 있다.

2. People with _____ differences are known as different races.
   생물학적인 차이가 있는 사람들은 다른 인종이라고 알려져 있다.

3. The enemy's attack _____ at dawn.
   적군은 공격을 새벽녘에 중단했다.

4. This is the most respectful way and is _____ only in formal situations.
   이것은 가장 존경어린 표현법이어서 예의를 갖추는 상황에만 쓰는 것이 적당합니다.

5. We gave a party in _____ of my grandfather's birthday.
   우리는 할아버지의 생신을 축하하는 파티를 열었다.

6. The nominee of our party is a man who has _____ his life to public service.
   우리 정당의 지명을 받은 사람은 공공의 봉사에 평생을 바친 사람이다.

7. She _____ that the questions were an invasion of privacy.
   그녀는 그 질문들이 사생활을 침해하는 것이라고 불평했다.

8. He's the owner of the house with _____ on the shore of the lake.
   그는 호숫가에 나무들이 있는 집의 주인이다.

9. The program can _____ music itself by analyzing a database.
   이 프로그램은 데이터베이스를 분석해 스스로 작곡을 할 수 있다.

10. Peach trees _____ in April.
    복숭아나무는 4월에 꽃을 피운다.

11. They also learn how to _____ and keep a clear mind.
    그들은 또한 집중하는 방법과 밝은 마음을 유지하는 방법을 배운다.

12. Who was the _____ of this Cathedral?
    이 성당을 지은 건축가는 누구입니까?

13. What's the _____ issue here?
    여기서 핵심 쟁점은 무엇입니까?

14. After sleeping in small roadside _____, they found their hotel suite comfortable.
    그들은 길가 작은 오두막에서 자고 나서 그들의 호텔방이 편안함을 알았다.

15. Put all your things in this basket and go through the inspection _____.
    소지품들은 이 바구니에 전부 담으시고 검사 장치를 통과하십시오.

16. We have moved on to better things only with the help of mechanical _____ and computers.
    우리는 기계식 계산기와 컴퓨터의 도움을 받고서야 더 향상된 방향으로 나아가게 되었다.

17. Maggots can invade the body from the _____ of mosquitos.
    구더기는 모기에 물린 상처를 통해서 인체에 침입할 수 있다.

18. Time is a herb that _____ all diseases.
    시간은 모든 병을 치료하는 약초이다.

Hint

appropriate biological calculator cease complain core devote cure concentrate
celebration architect blossom device account cabin arbor bite compose

Exercise

B. Fill in the word and meaning.

	Word	Meaning
01	arbor	
02	bite	
03	core	
04	account	
05	concentrate	
06	celebration	
07	biological	
08	device	
09	cease	
10	devote	
11	cabin	
12	calculator	
13	appropriate	
14	cure	
15	complain	
16	blossom	
17	compose	
18	architect	

	Meaning	Word
01	고려, 계산, 설명하다, 책임지다	
02	충당하다, 사유하다, 적절한, 적당한	
03	수목	
04	건축가, 설계사	
05	생물학적인, 생물학의	
06	물린 상처, 물다	
07	꽃을 피우다, 꽃, 개화	
08	중단하다, 멈추다	
09	축하, 의식, 칭찬	
10	불평하다, 하소연하다	
11	작곡하다, 작문하다	
12	집중하다, 집결시키다	
13	핵심, 속	
14	객실, 오두막	
15	계산기, 계산자	
16	치료하다, 구원하다, 치료	
17	장치, 도구, 책략	
18	바치다, 헌신하다	

🎧 C. Listen, write the word and meaning. (Track 111)

	Word	Meaning		Word	Meaning
01			10		
02			11		
03			12		
04			13		
05			14		
06			15		
07			16		
08			17		
09			18		

Unit 38

🎧 **Listen and repeat.** Track 112

01 dialect [dáiəlèkt]
n 방언, 사투리　a form of a language that is spoken in one part of a country
One of the most distinct **dialects** of North American English, Gullah is spoken by many people around South Caroline.
북미 영어에서 가장 독특한 방언들 중의 하나인 '굴라'는 사우스캐롤라이나 주위의 많은 사람들이 사용한다.

02 edition [idíʃən]
n 판, 간행　the form in which a book is published
I've only read the revised **edition** of her novel.
나는 그녀의 소설의 개정판만을 읽어보았다.

03 educate [édʒukèit]
v 교육하다, 육성하다　to teach or train somebody, especially in school
Schools and colleges have a strong influence on the future of society, because they **educate** the next generation.
학교와 대학들은 사회의 미래에 큰 영향력을 가지고 있는데 그 이유는 그들이 다음 세대를 교육하기 때문이다.

04 effective [iféktiv]
a 효과적인, 효력이 있는　successfully producing the result that you want
Gentle persuasion is more **effective** than force.
부드러운 설득이 강요보다 효과적이다.

05 explain [ikspléin]
v 설명하다, 해석하다, 해명하다　to make something clear or easy to understand
That **explains** his absence.
그것은 그가 왜 불참했는지를 설명해 준다.

06 expose [ikspóuz]
v 드러내다, 폭로하다　to show something that is usually hidden
The newspaper **exposed** the politician as a spy.
그 신문은 그 정치인이 스파이라고 폭로했다.

07 extent [ikstént]
n 정도, 범위　the length, area, size or importance of something
The **extent** of homelessness in the world is not fully known.
세계의 노숙자들이 어느 정도인지는 완전히 밝혀지지 않았다.

08 faucet [fɔ́:sit]
n 수도꼭지　a type of handle that you turn to let water out of a pipe
The paint is peeling, the **faucet** in the bathroom is leaking, and all the doors are broken.
페인트는 벗겨지고, 화장실 수도꼭지는 물이 새고, 모든 문들은 망가졌어요.

09 forbid [fəːrbíd]
v 금지하다, 방해하다　to not allow something
This bill not only **forbade** cloning human beings, but also cell cloning for research purposes.
이 법안은 인간의 복제뿐 아니라 연구목적의 체세포 복제까지 금지했다.

key words
distinct a 독특한 / revise v 개정하다 / generation n 세대 / persuasion n 설득, 확신
spy n 스파이, 간첩 / homelessness n 집 없는 사람 / leak v 새다

🎧 Listen and repeat. Track 113

10 formally [fɔ́ːrməli]
ad 정식으로, 공식으로   used when you want to appear serious or official
This is to **formally** invite you to lecture at our laboratory.
본 연구소에서의 강연에 정식으로 당신을 초청합니다.

11 grave [greiv]
n 무덤, 죽음   the place where a dead body is buried
We'll take this secret with us to our **graves**.
우리는 이 비밀을 무덤까지 갖고 가야 해.

12 greedy [gríːdi]
a 욕심 많은, 갈망하는   wanting more food, money, etc than you really need
He overcharges customers because he is **greedy**.
그는 욕심이 많아 고객들에게 바가지를 씌운다.

13 grocery [gróusəri]
n 식품점   the place where food is sold by a grocer
His acquaintance runs a **grocery** in the country.
그가 아는 사람이 시골에서 식품점을 운영하고 있다.

14 humanity [hjuːmǽnəti]
n 인류, 인간애, 인간성   the mind that is thinking of people in the world
Religions have helped greatly in the development of **humanity**.
종교는 인간애의 발달에 많은 도움을 주었다.

15 illegally [ilíːgəli]
ad 불법으로   not allowed by the law
The main reason for this decrease is hunters who kill gorillas **illegally**.
이렇게 수가 줄어든 가장 큰 원인은 고릴라를 불법으로 죽이는 사냥꾼들 때문이다.

16 imagination [imæ̀dʒənéiʃən]
n 상상(력), 창작력   the ability to create mental pictures or new ideas
A novel can be considered a work of **imagination** that is rooted in reality.
소설이란 것은, 현실에 바탕을 둔 상상력의 작품이라고 생각될 수 있다.

17 insurance [inʃúərəns]
n 보험, 보험금   an arrangement with a company in which you pay them regularly and they pay when you die or ill
When her husband died, she received 50,000 dollars in **insurance**.
남편이 죽었을 때 그녀는 보험금으로 5만 달러를 받았다.

18 intense [inténs]
a 격한, 강렬한   very strong or serious
The effects of the drug are **intense** but brief.
그 약의 효과는 강렬하지만 짧다.

key words
laboratory **n** 연구소 / overcharge **v** 부당한 값을 요구하다 / acquaintance **n** 아는 사람

Unit 38 191

Exercise

A. Complete the sentence.

1. This is to _____ invite you to lecture at our laboratory.
   본 연구소에서의 강연에 정식으로 당신을 초청합니다.

2. We'll take this secret with us to our _____.
   우리는 이 비밀을 무덤까지 갖고 가야 해.

3. Religions have helped greatly in the development of _____.
   종교는 인간애의 발달에 많은 도움을 주었다.

4. He overcharges customers because he is _____.
   그는 욕심이 많아 고객들에게 바가지를 씌운다.

5. The main reason for this decrease is hunters who kill gorillas _____.
   이렇게 수가 줄어든 가장 큰 원인은 고릴라를 불법으로 죽이는 사냥꾼들 때문이다.

6. His acquaintance runs a _____ in the country.
   그가 아는 사람이 시골에서 식품점을 운영하고 있다.

7. A novel can be considered a work of _____ that is rooted in reality.
   소설이란 것은, 현실에 바탕을 둔 상상력의 작품이라고 생각될 수 있다.

8. I've only read the revised _____ of her novel.
   나는 그녀의 소설의 개정판만을 읽어보았다.

9. When her husband died, she received 50,000 dollars in _____.
   남편이 죽었을 때 그녀는 보험금으로 5만 달러를 받았다.

10. The effects of the drug are _____ but brief.
    그 약의 효과는 강렬하지만 짧다.

11. Schools and colleges have a strong influence on the future of society, because they _____ the next generation.
    학교와 대학들은 사회의 미래에 큰 영향력을 가지고 있는데 그 이유는 그들이 다음 세대를 교육하기 때문이다.

12. Gentle persuasion is more _____ than force.
    부드러운 설득이 강요보다 효과적이다.

13. The paint is peeling, the _____ in the bathroom is leaking, and all the doors are broken.
    페인트는 벗겨지고, 화장실 수도꼭지는 물이 새고, 모든 문들은 망가졌어요.

14. That _____ his absence.
    그것은 그가 왜 불참했는지를 설명해 준다.

15. This bill not only _____ cloning human beings, but also cell cloning for research purposes.
    이 법안은 인간의 복제뿐 아니라 연구목적의 체세포 복제까지 금지했다.

16. The newspaper _____ the politician as a spy.
    그 신문은 그 정치인이 스파이라고 폭로했다.

17. The _____ of homelessness in the world is not fully known.
    세계의 노숙자들이 어느 정도인지는 완전히 밝혀지지 않았다.

18. One of the most distinct _____ of North American English, Gullah is spoken by many people around South Caroline.
    북미 영어에서 가장 독특한 방언들 중의 하나인 '굴라'는 사우스캐롤라이나 주위의 많은 사람들이 사용한다.

Hint

| humanity | insurance | edition | greedy | extent | imagination | effective | formally | intense |
| explain | grocery | dialect | forbid | grave | faucet | expose | illegally | educate |

Exercise

B. Fill in the word and meaning.

	Word	Meaning
01	edition	
02	faucet	
03	humanity	
04	grave	
05	dialect	
06	imagination	
07	grocery	
08	extent	
09	formally	
10	intense	
11	effective	
12	insurance	
13	explain	
14	illegally	
15	educate	
16	greedy	
17	forbid	
18	expose	

	Meaning	Word
01	방언, 사투리	
02	판, 간행	
03	교육하다, 육성하다	
04	효과적인, 효력이 있는	
05	설명하다, 해석하다, 해명하다	
06	드러내다, 폭로하다	
07	정도, 범위	
08	수도꼭지	
09	금지하다, 방해하다	
10	정식으로, 공식으로	
11	무덤, 죽음	
12	욕심 많은, 갈망하는	
13	식품점	
14	인류, 인간애, 인간성	
15	불법으로	
16	상상(력), 창작력	
17	보험, 보험금	
18	격한, 강렬한	

C. Listen, write the word and meaning. (Track 114)

	Word	Meaning		Word	Meaning
01			10		
02			11		
03			12		
04			13		
05			14		
06			15		
07			16		
08			17		
09			18		

Review 19

A. Read and fill in the word and meaning.

word	definition	meaning
	a tree-like structure	
	to write music, to produce a piece of writing	
	suitable or right for a particular situation, person, etc	
	to give all your attention or effort to something	
	to say that you are not satisfied with or happy about something	
	to give a lot of time, energy, etc	
	consideration about something	
	a tool or piece of equipment, a clever method	
	the act of doing something enjoyable because it is a special day	
	to make somebody healthy again after an illness	
	the central or most important part of something	
	to produce flowers	
	to stop or end	
	a person whose job is to design buildings	
	a small wooden house; a hut	
	connected with the scientific study of animals, plants, and other living things	
	a small electronic machine used for calculating figures	
	a painful place on the skin made by an insect, dog, etc	

Hint

appropriate biological calculator cease complain core devote cure concentrate
celebration architect blossom device account cabin arbor bite compose

Review 19

B. Read and fill in the word and meaning.

word	definition	meaning
	used when you want to appear serious or official	
	to teach or train somebody, especially in school	
	a type of handle that you turn to let water out of a pipe	
	the length, area, size or importance of something	
	wanting more food, money, etc than you really need	
	a form of a language that is spoken in one part of a country	
	to not allow something	
	to show something that is usually hidden	
	the place where food is sold by a grocer	
	not allowed by the law	
	the form in which a book is published	
	the mind that is thinking of people in the world	
	an arrangement with a company in which you pay them regularly and they pay when you die or ill	
	successfully producing the result that you want	
	the ability to create mental pictures or new ideas	
	to make something clear or easy to understand	
	very strong or serious	
	the place where a dead body is buried	

Hint

humanity insurance edition greedy extent imagination effective formally intense
explain grocery dialect forbid grave faucet expose illegally educate

Unit 39

🎧 Listen and repeat. Track 115

01	**interact**	v 상호작용하다　to have an effect on each other
	[íntərǽkt]	We're looking for another way to **interact**. 우리는 상호작용할 수 있는 다른 방법을 찾고 있습니다.

02	**international**	a 국제(상)의, 국제적인　involving two or more countries
	[ìntərnǽʃənəl]	I think it is necessary to study English, because English is the **international** language. 영어는 국제적인 언어이므로 영어를 공부하는 것은 필수라고 생각한다.

03	**lock**	v 잠그다, 가두다　to close or fasten so that it can only be open with a key
	[lɑk]	Does your family normally keep the doors **locked** at night? 당신의 가족들은 보통 밤에 현관문을 잠가두나요?

04	**logically**	ad 논리적으로　reasonably or sensibly
	[lάdʒikəli]	She thinks **logically**, with one idea following another. 그녀는 한 생각을 다음 생각과 연관 지어 논리적으로 생각한다.

05	**loose**	a 헐거운, 느슨한　not firmly fixed; not tight
	[luːs]	Wear comfortable, **loose** clothing to exercise class. 체육 시간에는 편하고 헐거운 옷을 입어라.

06	**metropolis**	n 대도시, 수도, 주요도시　a very large city
	[mitrάpəlis]	A recent survey reveals that population density in the **metropolis** is decreasing. 최근의 조사는 대도시 인구 밀도의 감소를 보여주고 있다.

07	**microwave**	n 전자레인지　a type of oven that cooks or heats food very quickly
	[máikrouwèiv]	Often my boss will make **microwave** lunches and leave the dirty dishes. 종종 사장은 전자레인지로 점심을 데워 먹고 접시를 그대로 두고 갈 거야.

08	**millionaire**	n 백만장자　a very rich person
	[mìljənɛ́ər]	The **millionaire** insisted on buying the masterpiece no matter how much it cost. 그 백만장자는 아무리 돈이 들더라도 그 걸작을 꼭 사고 말겠다고 고집했다.

09	**missionary**	n 선교사, 전도사 / a 전도(자)의　a person sent to a foreign country to teach about the Christian religion
	[míʃənèri]	As **missionaries** one of the things we do is to provide service such as teaching English. 선교사로서 우리가 하는 일 중 하나는 영어를 가르치는 일과 같은 봉사를 하는 것이다.

key words
firmly **ad** 단단히 / survey **n** 조사 / masterpiece **n** 걸작

🎧 Listen and repeat. Track 116

10 nuclear [njúːkliər]
a 핵의, 원자력의 — connected with the nucleus of an atom
Much of the coast has been polluted by **nuclear** waste.
해안의 많은 지역이 핵폐기물로 오염되었다.

11 nutritious [njutríʃəs]
a 영양분이 있는, 영양의 — containing substances which help your body to be healthy
For the most **nutritious** plate, choose dry vegetables of many colors.
가장 영양가 있는 요리를 위해서 다양한 색깔의 마른 야채를 고르세요.

12 occur [əkə́ːr]
v 일어나다, 생기다 — to happen, especially in a way that has not been planned
Heart failure **occurs** then the heart is unable to supply enough blood to meet the usual demands of the body.
심장 마비는 심장이 몸의 일상적 수요를 충족시킬 만큼 충분한 피를 공급하지 못하게 될 때 일어난다.

13 peer [piər]
v 응시하다, ~에 필적하다 — to look closely or carefully
They're **peering** outside through a telescope.
그들은 망원경을 통해 밖을 응시하고 있다.

14 penalty [pénəlti]
n 형벌, 벌금 — a punishment for breaking a law, rule or contract
Was there a **penalty** for being late?
지각하면 벌금이 있었나요?

15 perform [pərfɔ́ːrm]
v 실행하다, 공연하다 — to take part in a play or to sing, dance, etc in front of an audience
The most fun is to see magic **performed** on the streets.
가장 재미있는 것은 거리에서 공연되는 마술을 보는 것이다.

16 perhaps [pərhǽps]
ad 아마, 어쩌면 — possibly; maybe
We may **perhaps** enjoy, if we sit up late, a wonderful broadcast of opera from Rome.
우리는 아마 늦게까지 앉아서 로마에서 공연되는 오페라를 TV방송으로 즐길 수 있을 거야.

17 prefer [prifə́ːr]
v ~을 더 좋아하다 — to like something better
Would you **prefer** an aisle or a window seat?
복도 쪽 좌석과 창문 좌석 중 어느 쪽이 더 좋으십니까?

18 professor [prəfésər]
n 교수 — a teacher at a college or university
The **professor**'s lectures were very boring.
그 교수님의 강의는 매우 지루했다.

key words
nucleus **n** 핵, 중심 / dry **a** 마른 / aisle **n** 복도 / lecture **n** 강의

Unit 39 197

Exercise

A. Complete the sentence.

1. Much of the coast has been polluted by _____ waste.
   해안의 많은 지역이 핵폐기물로 오염되었다.
2. They're _____ outside through a telescope.
   그들은 망원경을 통해 밖을 응시하고 있다.
3. As _____, one of the things we do is to provide service such as teaching English.
   선교사로서 우리가 하는 일 중 하나는 영어를 가르치는 일과 같은 봉사를 하는 것이다.
4. Was there a _____ for being late?
   지각하면 벌금이 있었나요?
5. We may _____ enjoy, if we sit up late, a wonderful broadcast of opera from Rome.
   우리는 아마 늦게까지 앉아서 로마에서 공연되는 오페라를 TV방송으로 즐길 수 있을 거야.
6. Often my boss will make _____ lunches and leave the dirty dishes.
   종종 사장은 전자레인지로 점심을 데워 먹고 접시를 그대로 두고 갈 거야.
7. For the most _____ plate, choose dry vegetables of many colors.
   가장 영양가 있는 요리를 위해서 다양한 색깔의 마른 야채를 고르세요.
8. Would you _____ an aisle or a window seat?
   복도 쪽 좌석과 창문 좌석 중 어느 쪽이 더 좋으십니까?
9. We're looking for another way to _____.
   우리는 상호작용할 수 있는 다른 방법을 찾고 있습니다.
10. The _____'s lectures were very boring.
    그 교수님의 강의는 매우 지루했다.
11. I think it is necessary to study English, because English is the _____ language.
    영어는 국제적인 언어이므로 영어를 공부하는 것은 필수라고 생각한다.
12. She thinks _____, with one idea following another.
    그녀는 한 생각을 다음 생각과 연관 지어 논리적으로 생각한다.
13. The most fun is to see magic _____ on the streets.
    가장 재미있는 것은 거리에서 공연되는 마술을 보는 것이다..
14. Wear comfortable, _____ clothing to exercise class.
    체육 시간에는 편하고 헐거운 옷을 입어라.
15. A recent survey reveals that population density in the _____ is decreasing.
    최근의 조사는 대도시 인구 밀도의 감소를 보여주고 있다.
16. The _____ insisted on buying the masterpiece no matter how much it cost.
    그 백만장자는 아무리 돈이 들거라도 그 걸작을 꼭 사고 말겠다고 고집했다.
17. Does your family normally keep the doors _____ at night?
    당신의 가족들은 보통 밤에 현관문을 잠가두나요?
18. Heart failure _____ then the heart is unable to supply enough blood to meet the usual demands of the body.
    심장 마비는 심장이 몸의 일상적 수요를 충족시킬 만큼 충분한 피를 공급하지 못하게 될 때 일어난다.

Hint

metropolis interact peer nutritious logically professor loose penalty missionary
perhaps nuclear occur microwave perform millionaire prefer lock international

Exercise

B. Fill in the word and meaning.

	Word	Meaning
01	lock	
02	nuclear	
03	interact	
04	millionaire	
05	penalty	
06	microwave	
07	perhaps	
08	international	
09	professor	
10	missionary	
11	prefer	
12	metropolis	
13	occur	
14	perform	
15	loose	
16	peer	
17	nutritious	
18	logically	

	Meaning	Word
01	상호작용하다	
02	국제(상)의, 국제적인	
03	잠그다, 가두다	
04	논리적으로	
05	헐거운, 느슨한	
06	대도시, 수도, 주요도시	
07	전자레인지	
08	백만장자	
09	선교사, 전도사, 전도(자)의	
10	핵의, 원자력의	
11	영양분이 있는, 영양의	
12	일어나다, 생기다	
13	응시하다, ~에 필적하다	
14	형벌, 벌금	
15	실행하다, 공연하다	
16	아마, 어쩌면	
17	~을 더 좋아하다	
18	교수	

🎧 C. Listen, write the word and meaning. Track 117

	Word	Meaning		Word	Meaning
01			10		
02			11		
03			12		
04			13		
05			14		
06			15		
07			16		
08			17		
09			18		

Unit 40

🎧 Listen and repeat. Track 118

01 reflect
[riflékt]
v 반영하다, 반사하다   to show or express something
Life does not always **reflect** our ideals.
삶이 항상 우리의 이상을 반영하는 것은 아니다.

02 reform
[rifɔ́ːrm]
n 개혁, 개선 / v 개선하다   to change a system, the law, etc in order to make it better
I think we need to **reform** the examination system.
검사 시스템을 개선할 필요가 있다고 생각해요.

03 refund
[ríːfʌnd]
n 환불, 반환   a sum of money that is paid back to you
There's a scratch here so we won't be able to give you a **refund**.
여기 긁힌 자국이 있어서 환불해 줄 수가 없습니다.

04 regular
[régjələːr]
a 규칙적인   not having any individual part that is different from the rest
Don't you see the **regular** pattern in this paper?
이 포장지에 있는 규칙적인 무늬가 보이지 않니?

05 scare
[skɛəːr]
v 놀라게 하다, 위협하다   to make a person frightened
Another trick of being a clown is not to **scare** kids.
광대 노릇을 하는 또 다른 비결은 아이들을 놀라게 하지 않는 것이다.

06 scold
[skould]
v 꾸짖다, 잔소리하다   to speak angrily because somebody has done something wrong
Whenever she was **scolded** loudly, she pulled a face.
그녀는 큰 소리로 꾸짖음을 들을 때마다 얼굴을 찡그렸다.

07 society
[səsáiəti]
n 사회, 집단, 협회   an organization of people who live in a country and share customs and laws
Cellular phones are necessity in modern **society**.
현대 사회에서 휴대폰은 필수품이다.

08 sore
[sɔːr]
a 아픈, 화난   painful, especially when touched
My **sore** shoulder may go under the knife sooner than later.
저의 아픈 어깨는 곧 수술을 받을지도 몰라요.

09 source
[sɔːrs]
n 근원, 출처   a place, person or thing where something starts from
You need to list at least four **sources**, one being a survey list.
적어도 네 가지의 출처를 수록하되 그 중 하나는 설문지 목록이어야 합니다.

key words
examination n 검사 / scratch n 긁힌 자국 / trick n 비결, 요령 / clown n 광대

🎧 Listen and repeat. Track 119

10 tear [tɛəːr] — v 찢다, 째다 / n 눈물 — to damage something by pulling it apart or into pieces
Would you please **tear** off one of those plastic bags over there to put these mushrooms in?
이 버섯을 담을 수 있게 저기 있는 비닐봉지 한 장만 찢어다 줄래요?

11 theory [θíːəri] — n 이론, 학설 — the general idea or principles of a particular subject
Over the centuries, various **theories** have been advanced to explain the origin of alphabets.
수세기에 걸쳐서, 여러 가지 이론이 알파벳의 기원을 설명하기 위해서 제시되어왔다.

12 therapy [θérəpi] — n 치료, 요법 — treatment to cure a illness without drugs or operations
Even after years of music **therapy**, the feeling of fear is still with her.
수년간의 음악요법을 받은 후에도, 그녀는 여전히 두려움을 느끼고 있다.

13 unique [juːníːk] — a 독특한, 유일한 — not like anything else; being the only one of its type
As far as I know it's **unique** and therefore very valuable.
내가 아는 한 이것은 유일한 것으로 매우 귀중하다.

14 vacant [véikənt] — a 아무도 없는, 비어 있는 — not being used; empty
The bus was crowded and no **vacant** seat was to be found.
그 버스에는 사람들이 꽉 차서 비어있는 좌석이 없었다.

15 value [vǽljuː] — v 평가하다, 존중하다 — to think somebody / something is very important
She has always **valued** his independence.
그녀는 항상 그의 독립심을 존중해 왔다.

16 willing [wíliŋ] — a 기꺼이 ~하는 — happy to do something
He was **willing** to give up his bonus in exchange for a raise.
그는 급여 인상을 받는 대신 기꺼이 보너스를 포기했다.

17 wipe [waip] — v 닦다, 훔치다 — to clean something by rubbing it with a cloth, etc
I **wiped** my head with a towel and waited until the water came on again.
나는 수건으로 머리를 닦고 물이 다시 나올 때까지 기다렸다.

18 yell [jel] — v 소리 지르다, 굉음을 내다 — to shout very loudly
If you can't hear me I'll **yell** a little louder.
내 말이 안 들리면 좀 더 크게 소리칠게요.

key words
mushroom n 버섯 / therefore conj 그 결과

Unit 40

Exercise

A. Complete the sentence.

1. Would you please _____ off one of those plastic bags over there to put these mushrooms in?
   이 버섯을 담을 수 있게 저기 있는 비닐봉지 한 장만 찢어다 줄래요?

2. As far as I know it's _____ and therefore very valuable.
   내가 아는 한 이것은 유일한 것으로 매우 귀중하다.

3. She has always _____ his independence.
   그녀는 항상 그의 독립심을 존중해 왔다.

4. I _____ my head of with a towel and waited until the water came on again.
   나는 수건으로 머리를 닦고 물이 다시 나올 때까지 기다렸다.

5. If you can't hear me I'll _____ a little louder.
   내 말이 안 들리면 좀 더 크게 소리칠게요.

6. I think we need to _____ the examination system.
   검사 시스템을 개선할 필요가 있다고 생각해요.

7. There's a scratch here so we won't be able to give you a _____.
   여기 긁힌 자국이 있어서 환불해 줄 수가 없습니다.

8. Another trick of being a clown is not to _____ kids.
   광대 노릇을 하는 또 다른 비결은 아이들을 놀라게 하지 않는 것이다.

9. Over the centuries, various _____ have been advanced to explain the origin of alphabets.
   수세기에 걸쳐서, 여러 가지 이론이 알파벳의 기원을 설명하기 위해서 제시되어왔다.

10. The bus was crowded and no _____ seat was to be found.
    그 버스에는 사람들이 꽉 차서 비어있는 좌석이 없었다.

11. Whenever she was _____ loudly, she pulled a face.
    그녀는 큰 소리로 꾸짖음을 들을 때마다 얼굴을 찡그렸다.

12. He was _____ to give up his bonus in exchange for a raise.
    그는 급여 인상을 받는 대신 기꺼이 보너스를 포기했다.

13. Even after years of music _____, the feelings of fear is still with her.
    수년간의 음악요법을 받은 후에도, 그녀는 여전히 두려움을 느끼고 있다.

14. Don't you see the _____ pattern in this paper?
    이 포장지에 있는 규칙적인 무늬가 보이지 않니?

15. Cellular phones are necessity in modern _____.
    현대 사회에서 휴대폰은 필수품이다.

16. My _____ shoulder may go under the knife sooner than later.
    저의 아픈 어깨는 곧 수술을 받을지도 몰라요.

17. Life does not always _____ our ideals.
    삶이 항상 우리의 이상을 반영하는 것은 아니다.

18. You need to list at least four _____, one being a survey list.
    적어도 네 가지의 출처를 수록하되 그 중 하나는 설문지 목록이어야 합니다.

Hint

| yell | unique | sore | theory | reflect | scare | value | tear | reform |
| wipe | society | willing | vacant | therapy | source | refund | regular | scold |

Exercise

B. Fill in the word and meaning.

	Word	Meaning
01	reform	
02	tear	
03	scare	
04	unique	
05	scold	
06	value	
07	reflect	
08	willing	
09	society	
10	yell	
11	sore	
12	wipe	
13	regular	
14	vacant	
15	source	
16	therapy	
17	refund	
18	theory	

	Meaning	Word
01	반영하다, 반사하다	
02	개혁, 개선, 개선하다	
03	환불, 반환	
04	규칙적인	
05	놀라게 하다, 위협하다	
06	꾸짖다, 잔소리하다	
07	사회, 집단, 협회	
08	아픈, 화난	
09	근원, 출처	
10	찢다, 째다, 눈물	
11	이론, 학설	
12	치료, 요법	
13	독특한, 유일한	
14	아무도 없는, 비어 있는	
15	평가하다, 존중하다	
16	기꺼이 ~하는	
17	닦다, 훔치다	
18	소리 지르다, 굉음을 내다	

🎧 C. Listen, write the word and meaning. (Track 120)

	Word	Meaning		Word	Meaning
01			10		
02			11		
03			12		
04			13		
05			14		
06			15		
07			16		
08			17		
09			18		

Review 20

A. Read and fill in the word and meaning.

word	definition	meaning
	to take part in a play or to sing, dance, etc in front of an audience	
	not firmly fixed; not tight	
	a very large city	
	possibly; maybe	
	a type of oven that cooks or heats food very quickly	
	reasonably or sensibly	
	a person sent to a foreign country to teach about the Christian religion	
	connected with the nucleus of an atom	
	a very rich person	
	to have an effect on each other	
	to close or fasten so that it can only be open with a key	
	to happen, especially in a way that has not been planned	
	a teacher at a college or university	
	containing substances which help your body to be healthy	
	to look closely or carefully	
	involving two or more countries	
	to like something better	
	a punishment for breaking a law, rule or contract	

Hint

metropolis interact peer nutritious logically professor loose penalty missionary
perhaps nuclear occur microwave perform millionaire prefer lock international

B. Read and fill in the word and meaning.

word	definition	meaning
	to speak angrily because somebody has done something wrong	
	happy to do something	
	not having any individual part that is different from the rest	
	to make a person frightened	
	to think somebody / something is very important	
	to clean something by rubbing it with a cloth, etc	
	an organization of people who live in a country and share customs and laws	
	a sum of money that is paid back to you	
	not being used; empty	
	to shout very loudly	
	painful, especially when touched	
	to damage something by pulling it apart or into pieces	
	to show or express something	
	a place, person or thing where something starts from	
	not like anything else; being the only one of its type	
	the general idea or principles of a particular subject	
	to change a system, the law, etc in order to make it better	
	treatment to cure a illness without drugs or operations	

Hint

yell   unique   sore   theory   reflect   scare   value   tear   reform
wipe   society   willing   vacant   therapy   source   refund   regular   scold

Review 20

MEMO

Total Test

Test 1

Track 3

🎧 **Listen, write the word and meaning.**

	Word	Meaning
01		
02		
03		
04		
05		
06		
07		
08		
09		
10		
11		
12		
13		
14		
15		
16		
17		
18		

점수		점	확인	

Test 2

Track 6

🎧 **Listen, write the word and meaning.**

	Word	Meaning
01		
02		
03		
04		
05		
06		
07		
08		
09		
10		
11		
12		
13		
14		
15		
16		
17		
18		

점수		점	확인	

Test 3

Track 9

🎧 **Listen, write the word and meaning.**

	Word	Meaning
01		
02		
03		
04		
05		
06		
07		
08		
09		
10		
11		
12		
13		
14		
15		
16		
17		
18		

점수	점	확인	

Test 4

Track 12

🎧 **Listen, write the word and meaning.**

	Word	Meaning
01		
02		
03		
04		
05		
06		
07		
08		
09		
10		
11		
12		
13		
14		
15		
16		
17		
18		

점수	점	확인	

Test 5

Track 15

🎧 **Listen, write the word and meaning.**

	Word	Meaning
01		
02		
03		
04		
05		
06		
07		
08		
09		
10		
11		
12		
13		
14		
15		
16		
17		
18		

점수		점	확인	

Test 6

Track 18

🎧 **Listen, write the word and meaning.**

	Word	Meaning
01		
02		
03		
04		
05		
06		
07		
08		
09		
10		
11		
12		
13		
14		
15		
16		
17		
18		

점수		점	확인	

Test 7

Track 21

🎧 **Listen, write the word and meaning.**

	Word	Meaning
01		
02		
03		
04		
05		
06		
07		
08		
09		
10		
11		
12		
13		
14		
15		
16		
17		
18		

점수		확인	
	점		

Test 8

Track 24

🎧 **Listen, write the word and meaning.**

	Word	Meaning
01		
02		
03		
04		
05		
06		
07		
08		
09		
10		
11		
12		
13		
14		
15		
16		
17		
18		

점수		확인	
	점		

Test 9

Track 27

🎧 **Listen, write the word and meaning.**

	Word	Meaning
01		
02		
03		
04		
05		
06		
07		
08		
09		
10		
11		
12		
13		
14		
15		
16		
17		
18		

점수	점	확인	

Test 10

Track 30

🎧 **Listen, write the word and meaning.**

	Word	Meaning
01		
02		
03		
04		
05		
06		
07		
08		
09		
10		
11		
12		
13		
14		
15		
16		
17		
18		

점수	점	확인	

Test 11

Track 33

🎧 **Listen, write the word and meaning.**

	Word	Meaning
01		
02		
03		
04		
05		
06		
07		
08		
09		
10		
11		
12		
13		
14		
15		
16		
17		
18		

점수	점	확인	

Test 12

Track 36

🎧 **Listen, write the word and meaning.**

	Word	Meaning
01		
02		
03		
04		
05		
06		
07		
08		
09		
10		
11		
12		
13		
14		
15		
16		
17		
18		

점수	점	확인	

Test 13

Track 39

🎧 **Listen, write the word and meaning.**

	Word	Meaning
01		
02		
03		
04		
05		
06		
07		
08		
09		
10		
11		
12		
13		
14		
15		
16		
17		
18		

점수	점	확인	

Test 14

Track 42

🎧 **Listen, write the word and meaning.**

	Word	Meaning
01		
02		
03		
04		
05		
06		
07		
08		
09		
10		
11		
12		
13		
14		
15		
16		
17		
18		

점수	점	확인	

Test 15

Track 45

🎧 **Listen, write the word and meaning.**

	Word	Meaning
01		
02		
03		
04		
05		
06		
07		
08		
09		
10		
11		
12		
13		
14		
15		
16		
17		
18		

점수		확인	
	점		

Test 16

Track 48

🎧 **Listen, write the word and meaning.**

	Word	Meaning
01		
02		
03		
04		
05		
06		
07		
08		
09		
10		
11		
12		
13		
14		
15		
16		
17		
18		

점수		확인	
	점		

Test 17

Track 51

🎧 Listen, write the word and meaning.

	Word	Meaning
01		
02		
03		
04		
05		
06		
07		
08		
09		
10		
11		
12		
13		
14		
15		
16		
17		
18		

점수	점	확인	

Test 18

Track 54

🎧 Listen, write the word and meaning.

	Word	Meaning
01		
02		
03		
04		
05		
06		
07		
08		
09		
10		
11		
12		
13		
14		
15		
16		
17		
18		

점수	점	확인	

Test 19

Track 57

🎧 **Listen, write the word and meaning.**

	Word	Meaning
01		
02		
03		
04		
05		
06		
07		
08		
09		
10		
11		
12		
13		
14		
15		
16		
17		
18		

점수	점	확인	

Test 20

Track 60

🎧 **Listen, write the word and meaning.**

	Word	Meaning
01		
02		
03		
04		
05		
06		
07		
08		
09		
10		
11		
12		
13		
14		
15		
16		
17		
18		

점수	점	확인	

Test 21

Track 63

🎧 **Listen, write the word and meaning.**

	Word	Meaning
01		
02		
03		
04		
05		
06		
07		
08		
09		
10		
11		
12		
13		
14		
15		
16		
17		
18		

점수	점	확인	

Test 22

Track 66

🎧 **Listen, write the word and meaning.**

	Word	Meaning
01		
02		
03		
04		
05		
06		
07		
08		
09		
10		
11		
12		
13		
14		
15		
16		
17		
18		

점수	점	확인	

Test 23

Track 69

🎧 **Listen, write the word and meaning.**

	Word	Meaning
01		
02		
03		
04		
05		
06		
07		
08		
09		
10		
11		
12		
13		
14		
15		
16		
17		
18		

점수	점	확인	

Test 24

Track 72

🎧 **Listen, write the word and meaning.**

	Word	Meaning
01		
02		
03		
04		
05		
06		
07		
08		
09		
10		
11		
12		
13		
14		
15		
16		
17		
18		

점수	점	확인	

Test 25

Track 75

🎧 **Listen, write the word and meaning.**

	Word	Meaning
01		
02		
03		
04		
05		
06		
07		
08		
09		
10		
11		
12		
13		
14		
15		
16		
17		
18		

점수	점	확인	

Test 26

Track 78

🎧 **Listen, write the word and meaning.**

	Word	Meaning
01		
02		
03		
04		
05		
06		
07		
08		
09		
10		
11		
12		
13		
14		
15		
16		
17		
18		

점수	점	확인	

Test 27

Track 81

🎧 **Listen, write the word and meaning.**

	Word	Meaning
01		
02		
03		
04		
05		
06		
07		
08		
09		
10		
11		
12		
13		
14		
15		
16		
17		
18		

점수		점	확인	

Test 28

Track 84

🎧 **Listen, write the word and meaning.**

	Word	Meaning
01		
02		
03		
04		
05		
06		
07		
08		
09		
10		
11		
12		
13		
14		
15		
16		
17		
18		

점수		점	확인	

Test 29

🎧 **Listen, write the word and meaning.** (Track 87)

	Word	Meaning
01		
02		
03		
04		
05		
06		
07		
08		
09		
10		
11		
12		
13		
14		
15		
16		
17		
18		

점수	점	확인

Test 30

🎧 **Listen, write the word and meaning.** (Track 90)

	Word	Meaning
01		
02		
03		
04		
05		
06		
07		
08		
09		
10		
11		
12		
13		
14		
15		
16		
17		
18		

점수	점	확인

Test 31

Track 93

🎧 **Listen, write the word and meaning.**

	Word	Meaning
01		
02		
03		
04		
05		
06		
07		
08		
09		
10		
11		
12		
13		
14		
15		
16		
17		
18		

점수	점	확인	

Test 32

Track 96

🎧 **Listen, write the word and meaning.**

	Word	Meaning
01		
02		
03		
04		
05		
06		
07		
08		
09		
10		
11		
12		
13		
14		
15		
16		
17		
18		

점수	점	확인	

Test 33

Track 99

🎧 **Listen, write the word and meaning.**

	Word	Meaning
01		
02		
03		
04		
05		
06		
07		
08		
09		
10		
11		
12		
13		
14		
15		
16		
17		
18		

점수	점	확인	

Test 34

Track 102

🎧 **Listen, write the word and meaning.**

	Word	Meaning
01		
02		
03		
04		
05		
06		
07		
08		
09		
10		
11		
12		
13		
14		
15		
16		
17		
18		

점수	점	확인	

Test 35

Track 105

🎧 **Listen, write the word and meaning.**

	Word	Meaning
01		
02		
03		
04		
05		
06		
07		
08		
09		
10		
11		
12		
13		
14		
15		
16		
17		
18		

점수	점	확인

Test 36

Track 108

🎧 **Listen, write the word and meaning.**

	Word	Meaning
01		
02		
03		
04		
05		
06		
07		
08		
09		
10		
11		
12		
13		
14		
15		
16		
17		
18		

점수	점	확인

Test 37

Track 111

🎧 Listen, write the word and meaning.

	Word	Meaning
01		
02		
03		
04		
05		
06		
07		
08		
09		
10		
11		
12		
13		
14		
15		
16		
17		
18		

점수	점	확인	

Test 38

Track 114

🎧 Listen, write the word and meaning.

	Word	Meaning
01		
02		
03		
04		
05		
06		
07		
08		
09		
10		
11		
12		
13		
14		
15		
16		
17		
18		

점수	점	확인	

Test 39

Track 117

🎧 **Listen, write the word and meaning.**

	Word	Meaning
01		
02		
03		
04		
05		
06		
07		
08		
09		
10		
11		
12		
13		
14		
15		
16		
17		
18		

점수	점	확인	

Test 40

Track 120

🎧 **Listen, write the word and meaning.**

	Word	Meaning
01		
02		
03		
04		
05		
06		
07		
08		
09		
10		
11		
12		
13		
14		
15		
16		
17		
18		

점수	점	확인	

Answer Key

Unit 1

A
1. audience
2. conference
3. blank
4. anxious
5. apt
6. bloom
7. Cattle
8. decorations
9. celebrating
10. Abbey
11. control
12. convenient
13. awake
14. cope
15. abroad
16. definition
17. chemical
18. directions

B
1. 공백의, 백지의
2. 해외로, 널리
3. 장식, 훈장
4. 경축하다, 찬양하다
5. 대수도원, 대성당
6. 화학, 화학의
7. 정의, 한정
8. 열망하는
9. 대처하다, 극복하다
10. 꽃이 피다
11. 방향, 지도, 감독
12. 깨우다, 깨어 있는
13. 편리한
14. 청중, 관객
15. 소
16. 지배, 통제하다, 억제하다
17. 회당, 회의
18. ~하는 경향이 있는, 적절한

1. abbey
2. abroad
3. anxious
4. apt
5. audience
6. awake
7. blank
8. bloom
9. cattle
10. celebrate
11. chemical
12. conference
13. control
14. convenient
15. cope
16. decoration
17. definition
18. direction

C
1. cattle — 소
2. abbey — 대수도원, 대성당
3. direciton — 방향, 지도, 감독
4. celebrate — 경축하다, 찬양하다
5. abroad — 해외로, 널리
6. chemical — 화학, 화학의
7. cope — 대처하다, 극복하다
8. bloom — 꽃이 피다
9. convenient — 편리한
10. conference — 회당, 회의
11. anxious — 열망하는
12. control — 지배, 통제하다, 억제하다
13. definition — 정의, 한정
14. apt — ~하는 경향이 있는, 적절한
15. decoration — 장식, 훈장
16. blank — 공백의, 백지의
17. audience — 청중, 관객
18. awake — 깨우다, 깨어 있는

Unit 2

A
1. evil
2. distances
3. ignored
4. erupt
5. exactly
6. floated
7. grazing
8. knowledge
9. dizzy
10. folded
11. dislikes
12. grief
13. handicap
14. identification
15. flight
16. Imaginary
17. kingdom
18. knot

B
1. 현기증 나는, 현기증 나게 하다
2. 나쁜, 사악한
3. 싫어(미워)하다
4. 비상, 비행
5. 풀을 뜯어 먹(게 하)다
6. 거리, 간격
7. 무시하다
8. 매듭, 매다
9. 분출하다
10. 지식, 학식
11. 신분증명, 신원확인
12. 왕국
13. 정확하게, 엄밀히
14. 상상의, 가상의
15. 슬픔, 비탄
16. 접다
17. 신체장애, 불이익
18. 뜨다, 표류하다

1. dislike
2. distance
3. dizzy
4. erupt
5. evil
6. exactly
7. flight
8. float
9. fold
10. graze
11. grief
12. handicap
13. identification
14. ignore
15. imaginary
16. kingdom
17. knot
18. know

C
1. dislike — 싫어(미워)하다
2. identification — 신분증명, 신원확인
3. grief — 슬픔, 비탄
4. handicap — 신체장애, 불이익
5. ignore — 무시하다
6. distance — 거리, 간격
7. graze — 풀을 뜯어 먹(게 하)다
8. fold — 접다
9. imaginary — 상상의, 가상의
10. dizzy — 현기증 나는, 현기증 나게 하다
11. kingdom — 왕국
12. erupt — 분출하다
13. float — 뜨다, 표류하다
14. knot — 매듭, 매다
15. flight — 비상, 비행
16. evil — 나쁜, 사악한
17. knowledge — 지식, 학식
18. exactly — 정확하게, 엄밀히

Review 1

A
1. cattle — 소
2. abbey — 대수도원, 대성당
3. direciton — 방향, 지도, 감독
4. celebrate — 경축하다, 찬양하다
5. abroad — 해외로, 널리
6. chemical — 화학, 화학의
7. cope — 대처하다, 극복하다
8. bloom — 꽃이 피다
9. convenient — 편리한
10. conference — 회당, 회의
11. anxious — 열망하는
12. control — 지배, 통제하다, 억제하다
13. definition — 정의, 한정
14. apt — ~하는 경향이 있는, 적절한
15. decoration — 장식, 훈장
16. blank — 공백의, 백지의
17. audience — 청중, 관객
18. awake — 깨우다, 깨어 있는

B
1. dislike — 싫어(미워)하다
2. identification — 신분증명, 신원확인
3. grief — 슬픔, 비탄
4. handicap — 신체장애, 불이익
5. ignore — 무시하다
6. distance — 거리, 간격
7. graze — 풀을 뜯어 먹(게 하)다
8. fold — 접다
9. imaginary — 상상의, 가상의
10. dizzy — 현기증 나는, 현기증 나게 하다
11. kingdom — 왕국
12. erupt — 분출하다
13. float — 뜨다, 표류하다
14. knot — 매듭, 매다
15. flight — 비상, 비행
16. evil — 나쁜, 사악한
17. knowledge — 지식, 학식
18. exactly — 정확하게, 엄밀히

Unit 3

A
1. microphone
2. load
3. patches
4. noticed
5. preserve
6. message
7. rapidly
8. microscope
9. rather
10. normal
11. northern
12. lower
13. patients
14. percent
15. predicting
16. local
17. prepare
18. reaches

B
1. 정상의, 표준적인
2. 환자, 인내심이 강한
3. 보전하다, 보호하다
4. 짐, 짐을 싣다
5. 준비하다
6. 주의, 주목, 알아채다, 주의하다
7. 빠르게, 재빨리
8. 장소의, 지방의
9. 예언하다, 예보하다
10. 마이크
11. 북쪽에 있는
12. 현미경
13. 도착하다, 뻗치다
14. 헝겊조각, 부스러기
15. 전갈, 통신(문)
16. 오히려, 다소
17. 퍼센트
18. 낮추다, 낮은(아래)쪽의

1. load
2. local
3. lower
4. message
5. microphone
6. microscope
7. normal
8. northern
9. notice
10. patch
11. patient
12. percent
13. predict
14. prepare
15. preserve
16. rapidly
17. rather
18. reach

C
1. notice
2. local
3. patch
4. reach
5. load
6. patient
7. rather
8. lower
9. rapidly
10. percent
11. message
12. preserve
13. microphone
14. northern
15. predict
16. microscope
17. prepare
18. normal

주의, 주목, 알아채다, 주의하다
장소의, 지방의
헝겊조각, 부스러기
도착하다, 뻗치다
짐, 짐을 싣다
환자, 인내심이 강한
오히려, 다소
낮추다, 낮은(아래)쪽의
빠르게, 재빨리
퍼센트
전갈, 통신(문)
보전하다, 보호하다
마이크
북쪽에 있는
예언하다, 예보하다
현미경
준비하다
정상의, 표준적인

Unit 4

A
1. scary
2. request
3. stretches
4. upset
5. require
6. Soldiers
7. rescued
8. threaten
9. scientific
10. specialist
11. structures
12. textbook
13. screamed
14. twisted
15. streaming
16. thread
17. soul
18. upside

B
1. 구조, 구조하다
2. 과학적인
3. 요구, 요구하다
4. 흐르다
5. 구조, 조직
6. 요구하다, 필요로 하다
7. 영혼, 정신
8. 교과서
9. 윗면, 위쪽
10. 군인
11. 실, 바느질 실
12. 전문가, 전문의
13. 뒤집어엎다, 당황케 하다
14. 뒤틀다, 꼬다
15. 소리치다
16. 협박하다, 위협하다
17. 뻗다, 늘이다
18. 무서운

1. request
2. require
3. rescue
4. scary
5. scientific
6. scream
7. soldier
8. soul
9. specialist
10. stream
11. stretch
12. structure
13. textbook
14. thread
15. threaten
16. twist
17. upset
18. upside

C
1. request
2. stream
3. specialist
4. upside
5. require
6. soul
7. textbook
8. rescue
9. structure
10. thread
11. scary
12. threaten
13. soldier
14. stretch
15. twist
16. scientific
17. upset
18. scream

요구, 요구하다
흐르다
전문가, 전문의
윗면, 위쪽
요구하다, 필요로 하다
영혼, 정신
교과서
구조, 구조하다
구조, 조직
실, 바느질 실
무서운
협박하다, 위협하다
군인
뻗다, 늘이다
뒤틀다, 꼬다
과학적인
뒤집어엎다, 당황케 하다
소리치다

Review 2

A
1. notice
2. local
3. patch
4. reach
5. load
6. patient
7. rather
8. lower
9. rapidly
10. percent
11. message
12. preserve
13. microphone
14. northern
15. predict
16. microscope
17. prepare
18. normal

주의, 주목, 알아채다, 주의하다
장소의, 지방의
헝겊조각, 부스러기
도착하다, 뻗치다
짐, 짐을 싣다
환자, 인내심이 강한
오히려, 다소
낮추다, 낮은(아래)쪽의
빠르게, 재빨리
퍼센트
전갈, 통신(문)
보전하다, 보호하다
마이크
북쪽에 있는
예언하다, 예보하다
현미경
준비하다
정상의, 표준적인

B
1. request
2. stream
3. specialist
4. upside
5. require
6. soul
7. textbook
8. rescue
9. structure
10. thread
11. scary
12. threaten
13. soldier
14. stretch
15. twist
16. scientific
17. upset
18. scream

요구, 요구하다
흐르다
전문가, 전문의
윗면, 위쪽
요구하다, 필요로 하다
영혼, 정신
교과서
구조, 구조하다
구조, 조직
실, 바느질 실
무서운
협박하다, 위협하다
군인
뻗다, 늘이다
뒤틀다, 꼬다
과학적인
뒤집어엎다, 당황케 하다
소리치다

Unit 5

A
1. addition
2. cradle
3. boring
4. credit
5. appointment
6. depart
7. behavior
8. central
9. academy
10. certain
11. compact
12. bounds
13. Complaints
14. correct
15. approval
16. depend
17. bay
18. depressed

B
1. 만
2. 불평
3. 학교, 학원
4. 행동, 행실
5. 요람
6. 추가, 부가
7. 옳은, 정확한, 고치다
8. 지루한, 따분한
9. 출발하다
10. 경계, 범위, ~행의
11. 찬성, 승인
12. 신용거래, 칭찬, 믿다
13. 의지하다, 믿다
14. 밀집한, 압축하다
15. 우울한, 내리 눌린
16. 확실한, 일정한
17. 중앙의, 중심적인
18. 약속, 임명

1. academy
2. addition
3. appointment
4. approval
5. bay
6. behavior
7. boring
8. bound
9. central
10. certain
11. compact
12. complaint
13. correct
14. credit
15. cradle
16. depart
17. depend
18. depressed

C
1. bound — 경계, 범위, ~행의
2. cradle — 요람
3. central — 중앙의, 중심적인
4. addition — 추가, 부가
5. boring — 지루한, 따분한
6. academy — 학교, 학원
7. certain — 확실한, 일정한
8. depart — 출발하다
9. credit — 신용거래, 칭찬, 믿다
10. appointment — 약속, 임명
11. behavior — 행동, 행실
12. compact — 밀집한, 압축하다
13. approval — 찬성, 승인
14. depend — 의지하다, 믿다
15. complaint — 불평
16. bay — 만
17. correct — 옳은, 정확한, 고치다
18. depressed — 우울한, 내리 눌린

Unit 6

A
1. dough
2. harm
3. lawn
4. expecting
5. disagrees
6. impressive
7. experiment
8. lamb
9. force
10. doubted
11. forecast
12. frequent
13. Indeed
14. harmful
15. informal
16. forgive
17. exist
18. labor

B
1. 기대하다
2. 의견이 다르다
3. 빈번한
4. 예상, 예보
5. 참으로, 과연
6. 의심, 의혹, 의심하다
7. 용서하다
8. 비공식의, 약식의
9. 힘, 영향(력)
10. 어린양
11. 해로운
12. 잔디(밭)
13. 실험, 시험
14. 노동, 노동자
15. 인상적인, 감동을 주는
16. 존재하다, 생존하다
17. 해, 손해
18. 가루 반죽

1. disagree
2. doubt
3. dough
4. exist
5. expect
6. experiment
7. force
8. forecast
9. forgive
10. frequent
11. harm
12. harmful
13. impressive
14. indeed
15. informal
16. labor
17. lamb
18. lawn

C
1. forecast — 예상, 예보
2. frequent — 빈번한
3. forgive — 용서하다
4. harm — 해, 손해
5. disagree — 의견이 다르다
6. indeed — 참으로, 과연
7. experiment — 실험, 시험
8. force — 힘, 영향(력)
9. harmful — 해로운
10. impressive — 인상적인, 감동을 주는
11. expect — 기대하다
12. labor — 노동, 노동자
13. informal — 비공식의, 약식의
14. lamb — 어린양
15. doubt — 의심, 의혹, 의심하다
16. lawn — 잔디(밭)
17. exist — 존재하다, 생존하다
18. dough — 가루 반죽

Review 3

A
1. bound — 경계, 범위, ~행의
2. cradle — 요람
3. central — 중앙의, 중심적인
4. addition — 추가, 부가
5. boring — 지루한, 따분한
6. academy — 학교, 학원
7. certain — 확실한, 일정한
8. depart — 출발하다
9. credit — 신용거래, 칭찬, 믿다
10. appointment — 약속, 임명
11. behavior — 행동, 행실
12. compact — 밀집한, 압축하다
13. approval — 찬성, 승인
14. depend — 의지하다, 믿다
15. complaint — 불평
16. bay — 만
17. correct — 옳은, 정확한, 고치다
18. depressed — 우울한, 내리 눌린

B
1. forecast — 예상, 예보
2. frequent — 자주 일어나는, 빈번한
3. forgive — 용서하다
4. harm — 해, 손해
5. disagree — 의견이 다르다
6. indeed — 참으로, 과연
7. experiment — 실험, 시험
8. force — 힘, 영향(력)
9. harmful — 해로운
10. impressive — 인상적인, 감동을 주는
11. expect — 기대하다
12. labor — 노동, 노동자
13. informal — 비공식의, 약식의
14. lamb — 어린양
15. doubt — 의심, 의혹, 의심하다
16. lawn — 잔디(밭)
17. exist — 존재하다, 생존하다
18. dough — 가루 반죽

Unit 7

A
1. loyal
2. mild
3. prize
4. mission
5. personal
6. obey
7. Pirates
8. mistake
9. occupation
10. offered
11. phrase
12. reality
13. lumps
14. Press / press
15. probable
16. reaction
17. lunar
18. recipe

B
1. 임무, 사명
2. 성실한, 충실한
3. 누르다, 강조하다
4. 제공하다, 제안, 제공
5. 상품, 상
6. 온순한, 따뜻한
7. 반응, 반작용
8. 직업, 업무
9. 있음직한, 예상되는
10. 달의, 태음의
11. 진실, 사실
12. 개인의, 본인 스스로의
13. 처방(전), 조리법
14. 잘못, 틀림
15. 구, 관용구
16. 복종하다
17. 덩어리, 혹

1. loyal
2. lump
3. lunar
4. mild
5. mission
6. mistake
7. obey
8. occupation
9. offer
10. personal
11. phrase
12. pirate
13. press
14. prize
15. probable
16. reaction
17. reality
18. recipe

C
1. occupation — 직업, 업무
2. recipe — 처방(전), 조리법
3. mistake — 잘못, 틀림
4. reality — 진실, 사실
5. obey — 복종하다
6. offer — 제공하다, 제안, 제공
7. personal — 개인의, 본인 스스로의
8. loyal — 성실한, 충실한
9. phrase — 구, 관용구
10. lump — 덩어리, 혹
11. pirate — 해적
12. mission — 임무, 사명
13. press — 누르다, 강조하다
14. reaction — 반응, 반작용
15. mild — 온순한, 따뜻한
16. probable — 있음직한, 예상되는
17. lunar — 달의, 태음의
18. prize — 상품, 상

Unit 8

A
1. spank
2. reuse
3. Seals
4. tightly
5. species
6. Subtract
7. succeeded
8. tone
9. subjects
10. response
11. tour
12. senseless
13. valuable
14. spicy
15. secretary
16. result
17. via
18. volcano

B
1. 바다표범
2. 단단히
3. 응답, 반응
4. 향신료를 넣은, 향긋한
5. 음질, 음색, 어조
6. 비서, 서기
7. 귀중한, 값비싼
8. 화산
9. 무감각의, 인사불성의
10. 빼다, 감하다
11. 결과, 성과
12. 주제, 과목
13. ~경유로
14. 찰싹 때리다
15. 관광 여행
16. 종류, 종
17. 성공하다
18. 다시 이용하다, 재생하다

1. response
2. result
3. reuse
4. seal
5. secretary
6. senseless
7. spank
8. species
9. spicy
10. subject
11. subtract
12. succeed
13. tightly
14. tone
15. tour
16. valuable
17. via
18. volcano

C
1. spicy — 향신료를 넣은, 향긋한
2. via — ~경유로
3. species — 종류, 종
4. response — 응답, 반응
5. valuable — 귀중한, 값비싼
6. subject — 주제, 과목
7. subtract — 빼다, 감하다
8. result — 결과, 성과
9. spank — 찰싹 때리다
10. tour — 관광 여행
11. senseless — 무감각의, 인사불성의
12. volcano — 화산
13. reuse — 다시 이용하다, 재생하다
14. succeed — 성공하다
15. tightly — 단단히
16. seal — 바다표범
17. tone — 음질, 음색, 어조
18. secretary — 비서, 서기

Review 4

A
1. occupation — 직업, 업무
2. recipe — 처방(전), 조리법
3. mistake — 잘못, 틀림
4. reality — 진실, 사실
5. obey — 복종하다
6. offer — 제공하다, 제안, 제공
7. personal — 개인의, 본인 스스로의
8. loyal — 성실한, 충실한
9. phrase — 구, 관용구
10. lump — 덩어리, 혹
11. pirate — 해적
12. mission — 임무, 사명
13. press — 누르다, 강조하다
14. reaction — 반응, 반작용
15. mild — 온순한, 따뜻한
16. probable — 있음직한, 예상되는
17. lunar — 달의, 태음의
18. prize — 상품, 상

B
1. spicy — 향신료를 넣은, 향긋한
2. via — ~경유로
3. species — 종류, 종
4. response — 응답, 반응
5. valuable — 귀중한, 값비싼
6. subject — 주제, 과목
7. subtract — 빼다, 감하다
8. result — 결과, 성과
9. spank — 찰싹 때리다
10. tour — 관광 여행
11. senseless — 무감각의, 인사불성의
12. volcano — 화산
13. reuse — 다시 이용하다, 재생하다
14. succeed — 성공하다
15. tightly — 단단히
16. seal — 바다표범
17. tone — 음질, 음색, 어조
18. secretary — 비서, 서기

Unit 9

A
1. charity
2. completed
3. arrivals
4. crazy
5. assignment
6. badly
7. depth
8. cheated
9. branches
10. breathe
11. adjust
12. comprehension
13. create
14. better
15. cricket
16. depression
17. admiral
18. descendants

B
1. 기만하다, 속이다, 속임수
2. 조정하다, 맞추다
3. 대단히, 나쁘게
4. 해군 대장, 제독
5. 이해, 이해력
6. 가지
7. 완전한, 완성하다
8. 우울, 불경기
9. 보다 좋은, 보다 좋게
10. 자손, 후예
11. 창조하다, 고안하다
12. 깊이, 깊음
13. 호흡하다
14. 미친
15. 할당, 담당, 숙제
16. 크리켓
17. 자비, 자선
18. 도착, 도달

1. adjust
2. admiral
3. arrival
4. assignment
5. badly
6. better
7. branch
8. breathe
9. charity
10. cheat
11. complete
12. comprehension
13. crazy
14. create
15. cricket
16. depression
17. depth
18. descendant

C
1. descendant — 자손, 후예
2. charity — 자비, 자선
3. depth — 깊이, 깊음
4. breathe — 호흡하다
5. adjust — 조정하다, 맞추다
6. cheat — 기만하다, 속이다, 속임수
7. depression — 우울, 불경기
8. complete — 완전한, 완성하다
9. admiral — 해군 대장, 제독
10. comprehension — 이해, 이해력
11. branch — 가지
12. cricket — 크리켓
13. crazy — 미친
14. arrival — 도착, 도달
15. better — 보다 좋은, 보다 좋게
16. assignment — 할당, 담당, 숙제
17. create — 창조하다, 고안하다
18. badly — 대단히, 나쁘게

Unit 10

A
1. frank
2. earmuffs
3. education
4. Fables
5. inner
6. failure
7. friendship
8. harmony
9. lawyer
10. hatch
11. earn
12. health
13. ingredients
14. factual
15. insisted
16. least
17. freedom
18. lend

B
1. 솔직한, 명백한
2. 조화, 화합
3. (생활비를) 벌다, 획득하다
4. 까다, 부화하다
5. 교육, 양성
6. 안의, 정신적인
7. 우화, 전설, 꾸며낸 이야기
8. 가장 작은(적은), 최소, 최저
9. 우정
10. 빌려주다
11. 자유, 면제
12. 법률가, 변호사
13. 실패, 부족, 쇠약
14. 강요하다, 주장하다
15. 건강
16. 사실의, 실제의
17. 성분, 재료
18. 귀덮개

1. earmuff
2. earn
3. education
4. fable
5. factual
6. failure
7. frank
8. freedom
9. friendship
10. harmony
11. hatch
12. health
13. ingredient
14. inner
15. insist
16. lawyer
17. least
18. lend

C
1. earmuff — 귀덮개
2. failure — 실패, 부족, 쇠약
3. earn — 벌다, 획득하다
4. inner — 안의, 정신적인
5. frank — 솔직한, 명백한
6. ingredient — 성분, 재료
7. health — 건강
8. freedom — 자유, 면제
9. hatch — 까다, 부화하다
10. fable — 우화, 전설, 꾸며낸 이야기
11. education — 교육, 양성
12. lend — 빌려주다
13. factual — 사실의, 실제의
14. lawyer — 법률가, 변호사
15. insist — 강요하다, 주장하다
16. least — 가장 작은(적은), 최소, 최저
17. harmony — 조화, 화합
18. friendship — 우정

Review 5

A
1. descendant — 자손, 후예
2. charity — 자비, 자선
3. depth — 깊이, 깊음
4. breathe — 호흡하다
5. adjust — 조정하다, 맞추다
6. cheat — 기만하다, 속이다, 속임수
7. depression — 우울, 불경기
8. complete — 완전한, 완성하다
9. admiral — 해군 대장, 제독
10. comprehension — 이해, 이해력
11. branch — 가지
12. cricket — 크리켓
13. crazy — 미친
14. arrival — 도착, 도달
15. better — 보다 좋은, 보다 좋게
16. assignment — 할당, 담당, 숙제
17. create — 창조하다, 고안하다
18. badly — 대단히, 나쁘게

B
1. earmuff — 귀덮개
2. failure — 실패, 부족, 쇠약
3. earn — 벌다, 획득하다
4. inner — 안의, 정신적인
5. frank — 솔직한, 명백한
6. ingredient — 성분, 재료
7. health — 건강
8. freedom — 자유, 면제
9. hatch — 까다, 부화하다
10. fable — 우화, 전설, 꾸며낸 이야기
11. education — 교육, 양성
12. lend — 빌려주다
13. factual — 사실의, 실제의
14. lawyer — 법률가, 변호사
15. insist — 강요하다, 주장하다
16. least — 가장 작은(적은), 최소, 최저
17. harmony — 조화, 화합
18. friendship — 우정

Unit 11

A
1. prove
2. magazine
3. pleasant
4. mainly
5. orbit
6. marriage
7. reduction
8. modern
9. movements
10. operate
11. Oysters
12. pitched
13. referring
14. pity
15. major
16. proverb
17. recommend
18. professional

B
1. 결혼
2. 궤도, 궤도를 돌다
3. 잡지
4. 던지다, (천막을) 치다
5. 현대의, 근대의
6. 직업의, 전문의, 전문가
7. 추천하다, 권하다
8. 주요한, 큰
9. 속담, 격언
10. 굴
11. 증명하다, 시험하다
12. 감소, 축소
13. 동정, 애석한 일
14. 급하다, 지시하다
15. 운동, 활동
16. 즐거운, 좋은
17. 작동하다, 작용하다
18. 주로, 대개

C
1. reduction — 감소, 축소
2. professional — 직업의, 전문의, 전문가
3. magazine — 잡지
4. pleasant — 즐거운, 좋은
5. recommend — 추천하다, 권하다
6. prove — 증명하다, 시험하다
7. mainly — 주로, 대개
8. pitch — 던지다, (천막을) 치다
9. proverb — 속담, 격언
10. pity — 동정, 애석한 일
11. major — 주요한, 큰
12. oyster — 굴
13. refer — 언급하다, 지시하다
14. marriage — 결혼
15. orbit — 궤도, 궤도를 돌다
16. modern — 현대의, 근대의
17. operate — 작동하다, 작용하다
18. movement — 운동, 활동

Unit 12

A
1. series
2. traditional
3. serious
4. shared
5. reward
6. spilled
7. weighed
8. spoiled
9. squeezing
10. wealth
11. vow
12. Success
13. romance
14. sudden
15. tourists
16. summarized
17. roamed
18. Trade

B
1. 진지한, 중대한
2. 보수, 포상, 보답하다
3. 돌연한, 갑작스러운
4. 요약하다
5. 로맨스, 연애
6. 맹세놓다
7. 여행자, 관광객
8. 짜내다, 압착하다
9. 맹세, 서약
10. 연속, 시리즈
11. 부, 재산
12. 성공, 성취
13. 무게를 재다
14. 거닐다, 돌아다니다
15. 전통적인, 관습의
16. 엎지르다
17. 거래하다, 무역하다, 무역
18. 분배하다, 공유하다

C
1. share — 분배하다, 공유하다
2. reward — 보수, 포상, 보답하다
3. serious — 진지한, 중대한
4. traditional — 전통적인, 관습의
5. roam — 거닐다, 돌아다니다
6. series — 연속, 시리즈
7. romance — 로맨스, 연애
8. spill — 엎지르다
9. trade — 거래하다, 무역하다, 무역
10. summarize — 요약하다
11. tourist — 여행자, 관광객
12. spoil — 망쳐놓다
13. weigh — 무게를 재다
14. squeeze — 짜내다, 압착하다
15. wealth — 부, 재산
16. success — 성공, 성취
17. vow — 맹세, 서약
18. sudden — 돌연한, 갑작스러운

Review 6

A
1. reduction — 감소, 축소
2. professional — 직업의, 전문의, 전문가
3. magazine — 잡지
4. pleasant — 즐거운, 좋은
5. recommend — 추천하다, 권하다
6. prove — 증명하다, 시험하다
7. mainly — 주로, 대개
8. pitch — 던지다, (천막을) 치다
9. proverb — 속담, 격언
10. pity — 동정, 애석한 일
11. major — 주요한, 큰
12. oyster — 굴
13. refer — 언급하다, 지시하다
14. marriage — 결혼
15. orbit — 궤도, 궤도를 돌다
16. modern — 현대의, 근대의
17. operate — 작동하다, 작용하다
18. movement — 운동, 활동

B
1. share — 분배하다, 공유하다
2. reward — 보수, 포상, 보답하다
3. serious — 진지한, 중대한
4. traditional — 전통적인, 관습의
5. roam — 거닐다, 돌아다니다
6. series — 연속, 시리즈
7. romance — 로맨스, 연애
8. spill — 엎지르다
9. trade — 거래하다, 무역하다, 무역
10. summarize — 요약하다
11. tourist — 여행자, 관광객
12. spoil — 망쳐놓다
13. weigh — 무게를 재다
14. squeeze — 짜내다, 압착하다
15. wealth — 부, 재산
16. success — 성공, 성취
17. vow — 맹세, 서약
18. sudden — 돌연한, 갑작스러운

Unit 13

A
1. affect
2. childhood
3. billion
4. condition
5. against
6. dashed
7. agency
8. crosswalk
9. diligent
10. athletic
11. Biologists
12. bulbs
13. cheeks
14. crumb
15. difficulty
16. broadcast
17. dimensions
18. conductor

B
1. 10억
2. 영향을 주다, 감동시키다
3. 뺨, 볼
4. 돌진하다, 내던지다
5. ~에 기대어서, 반대하여
6. 방송하다, 방송
7. 곤란, 어려움
8. 안내자, 지휘자
9. 운동의, 체육의
10. 작은 조각, 빵부스러기
11. 구, 전구
12. 횡단보도
13. 생물학자
14. 근면한, 부지런한
15. 조건, 상태, 지위
16. 치수, 차원, 규모
17. 어린 시절
18. 대리점, 대리권

1. affect
2. against
3. agency
4. athletic
5. billion
6. biologist
7. broadcast
8. bulb
9. cheek
10. childhood
11. condition
12. conductor
13. crosswalk
14. crumb
15. dash
16. difficulty
17. diligent
18. dimension

C
1. diligent — 근면한, 부지런한
2. dimension — 치수, 차원, 규모
3. affect — 영향을 주다, 감동시키다
4. difficulty — 곤란, 어려움
5. condition — 조건, 상태, 지위
6. against — ~에 기대어서, 반대하여
7. crumb — 작은 조각, 빵부스러기
8. dash — 돌진하다, 내던지다
9. agency — 대리점, 대리권
10. crosswalk — 횡단보도
11. broadcast — 방송하다, 방송
12. conductor — 안내자, 지휘자
13. bulb — 구, 전구
14. biologist — 생물학자
15. cheek — 뺨, 볼
16. billion — 10억
17. athletic — 운동의, 체육의
18. childhood — 어린 시절

Unit 14

A
1. electronic
2. hire
3. intention
4. fashionable
5. Fasten
6. future
7. generations
8. helmet
9. length
10. identity
11. effect
12. interaction
13. invited
14. folk
15. level
16. elbows
17. liberty
18. favor

B
1. 팔꿈치
2. 사람들, 서민의, 민속의
3. 상호 작용
4. 효과, 영향, 초래하다
5. 초청하다, 권유하다
6. 미래, 장래
7. 전자(학)의
8. 길이
9. 동시대의 사람들, 세대
10. 고용하다, 임대하다, 고용
11. 묶다, 고정하다
12. 헬멧
13. 자유
14. 호의, 부탁, 호의를 보이다
15. 수평, 수준
16. 신원, 정체성
17. 의향, 의지, 목적
18. 유행의, 유행을 따른

1. effect
2. elbow
3. electronic
4. fashionable
5. fasten
6. favor
7. folk
8. future
9. generation
10. helmet
11. hire
12. identity
13. intention
14. interaction
15. invite
16. length
17. level
18. liberty

C
1. level — 수평, 수준
2. helmet — 헬멧
3. effect — 효과, 영향, 초래하다
4. hire — 고용하다, 임대하다, 고용
5. liberty — 자유
6. generation — 동시대의 사람들, 세대
7. future — 미래, 장래
8. identity — 신원, 정체성
9. elbow — 팔꿈치
10. intention — 의향, 의지, 목적
11. folk — 사람들, 서민의, 민속의
12. electronic — 전자(학)의
13. favor — 호의, 부탁, 호의를 보이다
14. interaction — 상호 작용
15. fashionable — 유행의, 유행을 따른
16. length — 길이
17. invite — 초청하다, 권유하다
18. fasten — 묶다, 고정하다

Review 7

A
1. diligent — 근면한, 부지런한
2. dimension — 치수, 차원, 규모
3. affect — 영향을 주다, 감동시키다
4. difficulty — 곤란, 어려움
5. condition — 조건, 상태, 지위
6. against — ~에 기대어서, 반대하여
7. crumb — 작은 조각, 빵부스러기
8. dash — 돌진하다, 내던지다
9. agency — 대리점, 대리권
10. crosswalk — 횡단보도
11. broadcast — 방송하다, 방송
12. conductor — 안내자, 지휘자
13. bulb — 구, 전구
14. biologist — 생물학자
15. cheek — 뺨, 볼
16. billion — 10억
17. athletic — 운동의, 체육의
18. childhood — 어린 시절

B
1. level — 수평, 수준
2. helmet — 헬멧
3. effect — 효과, 영향, 초래하다
4. hire — 고용하다, 임대하다, 고용, 임대료
5. liberty — 자유
6. generation — 동시대의 사람들, 세대
7. future — 미래, 장래
8. identity — 신원, 정체성
9. elbow — 팔꿈치
10. intention — 의향, 의지, 목적
11. folk — 사람들, 서민의, 민속의
12. electronic — 전자(학)의
13. favor — 호의, 부탁, 호의를 보이다
14. interaction — 상호 작용
15. fashionable — 유행의, 유행을 따른
16. length — 길이
17. invite — 초청하다, 권유하다
18. fasten — 묶다, 고정하다

Unit 15

A
1. nearby
2. motion
3. policy
4. mayor
5. ounces
6. Multiply
7. Public
8. refused
9. native
10. popular
11. operation
12. regard
13. organization
14. poet
15. measuring
16. provides
17. region
18. published

B
1. 운동, 활동
2. 시인
3. ~으로 여기다, 주목
4. 시장, 읍장
5. 대중적인, 인기 있는
6. (중량 단위의) 온스
7. 정책, 방침
8. 측정하다, 측정, 수단
9. 지방, 지역
10. 작용, 운영, 수술
11. 발표하다, 출판하다
12. 거절하다
13. 늘리다, 곱하다
14. 제공하다, 준비하다
15. 가까운, 가까이에
16. 공중의, 공적인
17. 조직, 기구, 체제
18. 출생지의, 타고난

C
1. mayor
2. measure
3. motion
4. multiply
5. native
6. nearby
7. operation
8. organization
9. ounce
10. poet
11. policy
12. popular
13. provide
14. public
15. publish
16. refuse
17. regard
18. region

1. native — 출생지의, 타고난
2. ounce — (중량 단위의) 온스
3. multiply — 늘리다, 곱하다
4. organization — 조직, 기구, 체제
5. mayor — 시장, 읍장
6. nearby — 가까운, 가까이에
7. motion — 운동, 활동
8. public — 공중의, 공적인
9. operation — 작용, 운영, 수술
10. measure — 측정하다, 측정, 수단
11. provide — 제공하다, 준비하다
12. publish — 발표하다, 출판하다
13. policy — 정책, 방침
14. region — 지방, 지역
15. popular — 대중적인, 인기 있는
16. regard — ~으로 여기다, 주목
17. poet — 시인
18. refuse — 거절하다

Unit 16

A
1. Unless
2. route
3. Statues
4. rubble
5. tax
6. shelter
7. shuttle
8. standard
9. trembled
10. statement
11. survey
12. trick
13. wheat
14. rude
15. whole
16. Suppose
17. wild
18. shock

B
1. 버릇없는, 무례한
2. 표준, 기준, 표준의, 일반적인
3. 도로, 길, 순서를 정하다
4. 가정하다, 추측하다
5. 왕복 운행
6. 세금, 조세
7. 밀, 소맥
8. 성명, 진술
9. 떨다, 흔들리다
10. 벽돌조각
11. ~하지 않으면
12. 상, 조상
13. 야생의, 거친, 사나운
14. 충격, 쇼크
15. 전부의, 모든
16. 묘기, 재주, 기술
17. 대피소, 은신처
18. 관찰, 조사, 측량

C
1. statement
2. trick
3. standard
4. statue
5. route
6. shuttle
7. rude
8. survey
9. rubble
10. shock
11. shelter
12. tremble
13. unless
14. wild
15. suppose
16. whole
17. tax
18. wheat

1. statement — 성명, 진술
2. trick — 묘기, 재주, 기술
3. standard — 표준, 기준, 표준의, 일반적인
4. statue — 상, 조상
5. route — 도로, 길, 순서를 정하다
6. shuttle — 왕복 운행
7. rude — 버릇없는, 무례한
8. survey — 관찰, 조사, 측량
9. rubble — 벽돌조각
10. shock — 충격, 쇼크
11. shelter — 대피소, 은신처
12. tremble — 떨다, 흔들리다
13. unless — ~하지 않으면
14. wild — 야생의, 거친, 사나운
15. suppose — 가정하다, 추측하다
16. whole — 전부의, 모든
17. tax — 세, 세금
18. wheat — 밀, 소맥

Review 8

A
1. native — 출생지의, 타고난
2. ounce — (중량 단위의) 온스
3. multiply — 늘리다, 곱하다
4. organization — 조직, 기구, 체제
5. mayor — 시장, 읍장
6. nearby — 가까운, 가까이에
7. motion — 운동, 활동
8. public — 공중의, 공적인
9. operation — 작용, 운영, 수술
10. measure — 측정하다, 측정, 수단
11. provide — 제공하다, 준비하다
12. publish — 발표하다, 출판하다
13. policy — 정책, 방침
14. region — 지방, 지역
15. popular — 대중적인, 인기 있는
16. regard — ~으로 여기다, 응시하다, 주목
17. poet — 시인
18. refuse — 거절하다

B
1. statement — 성명, 진술
2. trick — 묘기, 재주, 기술
3. standard — 표준, 기준, 표준의, 일반적인
4. statue — 상, 조상
5. route — 도로, 길, 순서를 정하다
6. shuttle — 왕복 운행
7. rude — 버릇없는, 무례한
8. survey — 관찰, 조사, 측량
9. rubble — 벽돌조각
10. shock — 충격, 쇼크
11. shelter — 대피소, 은신처
12. tremble — 떨다, 흔들리다
13. unless — ~하지 않으면
14. wild — 야생의, 거친, 사나운
15. suppose — 가정하다, 추측하다
16. whole — 전부의, 모든
17. tax — 세, 세금
18. wheat — 밀, 소맥

Unit 17

A
1. bitter
2. ambiguous
3. disappeared
4. career
5. deceived
6. ancestors
7. atoms
8. blamed
9. contact
10. contains
11. debate
12. decline
13. chores
14. attend
15. discovered
16. buds
17. disgusting
18. clues

B
1. 쓴, 괴로운
2. 모호한, 다의의
3. 싹, 봉오리
4. 토론, 논쟁, 토론하다, 숙고하다
5. 경력, 직업
6. 사라지다
7. 포함하다
8. 기울다, 사절하다
9. 조상, 선조
10. 구역질나는, 정말 싫은
11. 잡일, 허드렛일
12. 발견하다
13. 원자
14. 속이다
15. 실마리, 단서
16. 비난하다
17. 접촉, 교제, 접촉하다, 교제하다
18. 출석하다

1. ambiguous
2. ancestor
3. atom
4. attend
5. bitter
6. blame
7. bud
8. career
9. chore
10. clue
11. contact
12. contain
13. debate
14. deceive
15. decline
16. disappear
17. discover
18. disgusting

C
1. clue
2. debate
3. contact
4. ambiguous
5. contain
6. ancestor
7. chore
8. deceive
9. career
10. decline
11. discover
12. atom
13. bud
14. disappear
15. bitter
16. disgusting
17. attend
18. blame

실마리, 단서
토론, 논쟁, 토론하다, 숙고하다
접촉, 교제, 접촉하다, 교제하다
모호한, 다의의
포함하다
조상, 선조
잡일, 허드렛일
속이다
경력, 직업
기울다, 사절하다
발견하다
원자
싹, 봉오리
사라지다
쓴, 괴로운
구역질나는, 정말 싫은
출석하다
비난하다

Unit 18

A
1. figures
2. endangered
3. lifetime
4. Fellowship
5. flavors
6. jury
7. genius
8. emperor
9. grateful
10. horror
11. huge
12. hunted
13. issued
14. entrance
15. kindness
16. lifted
17. garbage
18. likely

B
1. 단체, 학회 회원
2. 황제, 제왕
3. 쓰레기
4. 일생, 생애의
5. 멸종위기에 처한
6. 감사하고 있는
7. 친절, 호의, 친절한 행위
8. 발행, 논쟁, 발행하다
9. 입구, 입장
10. 있음직한, 할 것 같은
11. 공포, 혐오
12. 들어올리다, 향상시키다
13. 사냥하다, 추적하다
14. 맛, 조미료, ~에 맛을 내다
15. 배심, 심사원
16. 천재
17. 거대한, 무한한
18. 숫자, 모양, 인물

1. emperor
2. endangered
3. entrance
4. fellowship
5. figure
6. flavor
7. garbage
8. genius
9. grateful
10. horror
11. hunt
12. hunt
13. issue
14. jury
15. kindness
16. lifetime
17. lift
18. likely

C
1. genius
2. emperor
3. garbage
4. likely
5. flavor
6. endangered
7. horror
8. grateful
9. lift
10. entrance
11. lifetime
12. huge
13. fellowship
14. hunt
15. issue
16. kindness
17. figure
18. jury

천재
황제, 제왕
쓰레기
있음직한, 할 것 같은
맛, 조미료, ~에 맛을 내다
멸종위기에 처한
공포, 혐오
감사하고 있는
들어 올리다, 향상시키다
입구, 입장
일생, 생애의
거대한, 무한한
단체, 학회 회원
사냥하다, 추적하다
발행, 논쟁, 발행하다
친절, 호희, 친절한 행위
숫자, 모양, 인물
배심, 심사원

Review 9

A
1. clue
2. debate
3. contact
4. ambiguous
5. contain
6. ancestor
7. chore
8. deceive
9. career
10. decline
11. discover
12. atom
13. bud
14. disappear
15. bitter
16. disgusting
17. attend
18. blame

실마리, 단서
토론, 논쟁, 토론하다, 숙고하다
접촉, 교제, 접촉하다, 교제하다
모호한, 다의의
포함하다
조상, 선조
잡일, 허드렛일
속이다
경력, 직업
기울다, 사절하다
발견하다
원자
싹, 봉오리
사라지다
쓴, 괴로운
구역질나는, 정말 싫은
출석하다
비난하다

B
1. genius
2. emperor
3. garbage
4. likely
5. flavor
6. endangered
7. horror
8. grateful
9. lift
10. entrance
11. lifetime
12. huge
13. fellowship
14. hunt
15. issue
16. kindness
17. figure
18. jury

천재
황제, 제왕
쓰레기
있음직한, 할 것 같은
맛, 조미료, ~에 맛을 내다
멸종위기에 처한
공포, 혐오
감사하고 있는
들어 올리다, 향상시키다
입구, 입장
일생, 생애의
거대한
단체, 학회 회원
사냥하다, 추적하다
발행, 논쟁, 발행하다
친절, 호의, 친절한 행위
숫자, 모양, 인물
배심, 심사원

Unit 19

A
1. relaxes
2. medium
3. package
4. possible
5. mess
6. Neither
7. nickname
8. races
9. nonsense
10. passengers
11. merry
12. praise
13. republic
14. prayed
15. raise
16. pardon
17. rapid
18. religious

B
1. 어느 쪽도 ~아니다
2. 용서, 용서하다
3. 인종, 종족
4. 명랑한, 축제 기분의
5. 기도하다, 빌다
6. 승객, 여객
7. 올리다, 일으키다, 기르다
8. 혼란, 어수선함, 불결
9. 칭찬, 칭찬하다
10. 별명
11. 종교(상)의, 신앙의
12. 가능한
13. 공화국
14. 무의미한 말, 허튼 소리
15. 빠른, 신속한
16. 포장, 꾸러미
17. 늦추다, 긴장을 풀다
18. 중간, 매개물, 중간의

1. medium
2. merry
3. mess
4. neither
5. nickname
6. nonsense
7. package
8. pardon
9. passenger
10. possible
11. praise
12. pray
13. race
14. raise
15. rapid
16. relax
17. religious
18. republic

C
1. merry — 명랑한, 축제 기분의
2. nickname — 별명
3. praise — 칭찬, 칭찬하다
4. neither — 어느 쪽도 ~아니다
5. republic — 공화국
6. pray — 기도하다, 빌다
7. mess — 혼란, 어수선함, 불결
8. race — 인종, 종족
9. medium — 중간, 매개물, 중간의
10. religious — 종교(상)의, 신앙의
11. passenger — 승객, 여객
12. raise — 올리다, 일으키다, 기르다
13. package — 포장, 꾸러미
14. nonsense — 무의미한 말, 허튼 소리
15. rapid — 빠른, 신속한
16. possible — 가능한
17. pardon — 용서, 용서하다
18. relax — 늦추다, 긴장을 풀다

Unit 20

A
1. truth
2. worth
3. ruin
4. saint
5. sightseeing
6. tumbled
7. slave
8. steal
9. steel
10. technique
11. zoologist
12. temperatures
13. terrific
14. rule
15. turkey
16. smart
17. storage
18. wisdom

B
1. 유람하다, 관광하다
2. 기술, 수법
3. 파괴하다, 망쳐놓다, 파괴, 몰락
4. 지혜, 슬기로움
5. 영리한, 세련된
6. 진실, 사실
7. 훔치다
8. 칠면조
9. 규칙, 통례, 다스리다, 규정하다
10. 넘어지다, 폭락하다, 넘어짐, 폭락
11. 동물학자
12. 강철
13. 대단한, 아주 좋은
14. 가치가 있는, 가치
15. 노예
16. 온도, 기온
17. 저장, 창고
18. 성인

1. ruin
2. rule
3. saint
4. sightsee
5. slave
6. smart
7. steal
8. steel
9. storage
10. technique
11. temperature
12. terrific
13. truth
14. tumble
15. turkey
16. wisdom
17. worth
18. zoologist

C
1. steel — 강철
2. technique — 기술, 수법
3. storage — 저장, 창고
4. ruin — 파괴하다, 망쳐놓다, 파괴, 몰락
5. temperature — 온도, 기온
6. rule — 규칙, 통례, 다스리다, 규정하다
7. terrific — 대단한, 아주 좋은
8. worth — 가치가 있는, 가치
9. saint — 성인
10. truth — 진실, 사실
11. steal — 훔치다
12. tumble — 넘어지다, 폭락하다, 넘어짐, 폭락
13. sightsee — 유람하다, 관광하다
14. turkey — 칠면조
15. smart — 영리한, 세련된
16. wisdom — 지혜, 슬기로움
17. slave — 노예
18. zoologist — 동물학자

Review 10

A
1. merry — 명랑한, 축제 기분의
2. nickname — 별명
3. praise — 칭찬, 칭찬하다
4. neither — 어느 쪽도 ~아니다
5. republic — 공화국
6. pray — 기도하다, 빌다
7. mess — 혼란, 어수선함, 불결
8. race — 인종, 종족
9. medium — 중간, 매개물, 중간의
10. religious — 종교(상)의, 신앙의
11. passenger — 승객, 여객
12. raise — 올리다, 일으키다, 기르다
13. package — 포장, 꾸러미
14. nonsense — 무의미한 말, 허튼 소리
15. rapid — 빠른, 신속한
16. possible — 가능한
17. pardon — 용서, 용서하다
18. relax — 늦추다, 긴장을 풀다

B
1. steel — 강철
2. technique — 기술, 수법
3. storage — 저장, 창고
4. ruin — 파괴하다, 망쳐놓다, 파괴, 몰락
5. temperature — 온도, 기온
6. rule — 규칙, 통례, 다스리다, 규정하다
7. terrific — 대단한, 아주 좋은
8. worth — 가치가 있는, 가치
9. saint — 성인
10. truth — 진실, 사실
11. steal — 훔치다
12. tumble — 넘어지다, 폭락하다, 넘어짐, 폭락
13. sightsee — 유람하다, 관광하다
14. turkey — 칠면조
15. smart — 영리한, 세련된
16. wisdom — 지혜, 슬기로움
17. slave — 노예
18. zoologist — 동물학자

Unit 21

A
1. argument
2. cushions
3. achieve
4. advanced
5. Arctic
6. connection
7. border
8. absolute
9. bundle
10. charged
11. chased
12. conducts
13. areas
14. adolescent
15. confusing
16. daily
17. cartons
18. ceremony

B
1. 지역, 지방, 구역
2. 의식, 의례, 예의
3. 완전한, 절대의, 순수한
4. 청구하다, 고발하다, 책임지다
5. 테두리, 국경, 접하다
6. 이루다, 성취하다
7. 수행하다, 인도하다, 지도하다
8. 논의, 토론, 요지
9. (충격을)흡수하다, 쿠션
10. 혼동하다, 혼란시키다
11. 앞으로 나온, 진보한, 상급의
12. 연결, 결합, 관계
13. 꾸러미, 묶음
14. 쫓다, 추적, 추구
15. 북극의, 북극 지방
16. 매일의, 매일
17. 용기, 상자
18. 사춘기의, 미숙한

1. absolute
2. achieve
3. adolescent
4. advanced
5. arctic
6. area
7. argument
8. border
9. bundle
10. carton
11. ceremony
12. charge
13. chase
14. conduct
15. confuse
16. connection
17. cushion
18. daily

C
1. confuse — 혼동하다, 혼란시키다
2. absolute — 완전한, 절대의, 순수한
3. conduct — 수행하다, 인도하다, 지도하다
4. daily — 매일의, 매일
5. connection — 연결, 결합, 관계
6. achieve — 이루다, 성취하다
7. cushion — (충격을)흡수하다, 쿠션
8. chase — 쫓다, 추적, 추구
9. bundle — 꾸러미, 묶음
10. adolescent — 사춘기의, 미숙한
11. border — 테두리, 국경, 접하다
12. arctic — 북극의, 북극 지방
13. argument — 논의, 토론, 요지
14. charge — 청구하다
15. advanced — 진보한, 상급의
16. ceremony — 의식, 의례, 예의
17. area — 지역, 지방, 구역
18. carton — 용기, 상자

Unit 22

A
1. decent
2. fail
3. extra
4. familiar
5. guards
6. harmoniously
7. hoop
8. imitate
9. digging
10. faithful
11. define
12. efforts
13. freezes
14. impact
15. elements
16. Emergency
17. disappointed
18. factor

B
1. 노력, 수고
2. 요인, 인자, 요소
3. 상당한, 제대로 된, 점잖은
4. 경계, 경호인, 지키다
5. 여분의, 임시의, 특별한
6. 실패하다, 못하다, 부족하다
7. 요소, 성분, 원소
8. 모방하다, 흉내 내다
9. 얼다, 동결
10. 파다, 파헤치다, 발굴하다
11. 영향(력), 충돌
12. 사이 좋게, 화목하게
13. 비상사태, 위급
14. 테, 후프, 테를 두르다
15. 충실한, 정확한
16. 실망한, 낙담한
17. 친밀한, 잘 알고 있는
18. 규정하다, 정의를 내리다

1. decent
2. dig
3. define
4. disappointed
5. effort
6. element
7. emergency
8. extra
9. factor
10. fail
11. familiar
12. faithful
13. freeze
14. guard
15. harmoniously
16. hoop
17. imitate
18. impact

C
1. dig — 파다, 파헤치다, 발굴하다
2. emergency — 비상사태, 위급
3. factor — 요인, 인자, 요소
4. hoop — 테, 후프, 테를 두르다
5. extra — 여분의, 임시의, 특별한
6. decent — 상당한, 제대로 된, 점잖은
7. element — 요소, 성분, 원소
8. fail — 실패하다, 못하다, 부족하다
9. define — 규정하다, 정의를 내리다
10. effort — 노력, 수고
11. familiar — 친밀한, 잘 알고 있는
12. disappointed — 실망한, 낙담한
13. imitate — 모방하다, 흉내 내다
14. freeze — 얼다, 동결
15. guard — 경계, 경호인, 지키다
16. faithful — 충실한, 정확한
17. impact — 영향(력), 충돌
18. harmoniously — 사이 좋게, 화목하게

Review 11

A
1. confuse — 혼동하다, 혼란시키다
2. absolute — 완전한, 절대의, 순수한
3. conduct — 수행하다, 인도하다, 지도하다
4. daily — 매일의, 매일
5. connection — 연결, 결합, 관계
6. achieve — 이루다, 성취하다
7. cushion — (충격을)흡수하다, 쿠션
8. chase — 쫓다, 추적, 추구
9. bundle — 꾸러미, 묶음
10. adolescent — 사춘기의, 미숙한
11. border — 테두리, 국경, 접하다
12. arctic — 북극의, 북극 지방
13. argument — 논의, 토론, 요지
14. charge — 청구하다
15. advanced — 진보한, 상급의
16. ceremony — 의식, 의례, 예의
17. area — 지역, 지방, 구역
18. carton — 용기, 상자

B
1. dig — 파다, 파헤치다, 발굴하다
2. emergency — 비상사태, 위급
3. factor — 요인, 인자, 요소
4. hoop — 테, 후프, 테를 두르다
5. extra — 여분의, 임시의, 특별한
6. decent — 상당한, 제대로 된, 점잖은
7. element — 요소, 성분, 원소
8. fail — 실패하다, 못하다
9. define — 규정하다, 정의를 내리다
10. effort — 노력, 수고
11. familiar — 친밀한, 잘 알고 있는
12. disappointed — 실망한, 낙담한
13. imitate — 모방하다, 흉내 내다
14. freeze — 얼다, 동결
15. guard — 경계, 경호인, 지키다
16. faithful — 충실한, 정확한
17. impact — 영향(력), 충돌
18. harmoniously — 사이 좋게, 화목하게

Answer Key

Unit 23

A
1. moment
2. impressed
3. mechanic
4. jaw
5. Lumberjacks
6. luxury
7. oppose
8. machine
9. permission
10. moral
11. movable
12. impossible
13. officials
14. personality
15. join
16. interpreted
17. omitted
18. physically

B
1. 감동시키다, ~에게 감명을 주다
2. 재목 벌채인
3. 순간, 단시간, 중요성
4. 불가능한, ~할 수 없는
5. 정비사, 수리공
6. 빼다, 빠뜨리다, 게을리하다
7. 사치(품), 사치스러운, 고급의
8. 공무상의, 공식의, 공무원
9. 허가, 면허
10. 해석하다, 통역하다
11. 육체적으로, 물질적으로
12. 기계, 기구, 기계의
13. 성격, 개성, 인물
14. 가입하다, 결합하다
15. 움직일 수 있는
16. 반대하다, 대항하다, 대비시키다
17. 도덕적인, 윤리적인, 교훈
18. 턱

1. impossible
2. impress
3. interpret
4. jaw
5. join
6. lumberjack
7. luxury
8. machine
9. mechanic
10. moment
11. moral
12. movable
13. official
14. omit
15. oppose
16. permission
17. personality
18. physically

C
1. moment
2. join
3. physically
4. impossible
5. jaw
6. interpret
7. moral
8. personality
9. impress
10. mechanic
11. omit
12. machine
13. official
14. permission
15. movable
16. lumberjack
17. oppose
18. luxury

순간, 단시간, 중요성
가입하다, 결합하다
육체적으로, 물질적으로
불가능한, ~할 수 없는
턱
해석하다, 통역하다
도덕적인, 윤리적인, 교훈
성격, 개성, 인물
감동시키다, ~에게 감명을 주다
정비사, 수리공
빼다, 빠뜨리다, 게을리 하다
기계, 기구, 기계의
공무상의, 공식의, 공무원
허가, 면허
움직일 수 있는
재목 벌채인
반대하다, 대항하다, 대비시키다
사치(품), 사치스러운, 고급의

Unit 24

A
1. thought
2. production
3. register
4. selfish
5. promises
6. specific
7. regrets
8. vehicles
9. repair
10. search
11. splits
12. stage
13. pressure
14. Therefore
15. vitamin
16. seldom
17. thorough
18. watercolors

B
1. 등록하다, 기록하다
2. 압박, 압력, 곤란
3. 특수한, 특정한, 명확한
4. 그런 까닭에, 그 결과
5. 수리하다, 회복하다
6. 무대, 단계, 상연하다
7. 생각, 사색, 사상
8. 찾다, 탐색하다
9. 비타민
10. 이기적인, 자기 본위의
11. 그림물감, 수채화
12. 생산, 제작, 생산량
13. 수송 수단, 탈것
14. 좀처럼 ~않는, 드물게
15. 철저한, 완벽주의자인
16. 쪼개다, 분리하다, 분리
17. 후회하다, 슬퍼하다, 유감
18. 약속, 계약, 약속하다

1. pressure
2. production
3. promise
4. register
5. regret
6. repair
7. search
8. seldom
9. selfish
10. specific
11. split
12. stage
13. therefore
14. thorough
15. thought
16. vehicle
17. vitamin
18. watercolor

C
1. promise
2. stage
3. pressure
4. production
5. vehicle
6. split
7. vitamin
8. therefore
9. specific
10. watercolor
11. register
12. thought
13. repair
14. selfish
15. thorough
16. search
17. seldom
18. regret

약속, 계약, 약속하다
무대, 단계, 상연하다
압박, 압력, 곤란
생산, 제작, 생산량
수송 수단, 탈것
쪼개다, 분리하다, 분리
비타민
그런 까닭에, 그 결과
특수한, 특정한, 명확한
그림물감, 수채화
등록하다, 기록하다
생각, 사색, 사상
수리하다, 회복하다
이기적인, 자기 본위의
철저한, 완벽주의자인
찾다, 탐색하다
좀처럼 ~않는, 드물게
후회하다, 슬퍼하다, 유감

Review 12

A
1. moment
2. join
3. physically
4. impossible
5. jaw
6. interpret
7. moral
8. personality
9. impress
10. mechanic
11. omit
12. machine
13. official
14. permission
15. movable
16. lumberjack
17. oppose
18. luxury

순간, 단시간, 중요성
가입하다, 결합하다
육체적으로, 물질적으로
불가능한, ~할 수 없는
턱
해석하다, 통역하다
도덕적인, 윤리적인, 교훈
성격, 개성, 인물
감동시키다, ~에게 감명을 주다
정비사, 수리공
빼다, 빠뜨리다, 게을리 하다
기계, 기구, 기계의
공무상의, 공식의, 공무원
허가, 면허
움직일 수 있는
재목 벌채인
반대하다, 대항하다, 대비시키다
사치(품), 사치스러운, 고급의

B
1. promise
2. stage
3. pressure
4. production
5. vehicle
6. split
7. vitamin
8. therefore
9. specific
10. watercolor
11. register
12. thought
13. repair
14. selfish
15. thorough
16. search
17. seldom
18. regret

약속, 계약, 약속하다
무대, 단계, 상연하다
압박, 압력, 곤란
생산, 제작, 생산량
수송 수단, 탈것
쪼개다, 분리하다, 분리
비타민
그런 까닭에, 그 결과
특수한, 특정한, 명확한
그림물감, 수채화
등록하다, 기록하다
생각, 사색, 사상
수리하다, 회복하다
이기적인, 자기 본위의
철저한, 완벽주의자인
찾다, 탐색하다
좀처럼 ~않는, 드물게
후회하다, 슬퍼하다, 유감

Unit 25

A
1. academic
2. chipped
3. aerobics
4. articles
5. consumer
6. demanded
7. assure
8. brief
9. astronauts
10. bronze
11. chief
12. Adventures
13. civil
14. brow
15. climate
16. consider
17. decreased
18. alarming

B
1. 짧은, 간단한, 간단히 알리다
2. 학구적인, 대학의
3. 이마
4. 모험(심), 위험을 무릅쓰다
5. 시민의, 민간인의
6. 우주비행사
7. 소비자, 수요자
8. 보증하다, 안심시키다
9. 감소하다, 감소
10. 얇은 조각, 토막, 잘게 썰다
11. 요구하다, 묻다, 요구, 수요
12. 기사, 물건, 조항
13. 고려하다, 숙고하다
14. 청동(제품), 청동(색)의
15. 기후, 풍토
16. 심각한, 불안하게 만드는
17. 최고의, 주요한, 장
18. 에어로빅스

C
1. assure — 보증하다, 안심 시키다
2. brief — 짧은, 간단한, 간단히 알리다
3. astronaut — 우주비행사
4. consumer — 소비자, 수요자
5. academic — 학구적인, 대학의
6. bronze — 청동(제품), 청동(색)의
7. chief — 최고의, 주요한, 장
8. brow — 이마
9. adventure — 모험(심), 위험을 무릅쓰다
10. decrease — 감소하다, 감소
11. chip — 얇은 조각, 토막, 잘게 썰다
12. demand — 요구하다, 묻다, 요구, 수요
13. civil — 시민의, 민간인의
14. aerobics — 에어로빅스
15. climate — 기후, 풍토
16. article — 기사, 물건, 조항
17. consider — 고려하다, 숙고하다
18. alarming — 심각한, 불안하게 만드는

Unit 26

A
1. disaster
2. harvest
3. discouraged
4. fund
5. emphasis
6. epidemic
7. improve
8. essence
9. fan
10. democracy
11. fright
12. funeral
13. Heaven
14. feed
15. fears
16. height
17. displayed
18. impulse

B
1. 부채, 선풍기, 부채로 부치다
2. 민주주의, 민주정치
3. 먹을 것을 주다, 부양하다
4. 수확, 추수, 수확하다
5. 보이다, 전시하다
6. 공포, 두려움, 두려워하다
7. 충격, 충동
8. 재해, 재난
9. 개선하다, 향상시키다
10. 강조, 중점
11. 자금, 기금 투자하다
12. 높이, 고도, 절정
13. 본질, 진수
14. 두려움, 공포
15. 천국, 하늘
16. 유행(병), 유행성의
17. 장례(식), 장례의, 장례식용의
18. 용기를 잃게 하다, 실망시키다

C
1. disaster — 재해, 재난
2. fan — 부채, 선풍기, 부채로 부치다
3. democracy — 민주주의, 민주정치
4. impulse — 충격, 충동
5. discourage — 용기를 잃게 하다, 실망시키다
6. fear — 공포, 두려움, 두려워하다
7. emphasis — 강조, 중점
8. improve — 개선하다, 향상시키다
9. feed — 먹을 것을 주다, 부양하다
10. display — 보이다, 전시하다
11. fright — 두려움, 공포
12. essence — 본질, 진수
13. height — 높이, 고도, 절정
14. fund — 자금, 기금, 투자하다
15. epidemic — 유행(병), 유행성의
16. harvest — 수확, 추수, 수확하다
17. funeral — 장례(식), 장례식의
18. heaven — 천국, 하늘

Review 13

A
1. assure — 보증하다, 안심 시키다
2. brief — 짧은, 간단한, 간단히 알리다
3. astronaut — 우주비행사
4. consumer — 소비자, 수요자
5. academic — 학구적인, 대학의
6. bronze — 청동(제품), 청동(색)의
7. chief — 최고의, 주요한, 장
8. brow — 이마
9. adventure — 모험(심), 위험을 무릅쓰다
10. decrease — 감소하다, 감소
11. chip — 얇은 조각, 토막, 잘게 썰다
12. demand — 요구하다, 묻다, 요구, 수요
13. civil — 시민의, 민간인의
14. aerobics — 에어로빅스
15. climate — 기후, 풍토
16. article — 기사, 물건, 조항
17. consider — 고려하다, 숙고하다
18. alarming — 심각한, 불안하게 만드는

B
1. disaster — 재해, 재난
2. fan — 부채, 선풍기, 부채로 부치다
3. democracy — 민주주의, 민주정치
4. impulse — 충격, 충동
5. discourage — 용기를 잃게 하다, 실망시키다
6. fear — 공포, 두려움, 두려워하다
7. emphasis — 강조, 중점
8. improve — 개선하다, 향상시키다
9. feed — 먹을 것을 주다
10. display — 보이다, 전시하다
11. fright — 두려움, 공포
12. essence — 본질, 진수
13. height — 높이, 고도, 절정
14. fund — 자금, 기금, 투자하다
15. epidemic — 유행(병), 유행성의
16. harvest — 수확, 추수, 수확하다
17. funeral — 장례(식), 장례식의
18. heaven — 천국, 하늘

Unit 27

A
1. managed
2. leaned
3. incredible
4. naked
5. journalism
6. kneel
7. increase
8. melting
9. national
10. origins
11. pace
12. merely
13. orphanage
14. Mammals
15. plain
16. otherwise
17. maintain
18. palm

B
1. 기대다, 의지하다
2. 늘리다, 증대하다, 증가
3. 국민의, 국가의
4. 무릎을 꿇다
5. 녹다, 녹이다
6. 고아원
7. 유지하다, 지속하다
8. 그렇지 않으면
9. 쉬운, 명백한, 단순한
10. 포유동물
11. (일, 걸음)속도, 걸음
12. 저널리즘, 신문 잡지업계
13. 단지, 전혀
14. 손바닥
15. 해내다, 경영하다, 다루다
16. 기원, 출생, 유래
17. 벌거벗은, 꾸밈 없는
18. 믿을 수 없는

1. increase
2. incredible
3. journalism
4. kneel
5. lean
6. maintain
7. mammal
8. manage
9. melt
10. merely
11. naked
12. national
13. origin
14. orphanage
15. otherwise
16. pace
17. plain
18. palm

C
1. origin — 기원, 출생, 유래
2. palm — 손바닥
3. increase — 늘리다, 증대하다, 증가
4. national — 국민의, 국가의
5. orphanage — 고아원
6. incredible — 믿을 수 없는
7. naked — 벌거벗은, 꾸밈 없는
8. otherwise — 그렇지 않으면
9. journalism — 저널리즘, 신문 잡지업계
10. manage — 해내다, 경영하다
11. melt — 녹다, 녹이다
12. kneel — 무릎을 꿇다
13. merely — 단지, 전혀
14. mammal — 포유동물
15. lean — 기대다, 의지하다
16. pace — (일, 걸음)속도, 걸음
17. maintain — 유지하다, 지속하다
18. plain — 쉬운, 명백한, 단순한

Unit 28

A
1. stroke
2. throughout
3. reply
4. steadily
5. promotes
6. Volunteers
7. tides
8. vocabulary
9. shelf
10. secret
11. wages
12. respect
13. steward
14. proper
15. tightly
16. protein
17. replaced
18. sensible

B
1. 대신하다, 대체하다
2. ~의 일을 보다, 집사
3. 대답하다, 응답하다
4. 증진하다, 촉진하다
5. 어휘, 단어집
6. 비밀의, 비밀
7. 임금, 보상
8. 적당한, 타당한, 고유의
9. 단단히, 꽉
10. 분별 있는, 현명한
11. 지원자, 지원하다, 자생하다
12. 한번 치기, 타격
13. 단백질, 단백질의
14. 조류, 흥망, 조류를 타다
15. 착실히, 확실하게, 꾸준히
16. ~동안, ~에 걸쳐서
17. 존경하다, 존경, 주의
18. 선반

1. promote
2. proper
3. protein
4. replace
5. reply
6. respect
7. secret
8. sensible
9. shelf
10. steadily
11. steward
12. stroke
13. throughout
14. tide
15. tightly
16. vocabulary
17. volunteer
18. wage

C
1. tide — 조류, 흥망, 조류를 타다
2. vocabulary — 어휘, 단어집
3. tightly — 단단히, 꽉
4. promote — 증진하다, 촉진하다
5. throughout — ~동안, ~에 걸쳐서
6. volunteer — 지원자, 지원하다, 자생하다
7. protein — 단백질, 단백질의
8. stroke — 한번 치기, 타격
9. proper — 적당한, 타당한, 고유의
10. wage — 임금, 보상
11. shelf — 선반
12. steadily — 착실히, 확실하게, 꾸준히
13. replace — 대신하다, 대체하다
14. steward — ~의 일을 보다, 집사
15. respect — 존경하다
16. secret — 비밀의, 비밀
17. reply — 대답하다, 응답하다
18. sensible — 분별 있는, 현명한

Review 14

A
1. origin — 기원, 출생, 유래
2. palm — 손바닥
3. increase — 늘리다, 증대하다, 증가
4. national — 국민의, 국가의
5. orphanage — 고아원
6. incredible — 믿을 수 없는
7. naked — 벌거벗은, 꾸밈 없는
8. otherwise — 그렇지 않으면
9. journalism — 저널리즘, 신문 잡지업계
10. manage — 해내다, 경영하다
11. melt — 녹다, 녹이다
12. kneel — 무릎을 꿇다
13. merely — 단지, 전혀
14. mammal — 포유동물
15. lean — 기대다, 의지하다
16. pace — (일, 걸음)속도, 걸음
17. maintain — 유지하다, 지속하다
18. plain — 쉬운, 명백한, 단순한

B
1. tide — 조류, 흥망, 조류를 타다
2. vocabulary — 어휘, 단어집
3. tightly — 단단히, 꽉
4. promote — 증진하다, 촉진하다
5. throughout — ~동안, ~에 걸쳐서
6. volunteer — 지원자, 지원하다, 자생하다
7. protein — 단백질, 단백질의
8. stroke — 한번 치기, 타격
9. proper — 적당한, 타당한, 고유의
10. wage — 임금, 보상
11. shelf — 선반
12. steadily — 착실히, 확실하게, 꾸준히
13. replace — 대신하다, 대체하다
14. steward — ~의 일을 보다, 집사
15. respect — 존경하다
16. secret — 비밀의, 비밀
17. reply — 대답하다, 응답하다
18. sensible — 분별 있는, 현명한

Unit 29

A
1. acceptable
2. combine
3. balanced
4. awkward
5. drugs
6. converting
7. contemporary
8. buried
9. Although
10. attitude
11. clay
12. burst
13. amuse
14. client
15. contrast
16. denied
17. accidental
18. buzzed

B
1. 균형이 잡힌
2. 받아들일 수 있는
3. 찰흙, 점토
4. 어색한, 서투른
5. 결합시키다, 결합하다
6. 우연한, 비본질적인
7. 대조, 대비
8. 묻다
9. 부정하다, 거절하다
10. 태도, 마음가짐, 자세
11. 약, 약품
12. 윙윙거리다
13. 동시대의, 현대의, 동시대사람
14. 비록 ~일지라도
15. 전환하다, 변화시키다
16. 소송 의뢰인, 고객
17. 폭발하다, 터지다, 폭발
18. 즐겁게 하다

1. acceptable
2. accidental
3. although
4. amuse
5. attitude
6. awkward
7. balanced
8. burst
9. bury
10. buzz
11. clay
12. client
13. combine
14. contemporary
15. contrast
16. convert
17. deny
18. drug

C
1. buzz — 윙윙거리다
2. accidental — 우연한, 비본질적인
3. drug — 약, 약품
4. clay — 찰흙, 점토
5. although — 비록 ~일지라도
6. client — 소송 의뢰인, 고객
7. acceptable — 받아들일 수 있는
8. deny — 부정하다, 거절하다
9. combine — 결합시키다, 결합하다
10. convert — 전환하다, 변화시키다
11. amuse — 즐겁게 하다
12. balanced — 균형이 잡힌
13. contemporary — 동시대의, 현대의, 동시대사람
14. awkward — 어색한, 서투른
15. burst — 폭발하다, 터지다, 폭발
16. attitude — 태도, 마음가짐, 자세
17. contrast — 대조, 대비
18. bury — 묻다

Unit 30

A
1. generosity
2. dragging
3. herb
4. else
5. fibers
6. evolution
7. excepted
8. Female
9. described
10. fist
11. independence
12. gathered
13. domestic
14. globalization
15. heroine
16. exact
17. historical
18. idioms

B
1. 진화, 발달
2. 묘사하다, 기술하다
3. 관대, 너그러움
4. 여성의, 암컷의
5. 세계화, 국제화
6. ~을 제외하다
7. 역사의, 역사적인
8. 그 밖에, 그 외에
9. 모으다, 모이다
10. 여걸, 여장부
11. 섬유, 섬유질식품
12. 숙어, 관용구
13. 주먹으로 치다, 주먹
14. 독립, 자주
15. 국내의, 가정의
16. 약용식물, 풀잎
17. 정확한, 정밀한, 꼼꼼한
18. 끌다, 질질 끌다

1. describe
2. domestic
3. drag
4. else
5. evolution
6. exact
7. except
8. female
9. fiber
10. fist
11. gather
12. generosity
13. globalization
14. herb
15. heroine
16. historical
17. idiom
18. independence

C
1. fist — 주먹으로 치다, 주먹
2. describe — 묘사하다, 기술하다
3. gather — 모으다, 모이다
4. fiber — 섬유, 섬유질식품
5. generosity — 관대, 너그러움
6. domestic — 국내의, 가정의
7. globalization — 세계화, 국제화
8. female — 여성의, 암컷의
9. drag — 끌다, 질질 끌다
10. except — ~을 제외하다
11. herb — 약용식물, 풀잎
12. else — 그 밖에, 그 외에
13. heroine — 여걸, 여장부
14. volution — 진화, 발달
15. idiom — 숙어, 관용구
16. historical — 역사의, 역사적인
17. exact — 정확한, 정밀한, 꼼꼼한
18. independence — 독립, 자주

Review 15

A
1. buzz — 윙윙거리다
2. accidental — 우연한, 비본질적인
3. drug — 약, 약품
4. clay — 찰흙, 점토
5. although — 비록 ~일지라도
6. client — 소송 의뢰인, 고객
7. acceptable — 받아들일 수 있는
8. deny — 부정하다, 거절하다
9. combine — 결합시키다, 결합하다
10. convert — 전환하다, 변화시키다
11. amuse — 즐겁게 하다
12. balanced — 균형이 잡힌
13. contemporary — 동시대의, 현대의, 동시대사람
14. awkward — 어색한, 서투른
15. burst — 폭발하다, 터지다, 폭발
16. attitude — 태도, 마음가짐, 자세
17. contrast — 대조, 대비
18. bury — 묻다

B
1. fist — 주먹으로 치다, 주먹
2. describe — 묘사하다, 기술하다
3. gather — 모으다, 모이다
4. fiber — 섬유, 섬유질식품
5. generosity — 관대, 너그러움
6. domestic — 국내의, 가정의
7. globalization — 세계화, 국제화
8. female — 여성의, 암컷의
9. drag — 끌다, 질질 끌다
10. except — ~을 제외하다
11. herb — 약용식물, 풀잎
12. else — 그 밖에, 그 외에
13. heroine — 여걸, 여장부
14. volution — 진화, 발달
15. idiom — 숙어, 관용구
16. historical — 역사의, 역사적인
17. exact — 정확한, 정밀한, 꼼꼼한
18. independence — 독립, 자주

Unit 31

A
1. negative
2. marginal
3. population
4. neighborhood
5. outline
6. politics
7. legal
8. pollution
9. individual
10. overcome
11. inflation
12. martial
13. navy
14. leaped
15. leisure
16. material
17. outlook
18. meal

B
1. 팽창, 인플레이션
2. 윤곽, 외형, 윤곽을 그리다
3. 가장자리의, 한계의
4. 해군, 군함
5. 정치, 정치학
6. 개개의, 개인적인, 개인
7. 식사, 식사를 하다
8. 시각, 태도, 통찰
9. 군인다운, 전쟁의
10. 인구, 주민
11. 뛰어 오르다, 도약
12. 오염
13. 부정적인, 소극적인
14. 틈, 여가, 한가한
15. 극복하다, 이기다
16. 이웃, 근처
17. 재료, 물질의, 구체적인
18. 법적인, 합법의

1. individual
2. inflation
3. leap
4. legal
5. leisure
6. marginal
7. martial
8. material
9. meal
10. navy
11. negative
12. neighborhood
13. outline
14. outlook
15. overcome
16. politics
17. pollution
18. population

C
1. meal — 식사, 식사를 하다
2. negative — 부정적인, 소극적인
3. individual — 개개의, 개인적인, 개인
4. navy — 해군, 군함
5. neighborhood — 이웃, 근처
6. material — 재료, 물질의, 구체적인
7. inflation — 팽창, 인플레이션
8. outlook — 시각, 태도, 통찰
9. outline — 윤곽, 외형, 윤곽을 그리다
10. population — 인구, 주민
11. martial — 군인다운, 전쟁의
12. leap — 뛰어 오르다, 도약
13. pollution — 오염
14. politics — 정치, 정치학
15. legal — 법적인, 합법의
16. overcome — 극복하다, 이기다
17. marginal — 가장자리의, 한계의
18. leisure — 틈, 여가, 한가한

Unit 32

A
1. responsibilities
2. purchase
3. welfare
4. reunified
5. scale
6. quite
7. shy
8. weapon
9. tray
10. suggestion
11. retire
12. sunset
13. reminds
14. survive
15. transportation
16. sigh
17. treated
18. weight

B
1. 책임, 의무
2. 일몰, 해질녘
3. 구입하다, 구입, 구입품
4. 수줍어하는
5. 운송, 교통수단
6. 눈금, 비율
7. 다루다, 대우하다, 치료하다
8. 제안, 제의, 암시
9. 복지, 복지 사업
10. 생각나게 하다
11. 살아남다, 생존하다
12. 다시 통일시키다
13. 무기
14. 한숨 쉬다, 탄식하다, 한숨
15. 무게, 체중, ~에 무게를 가하다
16. 퇴직하다, 물러가다
17. 쟁반, 음식 접시
18. 아주, 완전히

1. purchase
2. quite
3. remind
4. responsibility
5. retire
6. reunify
7. scale
8. shy
9. sigh
10. suggestion
11. sunset
12. survive
13. transportation
14. tray
15. treat
16. weapon
17. weight
18. welfare

C
1. weapon — 무기
2. purchase — 구입하다, 구입, 구입품
3. treat — 다루다, 대우하다, 치료하다
4. remind — 생각나게 하다
5. tray — 쟁반, 음식 접시
6. quite — 아주, 완전히
7. survive — 살아남다, 생존하다
8. transportation — 운송, 교통수단
9. retire — 퇴직하다, 물러가다
10. sigh — 한숨 쉬다, 탄식하다, 한숨
11. responsibility — 책임, 의무
12. suggestion — 제안, 제의, 암시
13. shy — 수줍어하는
14. weight — 무게, 체중, ~에 무게를 가하다
15. sunset — 일몰, 해질녘
16. scale — 눈금, 비율
17. reunify — 다시 통일시키다
18. welfare — 복지, 복지 사업

Review 16

A
1. meal — 식사, 식사를 하다
2. negative — 부정적인, 소극적인
3. individual — 개개의, 개인적인, 개인
4. navy — 해군, 군함
5. neighborhood — 이웃, 근처
6. material — 재료, 물질의, 구체적인
7. inflation — 팽창, 인플레이션
8. outlook — 시각, 태도, 통찰
9. outline — 윤곽, 외형, 윤곽을 그리다
10. population — 인구, 주민
11. martial — 군인다운, 전쟁의
12. leap — 뛰어 오르다, 도약
13. pollution — 오염
14. politics — 정치, 정치학
15. legal — 법적인, 합법의
16. overcome — 극복하다, 이기다
17. marginal — 가장자리의, 한계의
18. leisure — 틈, 여가

B
1. weapon — 무기
2. purchase — 구입하다, 구입, 구입품
3. treat — 다루다, 대우하다, 치료하다
4. remind — 생각나게 하다
5. tray — 쟁반, 음식 접시
6. quite — 아주, 완전히
7. survive — 살아남다, 생존하다
8. transportation — 운송, 교통수단
9. retire — 퇴직하다, 물러가다
10. sigh — 한숨 쉬다, 탄식하다, 한숨
11. responsibility — 책임, 의무
12. suggestion — 제안, 제의, 암시
13. shy — 수줍어하는
14. weight — 무게, 체중, ~에 무게를 가하다
15. sunset — 일몰, 해질녘
16. scale — 눈금, 비율
17. reunify — 다시 통일시키다
18. welfare — 복지, 복지 사업

Answer Key

Unit 33

A
1. citizen
2. bore
3. committee
4. appear
5. communicating
6. beads
7. competition
8. copper
9. apply
10. copyrights
11. description
12. claimed
13. destroyed
14. According
15. appointed
16. careless
17. benefits
18. cast

B
1. 이익, 수당, 이득을 보다
2. 저작권, 판권
3. 부주의한, 무관심한
4. 신청하다, 지원하다
5. 경쟁, 시합
6. ~에 따라서
7. 묘사, 서술
8. 던지다, 주조하다, 배역하다
9. 파괴하다, 부수다
10. 위원회
11. 임명하다, 지정하다, 정하다
12. 주장하다, 요구하다, 고소하다
13. 구리, 동전, 구릿(빛)의
14. 구슬, 염주
15. 시민
16. 전달하다, 통신하다
17. 나타나다
18. 낳다

1. according
2. appear
3. apply
4. appoint
5. bead
6. bear
7. benefit
8. careless
9. cast
10. citizen
11. claim
12. committee
13. communicate
14. competition
15. copper
16. copyright
17. description
18. destroy

C
1. citizen — 시민
2. copyright — 저작권, 판권
3. according — ~에 따라서
4. careless — 부주의한, 무관심한
5. benefit — 이익, 수당, 이득을 보다
6. competition — 경쟁, 시합
7. cast — 던지다, 주조하다, 배역하다
8. appear — 나타나다
9. bear — 낳다
10. appoint — 임명하다, 지정하다, 정하다
11. bead — 구슬, 염주
12. claim — 주장하다, 요구하다, 고소하다
13. apply — 신청하다, 지원하다
14. description — 묘사, 서술
15. committee — 위원회
16. destroy — 파괴하다, 부수다
17. communicate — 전달하다, 통신하다
18. copper — 구리, 동전, 구릿(빛)의

Unit 34

A
1. honest
2. flat
3. Gradually
4. experience
5. granted
6. humming
7. initial
8. developed
9. exhibition
10. insistent
11. earthquake
12. echo
13. dynamic
14. expenses
15. fix
16. hopeless
17. government
18. flames

B
1. 활기 있는, 동력의, 동적인
2. 불꽃, 불길, 타오르다
3. 정부, 통치(권)
4. 개발하다, 발전시키다
5. 희망 없는, 가망 없는
6. 지출, 비용, 경비
7. 정직한, 진실한
8. 최초의, 초기의
9. 지진
10. 고집 세우는, 주장하는
11. 시인하다, 인정하다
12. 경험, 체험, 경력
13. 평탄한, 편평한
14. 콧노래를 부르다
15. 전시, 전시회
16. 서서히, 점차로
17. 고치다, 붙이다, 응시하다
18. 메아리 치다, 모방하다, 메아리

1. develop
2. dynamic
3. earthquake
4. echo
5. exhibition
6. expense
7. experience
8. fix
9. flame
10. flat
11. government
12. gradually
13. grant
14. honest
15. hopeless
16. hum
17. initial
18. insistent

C
1. honest — 정직한, 진실한
2. develop — 개발하다, 발전시키다
3. grant — 시인하다, 인정하다
4. hopeless — 희망 없는, 가망 없는
5. insistent — 고집 세우는, 주장하는
6. echo — 메아리 치다, 모방하다, 메아리
7. gradually — 서서히, 점차로
8. earthquake — 지진
9. government — 정부, 통치(권)
10. dynamic — 활기 있는, 동력의, 동적인
11. flat — 평탄한, 편평한
12. expense — 지출, 비용, 경비
13. flame — 불꽃, 불길, 타오르다
14. exhibition — 전시, 전시회
15. hum — 콧노래를 부르다
16. initial — 최초의, 초기의
17. fix — 고치다, 붙이다, 응시하다
18. experience — 경험, 체험, 경력

Review 17

A
1. citizen — 시민
2. copyright — 저작권, 판권
3. according — ~에 따라서
4. careless — 부주의한, 무관심한
5. benefit — 이익, 수당, 이득을 보다
6. competition — 경쟁, 시합
7. cast — 던지다, 주조하다, 배역하다
8. appear — 나타나다
9. bear — 낳다
10. appoint — 임명하다, 지정하다, 정하다
11. bead — 구슬, 염주
12. claim — 주장하다, 요구하다, 고소하다
13. apply — 신청하다, 지원하다
14. description — 묘사, 서술
15. committee — 위원회
16. destroy — 파괴하다, 부수다
17. communicate — 전달하다, 통신하다
18. copper — 구리, 동전, 구릿(빛)의

B
1. honest — 정직한, 진실한
2. develop — 개발하다, 발전시키다
3. grant — 시인하다, 인정하다
4. hopeless — 희망 없는, 가망 없는
5. insistent — 고집 세우는, 주장하는
6. echo — 메아리 치다, 모방하다, 메아리
7. gradually — 서서히, 점차로
8. earthquake — 지진
9. government — 정부, 통치(권)
10. dynamic — 활기 있는, 동력의, 동적인
11. flat — 평탄한, 편평한
12. expense — 지출, 비용, 경비
13. flame — 불꽃, 불길, 타오르다
14. exhibition — 전시, 전시회
15. hum — 콧노래를 부르다
16. initial — 최초의, 초기의
17. fix — 고치다, 붙이다, 응시하다
18. experience — 경험, 체험, 경력

Answer Key

Unit 35

A
1. instant
2. patience
3. laundry
4. mention
5. instance
6. merits
7. nervous
8. licked
9. notice
10. partially
11. neutral
12. passage
13. merchants
14. portable
15. limit
16. priests
17. method
18. potential

B
1. 언급하다, 기재, 표창
2. 실례, 사례, 예를 들다
3. 부분적으로, 불공평하게
4. 방법, 순서
5. 즉석의, 즉시의
6. 인내(력), 참을성
7. 상인, 무역 상인
8. 성직자, 목사
9. 통행, 통과, 경과
10. 제한하다, 한계, 경계
11. 신경(성)의, 신경질적인, 불안한
12. 알아채다, 주의
13. 잠재적인, 잠재성
14. 핥다
15. 휴대용의
16. 장점, 공적
17. 중립의, 공평한
18. 세탁물, 세탁소

1. instance
2. instant
3. laundry
4. lick
5. limit
6. mention
7. merchant
8. merit
9. method
10. nervous
11. neutral
12. notice
13. partially
14. passage
15. patience
16. portable
17. priest
18. potential

C
1. method — 방법, 순서
2. neutral — 중립의, 공평한
3. passage — 통행, 통과, 경과
4. nervous — 신경(성)의, 신경질적인, 불안한
5. laundry — 세탁물, 세탁소
6. partially — 부분적으로, 불공평하게
7. notice — 알아채다, 주의
8. instance — 실례, 사례, 예를 들다
9. merit — 장점, 공적
10. patience — 인내(력), 참을성
11. instant — 즉석의, 즉시의
12. potential — 잠재적인, 잠재성
13. portable — 휴대용의
14. lick — 핥다
15. mention — 언급하다, 기재
16. priest — 성직자, 목사
17. limit — 제한하다, 한계, 경계
18. merchant — 상인, 무역상인

Unit 36

A
1. realistic
2. recent
3. widow
4. routine
5. taboo
6. similar
7. review
8. skipped
9. role
10. sweat
11. trial
12. typhoon
13. Unfortunately
14. whether
15. rejected
16. tangled
17. yield
18. situation

B
1. 거절하다, 무시하다
2. 빠뜨리다, 가볍게 뛰다, 거르다
3. 엉키게 하다, 혼란에 빠지다
4. 일상의, 판에 박힌
5. 금기, 금기의
6. 태풍
7. 현실주의의, 사실주의의
8. ~인지 어떤지, ~이든지(아니든지)
9. 유사한, 닮은
10. 생기게 하다, 산출하다, 산출
11. 근래의, 최근의, 새로운
12. 미망인, 과부
13. 불행하게
14. 상태, 사정, 입장
15. 공판, 시도, 시련
16. 역할, 배역
17. 땀, 땀을 흘리다
18. 재검토하다, 복습하다

1. realistic
2. recent
3. reject
4. review
5. role
6. routine
7. similar
8. situation
9. skip
10. sweat
11. taboo
12. tangle
13. trial
14. typhoon
15. unfortunately
16. whether
17. widow
18. yield

C
1. sweat — 땀, 땀을 흘리다
2. taboo — 금기, 금기의
3. realistic — 현실주의의, 사실주의의
4. unfortunately — 불행하게
5. tangle — 엉키게 하다, 혼란에 빠지다
6. reject — 거절하다, 무시하다
7. trial — 공판, 시도, 시련
8. recent — 근래의, 최근의, 새로운
9. typhoon — 태풍
10. role — 역할, 배역
11. whether — ~인지 어떤지, ~이든지(아니든지)
12. review — 재검토하다, 복습하다
13. skip — 빠뜨리다, 가볍게 뛰다, 거르다
14. situation — 상태, 사정, 입장
15. yield — 생기게 하다, 산출하다, 산출
16. routine — 일상의, 판에 박힌
17. similar — 유사한, 닮은
18. widow — 미망인, 과부

Review 18

A
1. method — 방법, 순서
2. neutral — 중립의, 공평한
3. passage — 통행, 통과, 경과
4. nervous — 신경(성)의, 신경질적인, 불안한
5. laundry — 세탁물, 세탁소
6. partially — 부분적으로, 불공평하게
7. notice — 알아채다, 주의
8. instance — 실례, 사례, 예를 들다
9. merit — 장점, 공적
10. patience — 인내(력), 참을성
11. instant — 즉석의, 즉시의
12. potential — 잠재적인, 잠재성
13. portable — 휴대용의
14. lick — 핥다
15. mention — 언급하다, 기재
16. priest — 성직자, 목사
17. limit — 제한하다, 한계, 경계
18. merchant — 상인, 무역상인

B
1. sweat — 땀, 땀을 흘리다
2. taboo — 금기, 금기의
3. realistic — 현실주의의, 사실주의의
4. unfortunately — 불행하게
5. tangle — 엉키게 하다, 혼란에 빠지다
6. reject — 거절하다, 무시하다
7. trial — 공판, 시도, 시련
8. recent — 근래의, 최근의, 새로운
9. typhoon — 태풍
10. role — 역할, 배역
11. whether — ~인지 어떤지, ~이든지(아니든지)
12. review — 재검토하다, 복습하다
13. skip — 빠뜨리다, 가볍게 뛰다, 거르다
14. situation — 상태, 사정, 입장
15. yield — 생기게 하다, 산출하다, 산출
16. routine — 일상의, 판에 박힌
17. similar — 유사한, 닮은
18. widow — 미망인, 과부

Unit 37

A
1. account
2. biological
3. ceased
4. appropriate
5. celebration
6. devoted
7. complained
8. arbores
9. compose
10. blossom
11. concentrate
12. architect
13. core
14. cabins
15. device
16. calculators
17. bite
18. cures

B
1. 수목
2. 물린 상처, 물다
3. 핵심, 속
4. 고려, 계산, 설명하다, 책임지다
5. 집중하다, 집결시키다
6. 축하, 의식, 칭찬
7. 생물학적인, 생물학의
8. 장치, 도구, 책략
9. 중단하다, 멈추다
10. 바치다, 헌신하다
11. 객실, 오두막
12. 계산기, 계산자
13. 충당하다, 사유하다, 적절한, 적당한
14. 치료하다, 구원하다, 치료
15. 불평하다, 하소연하다
16. 꽃을 피우다, 꽃, 개화
17. 작곡하다, 작문하다
18. 건축가, 설계사

1. account
2. appropriate
3. arbor
4. architect
5. biological
6. bite
7. blossom
8. cease
9. celebration
10. complain
11. compose
12. concentrate
13. core
14. cabin
15. calculator
16. cure
17. device
18. devote

C
1. arbor — 수목
2. compose — 작곡하다, 작문하다
3. appropriate — 충당하다, 적절한, 적당한
4. concentrate — 집중하다, 집결시키다
5. complain — 불평하다, 하소연하다
6. devote — 바치다, 헌신하다
7. account — 고려, 계산, 설명하다
8. device — 장치, 도구, 책략
9. celebration — 축하, 의식, 칭찬
10. cure — 치료하다, 구원하다, 치료
11. core — 핵심, 속
12. blossom — 꽃을 피우다, 꽃, 개화
13. cease — 중단하다, 멈추다
14. architect — 건축가, 설계사
15. cabin — 객실, 오두막
16. biological — 생물학적인, 생물학의
17. calculator — 계산기, 계산자
18. bite — 물린 상처, 물다

Unit 38

A
1. formally
2. graves
3. humanity
4. greedy
5. illegally
6. grocery
7. imagination
8. edition
9. insurance
10. intense
11. educate
12. effective
13. faucet
14. explains
15. forbade
16. exposed
17. extent
18. dialects

B
1. 판, 간행
2. 수도꼭지
3. 인류, 인간애, 인간성
4. 무덤, 죽음
5. 방언, 사투리
6. 상상(력), 창작력
7. 식품점
8. 정도, 범위
9. 정식으로, 공식으로
10. 격한, 강렬한
11. 효과적인, 효력이 있는
12. 보험, 보험금
13. 설명하다, 해석하다, 해명하다
14. 불법으로
15. 교육하다, 육성하다
16. 욕심 많은, 갈망하는
17. 금지하다, 방해하다
18. 드러내다, 폭로하다

1. dialect
2. edition
3. educate
4. effective
5. explain
6. expose
7. extent
8. faucet
9. forbid
10. formally
11. grave
12. greedy
13. grocery
14. humanity
15. illegally
16. imagination
17. insurance
18. intense

C
1. formally — 정식으로, 공식으로
2. educate — 교육하다, 육성하다
3. faucet — 수도꼭지
4. extent — 정도, 범위
5. greedy — 욕심 많은, 갈망하는
6. dialect — 방언, 사투리
7. forbid — 금지하다, 방해하다
8. expose — 드러내다, 폭로하다
9. grocery — 식품점
10. illegally — 불법으로
11. edition — 판, 간행
12. humanity — 인류, 인간애, 인간성
13. insurance — 보험, 보험금
14. effective — 효과적인, 효력이 있는
15. imagination — 상상(력), 창작력
16. explain — 설명하다, 해석하다, 해명하다
17. intense — 격한, 강렬한
18. grave — 무덤, 죽음

Review 19

A
1. arbor — 수목
2. compose — 작곡하다, 작문하다
3. appropriate — 충당하다, 적절한, 적당한
4. concentrate — 집중하다, 집결시키다
5. complain — 불평하다, 하소연하다
6. devote — 바치다, 헌신하다
7. account — 고려, 계산, 설명하다
8. device — 장치, 도구, 책략
9. celebration — 축하, 의식, 칭찬
10. cure — 치료하다, 구원하다, 치료
11. core — 핵심, 속
12. blossom — 꽃을 피우다, 꽃, 개화
13. cease — 중단하다, 멈추다
14. architect — 건축가, 설계사
15. cabin — 객실, 오두막
16. biological — 생물학적인, 생물학의
17. calculator — 계산기, 계산자
18. bite — 물린 상처, 물다

B
1. formally — 정식으로, 공식으로
2. educate — 교육하다, 육성하다
3. faucet — 수도꼭지
4. extent — 정도, 범위
5. greedy — 욕심 많은, 갈망하는
6. dialect — 방언, 사투리
7. forbid — 금지하다, 방해하다
8. expose — 드러내다, 폭로하다
9. grocery — 식품점
10. illegally — 불법으로
11. edition — 판, 간행
12. humanity — 인류, 인간애, 인간성
13. insurance — 보험, 보험금
14. effective — 효과적인, 효력이 있는
15. imagination — 상상(력), 창작력
16. explain — 설명하다, 해석하다, 해명하다
17. intense — 격한, 강렬한
18. grave — 무덤, 죽음

Answer Key

Unit 39

A
1. nuclear
2. peering
3. missionaries
4. penalty
5. perhaps
6. microwave
7. nutritious
8. prefer
9. interact
10. professor
11. international
12. logically
13. performed
14. loose
15. metropolis
16. millionaire
17. locked
18. occurs

B
1. 잠그다, 가두다
2. 핵의, 원자력의
3. 상호작용하다
4. 백만장자
5. 형벌, 벌금
6. 전자레인지
7. 아마, 어쩌면
8. 국제(상)의, 국제적인
9. 교수
10. 선교사, 전도사, 전도(장)의
11. ~을 더 좋아하다
12. 대도시, 수도, 주요도시
13. 일어나다, 생기다
14. 실행하다, 공연하다
15. 헐거운, 느슨한
16. 응시하다, ~에 필적하다
17. 영양분이 있는, 영양의
18. 논리적으로

1. interact
2. international
3. lock
4. logically
5. loose
6. metropolis
7. microwave
8. millionaire
9. missionary
10. nuclear
11. nutritious
12. occur
13. peer
14. penalty
15. perform
16. perhaps
17. prefer
18. professor

C
1. perform — 실행하다, 공연하다
2. loose — 헐거운, 느슨한
3. metropolis — 대도시, 수도
4. perhaps — 아마, 어쩌면
5. microwave — 전자레인지
6. logically — 논리적으로
7. missionary — 선교사, 전도사, 전도(자)의
8. nuclear — 핵의, 원자력의
9. millionaire — 백만장자
10. interact — 상호작용하다
11. lock — 잠그다, 가두다
12. occur — 일어나다, 생기다
13. professor — 교수
14. nutritious — 영양분이 있는, 영양의
15. peer — 응시하다, ~에 필적하다
16. international — 국제(상)의, 국제적인
17. prefer — ~을 더 좋아하다
18. penalty — 형벌, 벌금

Unit 40

A
1. tear
2. unique
3. valued
4. wiped
5. yell
6. reform
7. refund
8. scare
9. theories
10. vacant
11. scolded
12. willing
13. therapy
14. regular
15. society
16. sore
17. reflect
18. sources

B
1. 개혁, 개선, 개선하다
2. 찢다, 째다, 눈물
3. 놀라게 하다, 위협하다
4. 독특한, 유일한
5. 꾸짖다, 잔소리하다
6. 평가하다, 존중하다
7. 반영하다, 반사하다
8. 기꺼이 ~하는
9. 사회, 집단, 협회
10. 소리 지르다, 굉음을 내다
11. 아픈, 화난
12. 닦다, 훔치다
13. 규칙적인
14. 아무도 없는, 비어 있는
15. 근원, 출처
16. 치료, 요법
17. 환불, 반환
18. 이론, 학설

1. reflect
2. reform
3. refund
4. regular
5. scare
6. scold
7. society
8. sore
9. source
10. tear
11. theory
12. therapy
13. unique
14. vacant
15. value
16. willing
17. wipe
18. yell

C
1. scold — 꾸짖다, 잔소리하다
2. willing — 기꺼이 ~하는
3. regular — 규칙적인
4. scare — 놀라게 하다, 위협하다
5. value — 평가하다, 존중하다
6. wipe — 닦다, 훔치다
7. society — 사회, 집단, 협회
8. refund — 환불, 반환
9. vacant — 아무도 없는, 비어 있는
10. yell — 소리 지르다, 굉음을 내다
11. sore — 아픈, 화난
12. tear — 찢다, 째다, 눈물
13. reflect — 반영하다, 반사하다
14. source — 근원, 출처
15. unique — 독특한, 유일한
16. theory — 이론, 학설
17. reform — 개혁, 개선, 개선하다
18. therapy — 치료, 요법

Review 20

A
1. perform — 실행하다, 공연하다
2. loose — 헐거운, 느슨한
3. metropolis — 대도시, 수도
4. perhaps — 아마, 어쩌면
5. microwave — 전자레인지
6. logically — 논리적으로
7. missionary — 선교사, 전도사, 전도(자)의
8. nuclear — 핵의, 원자력의
9. millionaire — 백만장자
10. interact — 상호작용하다
11. lock — 잠그다, 가두다
12. occur — 일어나다, 생기다
13. professor — 교수
14. nutritious — 영양분이 있는, 영양의
15. peer — 응시하다, ~에 필적하다
16. international — 국제(상)의, 국제적인
17. prefer — ~을 더 좋아하다
18. penalty — 형벌, 벌금

B
1. scold — 꾸짖다, 잔소리하다
2. willing — 기꺼이 ~하는
3. rubber — 고무, 고무제품
4. scare — 놀라게 하다, 위협하다
5. value — 가치, 쓸모
6. wipe — 닦다, 훔치다
7. society — 사회, 집단, 협회
8. refund — 환불, 반환
9. vacant — 아무도 없는, 비어 있는
10. yell — 소리 지르다
11. sore — 아픈, 화난
12. tear — 찢다, 째다
13. reflect — 반영하다, 반사하다
14. source — 근원, 출처
15. unique — 독특한, 유일한
16. theory — 이론, 학설
17. reform — 개혁, 개선, 개선하다
18. therapy — 치료, 요법

Total Test — 해당 Unit별 Exercise 3번 문제의 정답과 일치

MEMO

MEMO